Overview

Contents

Wireless LANs, Second Edition

Jim Geier

SAMS

201 West 103rd St., Indianapolis, Indiana, 46290 USA

Wireless LANs, Second Edition

Copyright © 2002 by Sams Publishing

International Standard Book Number: 0-672-32058-4

Library of Congress Catalog Card Number: 2001087593

Printed in the United States of America

First Printing: July 2001

04   03   02   01   4   3   2   1

Trademarks

Warning and Disclaimer

ASSOCIATE PUBLISHER
Jeff Koch

ACQUISITIONS EDITOR
Katie Purdum

DEVELOPMENT EDITOR
Mark Renfrow

MANAGING EDITOR
Matt Purcell

PROJECT EDITOR
Christina Smith

COPY EDITORS
Krista Hansing
Gene Redding

INDEXER
Eric Schroeder

PROOFREADER
Benjamin Berg

TECHNICAL EDITOR
Ed Lamprecht

TEAM COORDINATOR
Vicki Harding

INTERIOR DESIGNER
Anne Jones

COVER DESIGNER
Aren Howell

PAGE LAYOUT
Ayanna Lacey

About the Author

Jim Geier is an independent consultant, assisting companies with the development of wireless network products and integration of wireless networks into corporate information systems. He is the principal consultant of his consulting firm, Wireless-Nets, Ltd.

Jim's 20 years of experience deals with the analysis, design, software development, installation, and support of numerous client/server and wireless network-based systems for retail, manufacturing, warehousing, health-care, education, and airline industries throughout the world. Jim is the author of three other books: *Wireless LANs* (1999, MTP), *Wireless Networking Handbook* (1996, New Riders), and *Network Reengineering* (1996, McGraw-Hill), as well as numerous articles for publications such as *Network World* and *Communications System Design*. Jim also speaks regularly at seminars, conferences, and trade shows in the United States, Europe, and Asia.

Jim has served as chairman of the Institute of Electrical and Electronic Engineers (IEEE) Computer Society, Dayton Section, and as chairman of the IEEE International Conference on Wireless LAN Implementation. He also was an active member of the IEEE 802.11 Working Group, responsible for developing international standards for wireless LANs. His education includes a bachelor's and master's degree in electrical engineering (with emphasis in computer networking and software development), and a master's degree in business administration.

As part of his Web site (http://www.wireless-nets.com), Jim maintains the *Online Guide to Wireless Networking*, which includes many of his articles and links to other sites. He is the editor of the monthly *Wireless-Nets Newsletter*, which is available free on his Web site at www.wireless-nets.com/newsletter.htm.

You can reach Jim via e-mail at jimgeier@wireless-nets.com.

About the Technical Editor

D. Ed Lamprecht is a manager of the Professional Services Group at Monarch Marking Systems which focuses on custom software and network solutions. He has more than 17 years of programming experience in applications, operating systems, and network programming. He received a bachelor's degree in 1983 from the University of Northern Iowa and started his career with NCR Corporation programming operating systems in assembly for retail computing systems. It was during this time that Ed also developed applications for other platforms, including UNIX and DOS.

In 1988, Ed joined Monarch Marking Systems, a company specializing in bar code printers and labels. Here he developed bar code applications for MS-DOS and Microsoft Windows as early as version 2.0, including PC drivers, TSRs, and connectivity software. Since 1996, Ed has been involved in data collection systems providing wireless network connectivity solutions of hand-held printers and data collection terminals for retail, industrial, manufacturing, and health care markets.

At Monarch, Ed has developed client/server applications, visited customer sites for analysis and problem solving, and provided international training on products and wireless connectivity. Ed holds seven patents in bar code software and handheld printer/data collectors. He lives with his wife, Michelle, and his son, Colin, in Dayton, Ohio. When not tinkering with PCs and networks at home, he enjoys model railroading, railroad memorabilia collecting, golfing, traveling, and spending time with his family.

Dedication

I dedicate this book to my wife, Debbie.

Acknowledgments

When writing this book, I was fortunate to work with an excellent team at Sams, whose contributions have greatly enhanced this book.

I'd like to give special thanks to Ed Lamprecht for performing the technical review of this book's manuscript. As usual, Ed's valuable suggestions greatly refined this book.

Tell Us What You Think!

As the reader of this book, *you* are our most important critic and commentator. We value your opinion and want to know what we're doing right, what we could do better, what areas you'd like to see us publish in, and any other words of wisdom you're willing to pass our way.

As an associate publisher for Sams Publishing, I welcome your comments. You can fax, e-mail, or write me directly to let me know what you did or didn't like about this book—as well as what we can do to make our books stronger.

Please note that I cannot help you with technical problems related to the topic of this book, and that due to the high volume of mail I receive, I might not be able to reply to every message.

When you write, please be sure to include this book's title and author's name as well as your name and phone or fax number. I will carefully review your comments and share them with the author and editors who worked on the book.

Fax: 317-581-4770

E-mail: feedback@samspublishing.com

Mail: Jeff Koch
            Associate Publisher
            Sams Publishing
            201 West 103rd Street
            Indianapolis, IN 46290 USA

Introduction

Wireless LAN technology is rapidly becoming a crucial component of computer networks and is growing by leaps and bounds. Thanks to the finalization of the IEEE 802.11 wireless LAN standard, wireless technology has emerged from the world of proprietary implementations to become an open solution for providing mobility as well as essential network services where wireline installations proved impractical. The inclusion of the newer IEEE 802.11a and 802.11b versions of the standard offers a firm basis for high-performance wireless LANs. Now companies and organizations are investing in wireless networks at a higher rate to take advantage of mobile, real-time access to information.

Most wireless LAN suppliers now have 802.11-compliant products, allowing companies to realize wireless network applications based on open systems. The move toward 802.11 standardization is lowering prices and enabling multivendor wireless LANs to interoperate. This is making the implementation of wireless networks more feasible than before, creating vast business opportunities for system implementation companies and consultants. However, many end-user companies and system integrators have limited knowledge and experience in developing and implementing wireless network systems. In many cases, there is also confusion over the capability and effectiveness of the 802.11 standard.

The implementation of wireless networks is much different than that of traditional wired networks. In contrast to ethernet, a wireless LAN has a large number of setup parameters that affect the performance and interoperability of the network. An engineer designing the network and the person installing the network must understand these parameters and how they affect the network. This book is full of implementation steps and notes as a guide when implementing wireless networks, especially ones that are 802.11-compliant.

This book provides a practical overview of wireless network technologies, with emphasis on the IEEE 802.11 wireless LAN standard and implementation steps and recommendations.

Audience

This book is intended for readers with knowledge of networking concepts and protocols. As examples, the reader should already be familiar with basic communications protocol handshaking processes and ethernet network infrastructures. Readers should also be conversant with basic computer terminology, such as *local area network*, *client/server*, and *application software*. Project managers can also benefit from the book by learning important project-planning steps for wireless network implementations.

The following constitutes the book's intended audience:

- Information system (IS) staff and system integrators involved with analyzing, designing, installing, and supporting wireless LANs
- Engineers developing wireless LAN-based products and solutions
- Managers planning and executing projects that develop wireless products or that implement wireless LAN systems

The Organization of This Book

This book follows a sequence of chapters that simplifies the learning process required in mastering wireless LAN technology. Chapters 1–3 address introductory material for the reader as a basis for understanding the more detailed elements. This portion will help the reader understand the concepts, benefits, and issues dealing with radio network systems, clearing up confusion of competing wireless solutions.

Chapter 4, "IEEE 802.11 Medium Access Control (MAC) Layer," and Chapter 5, "IEEE 802.11 Physical (PHY) Layer," discuss the details of the 802.11 Medium Access Control and physical layers. This helps readers understand details of 802.11 mechanisms (such as security and power management), examine frame structures, and determine which 802.11 physical layer best fits needs. Engineers designing wireless LAN solutions will find this part useful for understanding design options and tuning of an 802.11 network. This book includes detailed coverage of the 802.11a and 802.11b protocols, which was not available in the first edition of the book.

Chapter 6, "Wireless System Integration," discusses concepts related to integrating wireless LANs to existing systems. This includes technologies and components needed in addition to what 802.11 covers, such as MobileIP and application connectivity software. It's important to utilize these concepts to implement a complete and reliable wireless LAN solution.

Chapter 7, "Planning a Wireless LAN," and Chapter 8, "Implementing a Wireless LAN," describe the steps to follow when planning, analyzing, designing, and installing a wireless system. A single case study, threaded throughout these chapters, provides details of a real project to help you understand how to implement the ideas presented in the chapters' step-by-step procedures. In addition, special implementation notes enable readers to directly apply what they've read in earlier chapters to solving the needs for wireless networks within their companies or organization.

IS staff, system integrators, and project managers can strongly benefit by using this part of the book as a practical guide that is based on the experiences and lessons learned from many wireless network projects completed by the author.

Updates to This Book Compared to the First Edition

This book is a second edition to the initial *Wireless LANs* book published by Macmillan Technical Publishing (MTP) in 1999. This second edition is based on the initial edition and includes the following modifications:

- Detailed description of the IEEE 802.11b High-Rate Direct Sequence Physical Layer
- Detailed description of the IEEE 802.11a Orthogonal Frequency-Division Multiplexing (OFDM) Physical layer
- Updates on non-802.11 technologies, such as HiperLAN, HomeRF, and Bluetooth
- Focus on implementing wireless LANs for corporate information systems
- Discussion of interference potential between Bluetooth and 802.11 networks
- Description of the newer 802.11 standard efforts, such as IEEE 802.11e (QoS enhancements)
- Updated glossary that includes newer wireless LAN terms

Wireless Networks—
A First Look

PART
I

IN THIS PART

Introduction to Wireless Networks

IN THIS CHAPTER

Wireless LAN Benefits

The emergence and continual growth of wireless local area networks (LANs) are being driven by the need to lower the costs associated with network infrastructures and to support mobile networking applications that offer gains in process efficiency, accuracy, and lower business costs. The following sections explain the mobility and cost-saving benefits of wireless LANs.

Mobility

Mobility enables users to move physically while using an appliance, such as a handheld PC or data collector. Many jobs require workers to be mobile, such as inventory clerks, healthcare workers, policemen, and emergency care specialists. Of course, wireline networks require a physical tether between the user's workstation and the network's resources, which makes access to these resources impossible while roaming about the building or elsewhere. This freedom of movement results in significant return on investments due to gains in efficiency.

Mobile applications requiring wireless networking include those that depend on real-time access to data—usually stored in centralized databases (see Figure 1.1). If your application requires mobile users to be aware immediately of changes made to data, or if information put into the system must immediately be available to others, then you have a definite need for wireless networking. For accurate and efficient price markdowns, for example, many retail stores use wireless networks to interconnect handheld bar code scanners and printers to databases having current price information. This enables the printing of the correct prices on the items, making both the customer and the business owner more satisfied.

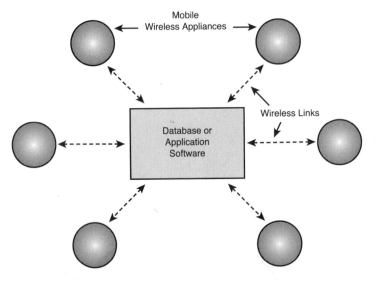

Figure 1.1

A wireless network supports mobile applications by providing access to real-time data.

Another example of the use of wireless networking is in auto racing. Formula 1 and Indy race-cars have sophisticated data acquisition systems that monitor the various onboard systems in the car. When the cars come around the track and pass their respective teams in the pit, this information is downloaded to a central computer, thereby enabling real-time analysis of the performance of the racecar.

Not all mobile applications, though, require wireless networking. Sometimes the business case doesn't support the need for mobile real-time access to information. If the application's data can be stored on the user's device and changes to the data are not significant, then the additional cost of wireless network hardware may not provide enough benefits to justify the additional expense. Keep in mind, though, that other needs for wireless networks may still exist.

Installation in Difficult-to-Wire Areas

The implementation of wireless networks offers many tangible cost savings when performing installations in difficult-to-wire areas. If rivers, freeways, or other obstacles separate buildings you want to connect (see Figure 1.2), a wireless solution may be much more economical than installing physical cable or leasing communications circuits, such as T1 service or 56Kbps lines. Some organizations spend thousands or even millions of dollars to install physical links with nearby facilities.

If you are facing this type of installation, consider wireless networking as an alternative. The deployment of wireless networking in these situations costs thousands of dollars, but it will result in a definite cost savings in the long run.

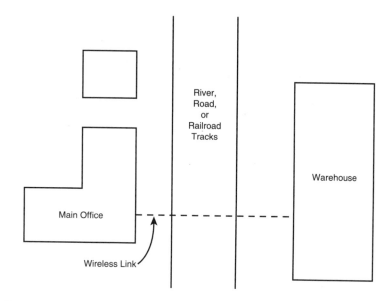

Figure 1.2

Wireless networks make it cost effective to provide network connectivity in situations that are difficult to wire.

Case Study 1.1:

Replacing a Dial-Up System with a Wireless Network

A grain handling firm based in Canada trimmed overhead and boosted customer service levels by replacing its slow and expensive modem-based dial-up links to a nearby satellite facility with a low-cost wireless network. This enables remote workstations to access the company's LAN swiftly and seamlessly. The result: Communication costs have dropped dramatically, and customer transactions at a remote facility are completed much faster.

The firm buys wheat, barley, flax, and canola from farmers and ships the grains to export markets. The company accepts delivery of the grain from farmers at grain elevators and then, based on the type of grain and its grade, pays for the delivery and logs the transaction into a settlement system.

In a particular city in Canada, farmers deliver large quantities of grain to an inland terminal that also houses business offices; smaller deliveries are made to a smaller grain elevator, called Elevator A, 700 feet away. With 12 staff members at the main business office and only 2 at Elevator A, implementing separate networks at each site to support the settlement system was not cost effective.

Faced with the problems of optimizing transaction speed for farmers at Elevator A, enhancing overall network operation control, minimizing capital expenditures, and controlling ongoing communication costs, the firm looked for a way to integrate workers at this remote facility with a new LAN implemented at the main business office. The most obvious solution was a leased telephone line. Because traffic is so light between the two sites, however, the cost could not be justified. Similarly, linking the sites with fiber optic or coaxial cable was also too expensive, due in part to the costs of obtaining permits to lay cable under the railroad lines that separate the facilities. The company then considered using the same frame relay network that links offices and elevators at its other facilities, but the cost of this option would have been $600 per month and low data speeds.

With no conventional communications alternatives meeting their needs, the firm began a market search for a low-cost, easy-to-install wireless link between the two sites that would not be affected by extreme climatic conditions—including temperatures that vary from 104 degrees Fahrenheit (40 degrees Celsius) in the summer to minus 40 degrees Fahrenheit (minus 40 degrees Celsius) in winter. The firm decided to use Proxim's RangeLINK product. RangeLINK has been operating flawlessly throughout Canada's harsh winter climate at speeds that enable transactions at Elevator A to be completed four times faster than with the modem-based dial-up system that the firm previously used.

The asbestos found in older facilities is another problem that many organizations encounter. The inhalation of asbestos particles is extremely hazardous to your health; therefore, you must take great care when installing network cabling within these areas. When taking necessary precautions, the resulting cost of cable installations in these facilities can be prohibitive.

Some organizations, for example, remove the asbestos, making it safe to install cabling. This process is very expensive because you must protect the building's occupants from breathing the asbestos particles agitated during removal. The cost of removing asbestos covering just a few flights of stairs can be tens of thousands of dollars. Obviously, the advantage of wireless networking in asbestos-contaminated buildings is that you can avoid the asbestos removal process, resulting in tremendous cost savings.

In some cases, it might be impossible to install cabling. Some municipalities, for example, may restrict you from permanently modifying older facilities with historical value. This could limit the drilling of holes in walls during the installation of network cabling and outlets. In that situation, a wireless network might be the only solution. Right-of-way restrictions within cities and counties may also block the digging of trenches in the ground to lay optical fiber for networked sites. Again, in this situation, a wireless network might be the best alternative.

Case Study 1.2:

A Wireless Solution in a Historic Building

An observatory in Australia has provided stargazing to astronomy enthusiasts for more than 140 years. Built in 1858, the observatory is classified by the National Trust as one of Australia's historical buildings.

When the observatory began investigating ways to share these views of space with a much broader audience, the obvious solution was to download images to multiple PCs and large screens via a local area network. Due to the historical nature of the building, however, cabling was not an option. Very thick sandstone walls and historic plaster ceilings could not be easily drilled into, and strings of cable would have been unsightly and unsafe to the public. The only feasible solution was a wireless LAN.

The observatory installed Lucent WaveLAN (now Agere's ORiNOCO) radio cards in each of its eight PCs and the network server. Telescopic images are downloaded from the Internet or from electronic cameras housed in the observatory's telescopes. These images are then displayed on the various PCs for individual viewing or on larger monitors for group viewing.

Increased Reliability

A problem inherent to wired networks is downtime due to cable faults. In fact, a cable fault is often the primary cause of system downtime. Moisture erodes metallic conductors via water intrusion during storms and accidental spillage or leakage of liquids. With wired networks, a user might accidentally break his network connector when trying to disconnect his PC from the network to move it to a different location. Imperfect cable splices can cause signal reflections that result in unexplainable errors. The accidental cutting of cables can bring down a network immediately. Wires and connectors can easily break through misuse and normal use. These problems interfere with users' ability to use network resources, causing havoc for network managers. An advantage of wireless networking, therefore, results from the use of less cable. This reduces the downtime of the network and the costs associated with replacing cables.

Reduced Installation Time

The installation of cabling is often a time-consuming activity. For LANs, installers must pull twisted-pair wires or optical fiber above the ceiling and drop cables through walls to network outlets that they must affix to the wall. These tasks can take days or weeks, depending on the size of the installation. The installation of optical fiber between buildings within the same geographical area consists of digging trenches to lay the fiber or pulling the fiber through an existing conduit. You might need weeks or possibly months to receive right-of-way approvals and dig through ground and asphalt.

The deployment of wireless networks greatly reduces the need for cable installation, making the network available for use much sooner. Thus, many countries lacking a network infrastructure have turned to wireless networking as a method of providing connectivity among computers without the expense and time associated with installing physical media. This is also necessary within the U.S. to set up temporary offices and rewire renovated facilities.

Case Study 1.3:

Using a Wireless Network for Disaster Recovery

A manufacturer in Sweden distributes auto safety equipment such as airbags, seat belts, and child seats. With factories in virtually all major European manufacturing countries, the manufacturer has positioned itself as one of the largest suppliers of safety equipment in Europe.

A fire in one of its facilities caused extensive damage to over 6,000 square meters (65,000 square feet) of production and storage facilities. Furthermore, existing network cabling and a majority of the manufacturing terminals were damaged in the blaze. Given the severity of the fire and the company's dedication to customer satisfaction, a solution was needed to fill existing customer orders rapidly.

By incorporating a configuration of Lucent WaveLAN–equipped PCs and WavePOINT access points (now Agere's ORiNOCO), the manufacturer was able to rebound from the disaster successfully and rapidly. Within a matter of days, the WaveLAN wireless local area network was installed. The WaveLAN solution helps track approximately 800,000 pieces of equipment delivered to customers daily.

In addition to the swift and easy installation, WaveLAN is providing the company with flexibility and mobility it lacked with a traditional wired LAN environment. Inventory control, materials tracking, and delivery information are available online from various locations on the production floor. WaveLAN's 2Mbps data speed helps to increase productivity further by handling this critical information easier than the 9600 baud speed of the old system. The cost effectiveness of the wireless LAN is also becoming apparent by helping the company save on reconfiguration and rewiring costs that average nearly 3,500 Swedish Kronas ($500) per terminal.

Long-Term Cost Savings

Companies reorganize, resulting in the movement of people, new floor plans, office partitions, and other renovations. These changes often require recabling the network, incurring both labor and material costs. In some cases, the recabling costs of organizational changes are substantial, especially with large enterprise networks. A reorganization rate of 15% each year can result in yearly reconfiguration expenses as high as $250,000 for networks that have 6,000 interconnected devices. The advantage of wireless networking is again based on the lack of cable: You can move the network connection by simply relocating an employee's PC.

Wireless LAN Applications

Wireless LANs are applicable to all industries with a need for mobile computer use or when the installation of physical media is not feasible. Wireless LANs are especially useful when employees must process information on the spot, directly in front of customers or co-workers, via electronic-based forms and interactive menus. Wireless networking makes it possible to place portable computers in the hands of mobile front-line workers such as doctors, nurses, warehouse clerks, inspectors, claims adjusters, real estate agents, and insurance salespeople.

The coupling of portable devices with wireless connectivity to a common database and specific applications, as Figure 1.1 illustrates, meets mobility needs, eliminates paperwork, decreases errors, reduces process costs, and improves efficiency. The alternative to this, which many companies still employ today, is using paperwork to update records, process inventories, and file claims. This method processes information slowly, produces redundant data, and is subject to errors caused by illegible handwriting. The wireless computer approach using a centralized database is clearly superior.

Retail

Retail organizations need to order, price, sell, and keep inventories of merchandise. A wireless network in a retail environment enables clerks and storeroom personnel to perform their functions directly from the sales floor. Salespeople are equipped with a pen-based computer or a small computing device with bar code reading and printing capability, with the wireless link to the store's database. They are then able to complete transactions such as pricing, bin labeling, placing special orders, and taking inventory from anywhere within the store.

When printing price labels that will be affixed to the item or shelves, retailers often use a hand-held bar code scanner and printer to produce bar coded or human-readable labels. A database or file contains the price information located either on the handheld device, often called a *batch* device, or on a server somewhere in the store. In batch mode, the price clerk scans the bar code (typically the product code) located on the item or shelf edge, the application software uses the product code to look up the new price, and then the printer produces a new label that the clerk affixes to the item.

In some cases, the batch-based scanner/printer has enough memory to store all the price information needed to perform the pricing function throughout a shift or an entire day. This situation makes sense if you update price information in the database once a day, typically during the evening. The clerks load the data onto the device at the beginning of their shifts, then walk throughout the store pricing items. However, if the memory in the device is not large enough to store all the data, a wireless network is probably necessary. If the handheld unit is equipped with a wireless network connection, then the data can be stored in the much larger memory capabilities of a centralized PC server or mainframe and accessed each time an item's bar code is scanned. In addition, a wireless network–based solution has merit if it is too time consuming to download information to a batch device.

Warehousing

Warehouse staff must manage the receiving, shelving, inventorying, picking, and shipping of goods. These responsibilities require the staff to be mobile. Warehouse operations traditionally have been paper intensive and time consuming. An organization can eliminate paper, reduce errors, and decrease the time necessary to move items in and out by giving each warehouse employee a handheld computing device with a bar code scanner interfaced via a wireless network to a warehouse inventory system.

Upon receiving an item for storage within the warehouse, a clerk can scan the item's bar-coded item number and enter other information from a small keypad into the database via the handheld device. The system can respond with a location by printing a put-away label. A forklift operator can then move the item to a storage place and account for the procedure by scanning the item's bar code. The inventory system keeps track of all transactions, making it very easy to produce accurate inventory reports. In addition, the online interaction with a database will identify mistakes immediately, enabling the operator to correct the mistake before it becomes a problem.

As shipping orders enter the warehouse, the inventory system produces a list of the items and their locations. A clerk can view this list from the database via a handheld device and locate the items needed to assemble a shipment. As the clerk removes the items from the storage bins, the database can be updated via the handheld device. All of these functions depend heavily on wireless networks to maintain real-time access to data stored in a central database.

Healthcare

Healthcare centers, such as hospitals and doctor's offices, must maintain accurate records to ensure effective patient care. A simple mistake can cost someone's life. As a result, doctors and nurses must carefully record test results, physical data, pharmaceutical orders, and surgical procedures. This paperwork often overwhelms healthcare staff, taking 50%–70% of their time.

Doctors and nurses are also extremely mobile, going from room to room caring for patients. The use of electronic patient records, with the capability to input, view, and update patient data from anywhere in the hospital, increases the accuracy and speed of healthcare. This improvement is made possible by providing each nurse and doctor with a wireless pen–based computer, coupled with a wireless network to databases that store critical medical information about the patients.

A doctor caring for someone in the hospital, for example, can place an order for a blood test by keying the request into a handheld computer. The laboratory will receive the order electronically and dispatch a lab technician to draw blood from the patient. The laboratory will run the tests requested by the doctor and enter the results into the patient's electronic medical record. The doctor can then check the results via the handheld appliance from anywhere in the hospital.

Another application for wireless networks in hospitals is the tracking of pharmaceuticals. The use of mobile handheld bar code printing and scanning devices dramatically increases the efficiency and accuracy of all drug transactions, such as receiving, picking, dispensing, inventory taking, and tracking drug expiration dates. Most importantly, though, it ensures that hospital staff are able to administer the right drug to the right person at the right time. This would not be possible without the use of wireless networks to support a centralized database and mobile data collection devices.

NOTE

In the war against drugs, President Bill Clinton signed into law the Controlled Substance Act, which pushes hospitals to keep better records of the intake, use, and distribution of controlled drugs. In most cases, the use of handheld computers increases productivity of pharmacy staff by 50%–75%, enables them to produce management reports rapidly, and eliminates errors due to math computations, transcriptions, and accounting.

Hospital Uses Wireless LAN to Speed Up Emergency Room Registration[1]

Indiana's Methodist Hospital installed Proxim's RangeLAN2 wireless communications technology to enable faster patient intake in the emergency room. The new system gives medical staff the ability to take patients straight back to the treatment rooms, giving them immediate treatment and more privacy in divulging insurance information and medical problems.

Methodist Hospital of Indianapolis, Indiana, is an 1,100-bed private hospital with a 45-bed emergency room that features a state-approved, Level-1 trauma center. Approximately 85,000–90,000 patients pass through the hospital's emergency room each year, and many are in need of immediate treatment. For these patients, there's no time to wait in a room full of people while a registration clerk collects information on the reason for the visit, type of insurance coverage, and health history. Sometimes information must be recorded as the patient is being transported to a room, or even while being treated.

To expedite the registration process, Methodist Hospital worked with Datacom for Business, a value-added reseller based in Champaign, Illinois. As a result, the hospital remodeled its 65,000-square-foot emergency room, eliminating all but two registration tables and replacing the rest with Compaq Contura notebook computers outfitted with wireless LAN adapters. Now patients can go directly to treatment rooms, where registration clerks gather the necessary intake data and enter it into the database on the host computer.

Methodist Hospital's wireless communications are made possible by RangeLAN2/PCMCIA adapters from Proxim, Inc. The wireless PCMCIA adapters enable the Compaq notebook computers running TN3270 terminal emulation to access the clinic's existing wired client/server network or communicate on a peer-to-peer basis with other mobile systems within the same clinic site.

---

[1] *Reprinted by permission from Proxim, Inc.*

The adapters operate at an average power output of about 100 milliwatts and use advanced power management to minimize the drain on the mobile systems' batteries. RangeLAN2 provides transparent access to standard wired LAN environments, including the hospital's existing TCP/IP network. This is accomplished through the use of three Proxim RangeLAN2/Access Points, which act as wireless bridges and enable mobile users anywhere in the emergency room to send information to the Telnet LAN server. The terminal emulation is then transferred in real-time over a TCP/IP enterprise backbone to the hospital's database in the mainframe computer.

Hospitality

Hospitality establishments check customers in and out and keep track of needs such as room service orders and laundry requests. Restaurants need to keep track of the names and numbers of people waiting for entry, table status, and drink and food orders. Restaurant staff must perform these activities quickly and accurately to avoid making patrons unhappy. Wireless networking satisfies these needs very well.

Wireless computers are very useful in situations where there is a large crowd, such as a sports bar restaurant. For example, someone can greet a restaurant patron at the door and enter his name, the size of the party, and smoking preferences into a common database via a wireless device. The greeter can then query the database and determine the availability of an appropriate table. Those who oversee the tables use a wireless device to update the database to show whether the table is occupied, being cleaned, or available. After obtaining a table, the waiter transmits the order to the kitchen via the wireless device, eliminating the need for paper order tickets. Keep in mind, however, that the wireless network approach in finer restaurants may not be appealing to patrons. In that case, the patrons may expect waiters to memorize their orders.

In addition, some companies are turning around the benefits of a wireless LAN to focus more directly on customers. For example, Starbuck's is installing an IEEE 802.11b wireless LAN system with Internet access in every store as a service to its customers. Starbuck's is taking the "Internet cafe" a step further, allowing the customer to use his own computer with his own software rather than be limited to the dedicated systems at the site.

Home and Small Office

For homeowners and small office inhabitants, a wireless LAN is becoming an effective option as compared to ethernet for sharing printers, scanners, and high-speed Internet connections. It's often less expensive to set up a wireless LAN and avoid having to install ethernet cabling throughout a home or small office. The cost savings in addition to mobility benefits are causing many homeowners to take this approach, especially as wireless LAN prices continue to drop and the fears of wireless subside. In the case of leasing a home or office, wireless may be the only alternative if the landlord has restrictions on changing the wiring.

A wireless LAN solution for the home and small office is very simple, generally consisting of a single access point that connects directly to the Internet connection (such as ISDN, DSL, or cable modem) via a router. Additionally, as soon as you install a wireless LAN radio in each laptop and PC, you're ready to use the network. You can browse the Web from your favorite chair while watching television or sitting in the backyard next to the pool.

General Enterprise Systems

In the past, the implementation of a wireless LAN was relatively expensive, compared to the higher-performing ethernet networks. This required a wireless LAN application to provide a tremendous gain in efficiency to make it cost-effective. As a result, most existing applications of wireless LANs are in markets such as healthcare, warehousing, and retail, where mobility provided efficiency gains capable of significantly lowering operational costs. With wireless LAN prices continuing to drop and performance increasing, however, many enterprise information system managers are beginning to consider seriously the use of wireless LANs instead of traditional ethernet. The benefits are to provide mobile and portable access to general network functions such as e-mail, Internet browsing, access to databases, and so on and eliminate the time and expense of installing and supporting physical cable. Thus, wireless LANs are now effectively satisfying applications in horizontal markets.

Wireless Services

Most wireless LAN applications reside inside buildings and are privately owned. Many companies, however, are in the process of constructing wireless networks in metropolitan areas to offer non–point-to-point wireless connectivity to subscribers in fixed locations. As a result, these companies are offering wireless services to provide options to traditional wire-based technologies such as ISDN, DSL, and cable modems. Because of the lack of wires, the wireless systems tend to be more reliable, and subscribers can initiate service much faster.

> **NOTE**
>
> The author's Web site at http://www.wireless-nets.com/cases.htm includes a collection of wireless network case studies.

Wireless LAN Technologies

There are several wireless LAN specifications and standards that you can choose from when developing wireless LAN products or integrating wireless LAN solutions into corporate information systems. The following sections provide a brief overview of these specifications and standards. The emphasis of this book is on IEEE 802.11–compliant wireless LANs because 802.11 is expected to continue being the preferred standard for supporting wireless LAN applications. Other technologies, such as HiperLAN, HomeRF SWAP, and Bluetooth, may become stronger competitors to 802.11 in the future.

IEEE 802.11

In June 1997, the IEEE finalized the initial standard for wireless LANs: IEEE 802.11. This standard specifies a 2.4GHz operating frequency with data rates of 1Mbps and 2Mbps. The initial 802.11 standard defines two forms of spread spectrum modulation: frequency hopping (802.11 FHSS) and direct sequence (802.11 DSSS).

In late 1999, the IEEE published two supplements to the 802.11 standard: 802.11a and 802.11b. IEEE 802.11b is a data rate extension of the initial 802.11 DSSS, providing operation in the 2.4GHz band at up to 11Mbps. Most wireless LANs implemented today comply with the 802.11b version of the standard.

The 802.11a standard defines operation at up to 54Mbps using orthogonal frequency division multiplexing (OFDM) modulation in the roomy 5GHz frequency band. The 802.11a standard has a wide variety of high-speed data rates available: 6, 9, 12, 18, 24, 36, 48, and 54Mbps; it is mandatory for all products to have 6Mbps, 12Mbps, and 24Mbps rates. Products implementing the 802.11a standard should begin appearing on the market in late 2001.

> **NOTE**
>
> Refer to Chapter 3, "Overview of the IEEE 802.11 Standard," Chapter 4, "IEEE 802.11 Medium Access Control (MAC) Layer," and Chapter 5, "IEEE 802.11 Physical (PHY) Layer," for details on the 802.11 standard.

HiperLAN

HiperLAN began in Europe as a specification (EN 300 652) ratified in 1996 by the European Telecommunications Standards Institute (ETSI) Broadband Radio Access Network (BRAN) organization. HiperLAN/1, the current version, operates in the 5GHz radio band at up to 24Mbps. Similar to ethernet, HiperLAN/1 shares access to the wireless LAN among end user devices via a connectionless protocol. HiperLAN/1 also provides quality of service (QoS) support for various needs of data, video, voice, and images.

ETSI is currently developing HiperLAN/2 under an organization called the HiperLAN/2 Global Forum (H2GF). HiperLAN/2 will operate in the 5GHz band at up to 54Mbps using a connection-oriented protocol for sharing access among end user devices. HiperLAN/2 will include QoS support and be capable of carrying ethernet frames, ATM cells, and IP packets.

> **NOTE**
>
> Refer to the HiperLAN/2 Global Forum Web site at http://www.hiperlan2.com for additional details on the HiperLAN/2 specification.

HomeRF SWAP

In March 1998, the HomeRF Working Group (HRFWG) announced its existence and set out to provide an open industry specification, Shared Wireless Access Protocol (SWAP), for wireless digital communication between PCs and consumer electronic devices within the home. The SWAP specification defines a common wireless interface supporting voice and data at 1MBps and 2MBps data rates using frequency hopping spread spectrum modulation in the 2.4GHz frequency band. HRFWG is currently developing a 10Mbps version of SWAP based on recent Federal Communications Commission (FCC) approval for wider bandwidth for frequency hopping systems.

> **NOTE**
>
> Refer to the HomeRF Web site at http://www.homerf.org for more details on the SWAP specification.

Bluetooth

Bluetooth is a specification published by the Bluetooth Special Interest Group (SIG), with some big promoters including 3Com, Ericsson, IBM, Intel, Lucent, Microsoft, Motorola, Nokia, and Toshiba. Bluetooth isn't a wireless LAN. Instead, it is a wireless personal area network (PAN), which is a subset of a wireless LAN. Bluetooth operates at 1Mbps, with relatively low power over short ranges using frequency hopping spread spectrum in the 2.4GHz frequency band.

> **NOTE**
>
> Refer to the Bluetooth SIG Web site at http://www.bluetooth.com for more details on the Bluetooth specification.

Wireless LAN Implications

Wireless LANs offer tremendous benefits, as described in an earlier section of this chapter. Project managers and design engineers should be aware, however, of the following potential problems from the implementation and use of wireless networking:

- Multipath propagation
- Path loss
- Radio signal interference
- Battery longevity
- System interoperability
- Network security
- Connection problems
- Installation issues
- Health risks

Multipath Propagation

As Figure 1.3 illustrates, transmitted signals can combine with reflected ones to corrupt the signal detected by the receiver. This is known as *multipath propagation. Delay spread* is the amount of delay experienced by the reflected signals compared to the primary signal. As delay spread increases, the signal at the receiver becomes more distorted and possibly undetectable even when the transmitter and receiver are within close range.

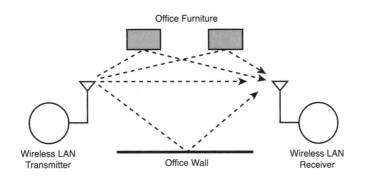

FIGURE 1.3
Multipath propagation decreases the quality of the signal at the receiver.

Multipath propagation can be a significant problem, especially with indoor applications. Office furniture, walls, and machinery are obstacles that can redirect parts of the transmitted signal. Wireless LAN manufacturers compensate for the effects of multipath propagation by using special processing techniques. As examples, equalization and antenna diversity are methods for reducing the number of problems arising from multipath propagation.

Path Loss

Path loss between the transmitter and receiver is a key consideration when designing a wireless LAN solution. Expected levels of path loss, based on the range between the transmitter and receiver, provide valuable information when determining requirements for transmit power levels, receiver sensitivity, and signal-to-noise ratio (SNR). Actual path loss depends on the transmit frequency, and it grows exponentially as the distance increases between the transmitter and receiver. With typical indoor applications, the path loss increases approximately 20dB every 100 feet.

Radio Signal Interference

The process of transmitting and receiving radio and laser signals through the air makes wireless systems vulnerable to atmospheric noise and transmissions from other systems. In addition, wireless networks can interfere with other nearby wireless networks and radio wave equipment. As shown in Figure 1.4, interference can be inward or outward.

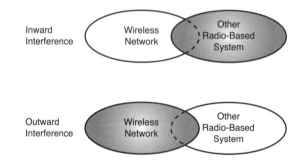

FIGURE 1.4

Inward and outward interference are problems for wireless networks.

Inward Interference

A radio-based LAN can experience inward interference from the harmonics of transmission systems or other products using similar radio frequencies in the local area. Microwave ovens operate in the S band (2.4GHz) that many wireless LANs use to transmit and receive. These signals result in delays to the user by either blocking transmissions from stations on the LAN or causing bit errors to occur in data being sent. These types of interference can limit the areas in which you can deploy a wireless network.

Case Study 1.4:

Radio Interference

When deploying a wireless network at a site located in Washington, D.C., along the Potomac River, a consulting firm occasionally experienced a great deal of delay from stations located on the side of the building facing the river. The implementation team found through radio propagation tests that a military base on the opposite side of the river was periodically transmitting radio signals. The interfering signals were strong enough for the LAN stations to misinterpret them as data traffic, forcing the stations to wait.

NOTE

Most radio-based products operate within public license-free bands. These products do not require users to obtain FCC licenses, which means the FCC does not manage the use of the products. If you experience interference resulting from another product operating within the public band, you have no recourse. The FCC is not required to step in and resolve the matter, which leaves you with the choice of dealing with delays the interface causes or looking for a different technology to support your needs. This type of interference, though, is rare.

Interference with radio-based networks is not as bad as it might seem. Products using the public radio frequencies incorporate spread spectrum modulation that limits the amount of harm an interfering signal causes. The spread spectrum signal operates over a wide bandwidth, and typical narrow bandwidth interference affects only a small part of the spread information signal, resulting in few or no errors. Thus, spread spectrum–type products are highly resistant to interference.

Narrowband interference with a signal-to-interference ratio of less than 10dB does not usually affect a spread spectrum transmission. However, wideband interference can have damaging effects on any type of radio transmission. The primary source of wideband interference is a domestic microwave oven, most of which operate in the 2.4GHz band. This could corrupt a wireless data signal transmitting from within 50 feet of the oven. Other interference may result from elevator motors, duplicating machines, theft protection equipment, and cordless phones.

Outward Interference

Outward interference occurs when a wireless network's signal disrupts other systems, such as adjacent wireless LANs and navigation equipment on aircraft. This disruption results in the loss of some or all of the system's functionality. Interference is uncommon with wireless LAN products operating in the public spread spectrum bands because they operate on such little power (less than 1 watt). The transmitting components must be very close and operating in the same band for either one to experience inward or outward interference.

Techniques for Reducing Interference

When dealing with interference, you should coordinate the operation of radio-based wireless network products with your company's frequency management organization, if one exists. Government organizations and most hospitals generally have people who manage the use of transmitting devices. This coordination will avoid potential interference problems.

In fact, coordination with frequency management officials is a mandatory requirement before operating radio-based wireless devices of any kind on a U.S. military base. The military does not follow the same frequency allocations issued by the FCC. The FCC deals with commercial sectors of the U.S., and the military has its own frequency management process. You must obtain special approval from the government to operate wireless LAN products on military bases and some government locations because they may interfere with some of the military's systems. The approval process can take several months to complete.

Potential Frequency Interference Between 802.11 and Bluetooth

A current problem is that both Bluetooth and 802.11 products operate in the same 2.4GHz unlicensed radio band. This poses a strong potential for radio frequency interference between products based on both technologies. The likelihood is that Bluetooth products will jam the operation of 802.11, not the other way around. The reason is that Bluetooth hops through frequencies 600 times faster than 802.11. While an 802.11 device is transmitting on a particular frequency, a nearby Bluetooth product will most likely interfere with the 802.11 transmission many times before the 802.11 device hops to the next frequency. This barrage of radio signals emanating from Bluetooth products could seriously degrade the operation of an 802.11 network.

Because the FCC doesn't directly mediate frequency conflicts between products within unlicensed ISM bands, Bluetooth and IEEE standards groups are left on their own to haggle over resolving the interference problems. The IEEE has taken a positive step forward by forming the 802.15 Coexistence Task Group 2. This group is developing recommended practices for coexistence of wireless personal access networks (PANs) that operate in the 2.4GHz frequency spectrum, and they've done preliminary analysis of the interference potential between 802.11 and Bluetooth. In addition, the group has made preliminary recommendations on how to solve the problem. The ultimate goal is to decrease the probability of Bluetooth and 802.11 devices transmitting at the same time. Refer to IEEE 802.15's Web site at `http://grouper.ieee.org/groups/802/15/pub/TG2.html` for more information on progress this group is making.

TIP

If no frequency management organization exists within your company, run some tests to determine the propagation patterns within your building. These tests let you know whether existing systems might interfere with, and thus block and cause delay to, your network. You will also discover whether your signal will disturb other systems. See Chapter 6, "Wireless System Integration," for details on ways to perform propagation tests (RF site survey).

Limited Battery Longevity

If you are using a portable computer in an automobile, performing an inventory in a warehouse, or caring for patients in a hospital, it's probably too cumbersome or impossible to plug your computer into an electrical outlet. Thus, you will depend on the computer's battery. The extra load of the wireless NIC in this situation can significantly decrease the amount of time you have available to operate the computer before needing to recharge the batteries. Your operating time, therefore, might decrease to less than an hour if you access the network often or perform other functions, such as printing.

To counter this problem, most vendors implement power management techniques in their radio cards and access points. Without power management, radio-based wireless components normally remain in a receptive state waiting for any information. For example, some vendors incorporate two modes to help conserve power: the Doze Mode and the Sleep Mode. The Doze Mode, which is the default state of the product, keeps the radio off most of the time and wakes it up periodically to determine if any messages await in a special mailbox. This mode alone uses approximately 50% less battery power. The Sleep Mode causes the radio to remain in a transmit-only standby mode. In other words, the radio wakes up and sends information if necessary, but it is not capable of receiving any information. Other products offer similar power management features.

> **NOTE**
>
> The typical current draw of an IEEE 802.11b product is as follows:
>
> Transmit: 350mA
>
> Receive: 250mA
>
> Sleep: less than 10mA
>
> The aggregate power consumption of the wireless LAN device is dependent on utilization and configuration parameter settings. Higher utilization and settings resulting in higher rates of transmission will increase power consumption.

System Interoperability

When implementing an ethernet network, network managers and engineers can deploy NICs from a variety of vendors on the same network. Because of the stable IEEE 802.3 standard that specifies the protocols and electrical characteristics that manufacturers must follow for ethernet, these products all speak exactly the same language. This uniformity enables you to select products meeting your requirements at the lowest cost from a variety of manufacturers.

With wireless LANs, you can't assume interoperability in all situations. There are still pre-802.11 (proprietary) wireless LANs, both frequency hopping and direct sequence 802.11 versions, and vendor-specific enhancements to 802.11-compliant products that make interoperability questionable. In order to ensure interoperability with wireless LANs, it's best to implement radio cards and access points from the same vendor if possible. You can implement multivendor wireless LANs successfully, but wireless LAN features are reduced to the lowest common denominator and may not make use of special vendor-specific enhancements of their wireless LAN products.

> **NOTE**
>
> Wireless Ethernet Compatibility Alliance (WECA) is an organization that ensures compliance among IEEE 802.11 wireless LANs through their Wi-Fi certification tests. You can learn more about WECA and the Wi-Fi compliance program at http://www.wi-fi.org. You can view a current list of Wi-Fi–compliant products at http://www.wi-fi.org/certified_products.asp.

Network Security

Network security refers to the protection of information and resources from loss, corruption, and improper use. Are wireless networks secure? Among businesses considering the implementation of a wireless system, this is a common and very important question. To answer this question, you must consider the functionality a wireless network performs.

A wireless network provides a bit pipe, consisting of a medium, synchronization, and error control that supports the flow of data bits from one point to another. The functionality of a wireless network corresponds to the lowest levels of the network architecture and does not include other functions, such as end-to-end connection establishment or login services that higher layers satisfy. Therefore, the only security issues relevant to wireless networks are those dealing with these lower architectural layers, such as data encryption.

Security Threats

The main security issue with wireless networks, especially radio networks, is that they intentionally propagate data over an area that may exceed the limits of the area the organization physically controls. For instance, radio waves easily penetrate building walls and are receivable from the facility's parking lot and possibly a few blocks away. Someone can passively retrieve your company's sensitive information by using the same wireless NIC from this distance without being noticed by network security personnel (see Figure 1.5). This requires, though, that the intruder obtain the network access code necessary to join the network.

This problem also exists with wired ethernet networks, but to a lesser degree. Current flow through the wires emits electromagnetic waves that someone could receive by using sensitive listening equipment. The person must be much closer to the cable, though, to receive the signal.

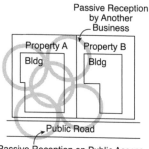

FIGURE 1.5

The passive reception of wireless network data is much easier than with wired networks.

Another security problem is the potential for electronic sabotage, in which someone maliciously jams the radio-based network and keeps you from using the network. Remember, most wireless networks utilize a carrier sense protocol to share the use of the common medium. If one station is transmitting, all others must wait. Someone can easily jam your network by using a wireless product of the same manufacturer that you have within your network and setting up a station to resend packets continually. These transmissions block all stations in that area from transmitting, thereby making the network inoperable. In such cases, the company stands to incur a loss.

Security Safeguards

Wireless network vendors solve most security problems by restricting access to the data. Most products require you to establish a network access code and set the code within each workstation. A wireless station will not process the data unless its code is set to the same number as the network. Some vendors also offer encryption as an option (see Figure 1.6).

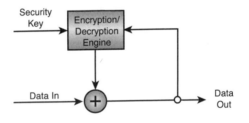

FIGURE 1.6

A data encryption process improves the security of wireless networks.

Application Connectivity Problems

The use of traditional wire-based protocols over wireless networks introduces problems with maintaining connections between the user's appliance and the application residing on a server. TCP/IP, for example, provides very reliable connections over wired networks such as ethernet and token ring. Over wireless networks, however, TCP/IP is susceptible to losing connections, especially when the appliance is operating in an area with marginal wireless network coverage.

A solution to this problem is to use wireless middleware software, which provides intermediate communications between the end user devices and the application software located on a host or server. The middleware enables highly efficient and reliable communications over the wireless network, while maintaining appropriate connections to application software and databases on the server/host via the more reliable wired LAN.

The mobile nature of wireless networks can offer addressing problems as well. Most networks require the IP address loaded in the user's appliance to be within a specific address range to maintain proper connections with applications. When a user roams from one IP subnet to another with a wireless appliance, the appliance and the application may lose the capability to connect with each other. As a result, implementers should consider the use of MobileIP as a means of maintaining connectivity while traversing different IP domains.

Installation Issues

With wired networks, planning the installation of cabling is fairly straightforward. You can survey the site and look for routes where installers can run the cable. You can measure the distances and quickly determine whether cable runs are possible. If some users are too far away from the network, you can design a remote networking solution or extend the length of the cable by using repeaters. Once the design is complete, installers can run the cables, and the cable plant will most likely support the transmission of data as planned.

A radio-based wireless LAN installation is not as predictable. It is difficult if not impossible to design the wireless system by merely inspecting the facility. Predicting the way in which the contour of the building will affect the propagation of radio waves is difficult. Omnidirectional antennas propagate radio waves in all directions if nothing gets in the way. Walls, ceilings, and other obstacles attenuate the signals more in one direction than the other and even cause some waves to change their paths of transmission. Even the opening of a bathroom door can change the propagation pattern. These events cause the actual radiation pattern to distort, taking on a jagged appearance, as shown in Figure 1.7.

Wireless metropolitan area networks (MANs) also are difficult to plan. What looks like a clear line-of-site path between two buildings separated by 1,500 feet might be cluttered with other radio transmitting devices.

To avoid installation problems, an organization should perform propagation tests to assess the coverage of the network. Neglecting to do so may leave some users outside of the propagation area of wireless servers and access points. Propagation tests give you the information necessary to plan wired connections between access points, allowing coverage over applicable areas.

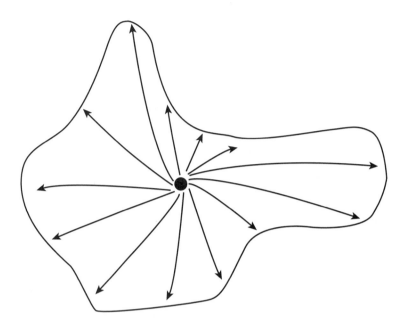

FIGURE 1.7

The resulting radiation pattern of an omnidirectional antenna within an office building is irregular and unpredictable.

Health Risks

Another common concern is whether wireless networks pose any form of health risk. So far, there has been no conclusive answer. Radio-based networks, however, appear to be just as safe or safer than cellular phones. There is little or no risk in using cellular phones, which operate in frequency bands immediately below wireless networks. Wireless network components should be even safer than cellular phones because they operate at lower power levels, typically between 50 and 100 milliwatts, compared to the 600 milliwatts to 3 watt range of cellular phones. In addition, wireless network components usually transmit for shorter periods of time.

Laser-based products, found in both wireless LANs and MANs, offer very little or no health risk. In the U.S., the Center for Devices and Radiological Health (CDRH), a department of the U.S. Food and Drug Administration, evaluates and certifies laser products for public use. The CDRH categorizes lasers into four classes, depending on the amount of harm they can cause to humans.

Supermarket scanners and most diffused infrared wireless LANs satisfy Class I requirements, under which there is no hazard under any circumstance. Class IV specifies devices such as laser scalpels that can cause grave danger if the operator handles them improperly. Most long-range, laser-based wireless networks are rated as Class III devices, whereby someone could

INTRODUCTION
TO WIRELESS
NETWORKS

damage his eyes by looking directly at the laser beam. Thus, care should be taken when orienting lasers between buildings.

Wireless LANs: A Historical Perspective

Network technologies and radio communications were brought together for the first time in 1971 at the University of Hawaii as a research project called ALOHANET. The ALOHANET system enabled computer sites at seven campuses spread out over four islands to communicate with the central computer on Oahu without using the existing unreliable and expensive phone lines. ALOHANET offered bidirectional communications in a star topology between the central computer and each of the remote stations. The remote stations had to communicate with each other via the centralized computer.

In the 1980s, amateur radio hobbyists, *hams,* kept radio networking alive within the U.S. and Canada by designing and building *terminal node controllers (TNCs)* to interface their computers through ham radio equipment (see Figure 1.8). A TNC acts much like a telephone modem, converting the computer's digital signal into one that a ham radio can modulate and send over the airwaves by using a packet switching technique. In fact, the American Radio Relay League (ARRL) and the Canadian Radio Relay League (CRRL) have been sponsoring the Computer Networking Conference since the early 1980s to provide a forum for the development of wireless WANs. Thus, hams have been using wireless networking for years, much earlier than the commercial market.

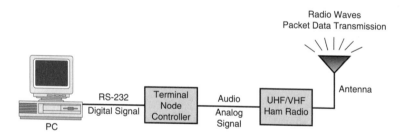

FIGURE 1.8

Terminal node controllers enable a PC to interface with a ham radio to form a packet radio network.

In 1985, the Federal Communications Commission (FCC) made the commercial development of radio-based LAN components possible by authorizing the public use of the Industrial, Scientific, and Medical (ISM) bands. These frequencies reside between 902MHz and 5.85GHz, just above the cellular phone operating frequencies. The ISM band is very attractive to wireless network vendors because it provides a part of the spectrum upon which to base their products, and end users do not have to obtain FCC licenses to operate the products. The ISM band allocation has had a dramatic effect on the wireless industry, prompting the development of wireless LAN components. Without a standard, though, vendors began developing proprietary radios and access points.

In the late 1980s the Institute for Electrical and Electronic Engineers (IEEE) 802 Working Group, responsible for the development of LAN standards such as ethernet and token ring, began development of standards for wireless LANs. Under the chairmanship of Vic Hayes from NCR, the IEEE 802.11 Working Group developed the Wireless LAN Medium Access Control and Physical Layer specifications. Before the ratification of the standard, companies began shipping proprietary wireless LAN radio cards and access points operating in the 902MHz ISM band. These products were initially relatively expensive, at US$1,400 per radio card. As a result, wireless LANs at that time were feasible only for satisfying network requirements when mobility provided tremendous gains in efficiency and resulting cost savings.

The IEEE Standards Board approved the standard on June 26, 1997, and the IEEE published the standard on November 18, 1997. The finalization of this standard prompted vendors to release 1Mbps and 2Mbps 802.11-compliant radio cards and access points throughout 1998. In December 1999, the IEEE released supplements (802.11a and 802.11b) to the 802.11 standard in order to increase performance of wireless LANs up to 54Mbps. Vendors began shipping wireless LANs operating at 11Mbps throughout 2000 (at prices of less than $200 per radio card) and at 22Mbps starting in 2001. The 54Mbps wireless LANs (IEEE 802.11a–compliant) will be available toward the end of 2001, slightly ahead of HiperLAN/2 systems (802.11's competitor).

Because of falling prices and increasing performance, wireless LANs today are taking on a much larger role in horizontal enterprise applications. The price and performance of wireless LANs are getting much closer to traditional wired, ethernet networks. Prices for wireless LAN radio cards are expected to decrease by at least 50% during 2001. It's very likely that the average price for wireless LAN radio cards will match the price of equivalent (performance and form factor) ethernet cards as we enter 2002. As a result, an information system manager is now in a position to give serious consideration to IEEE 802.11 wireless LANs for supporting high-speed network connections to PC and laptop users within his facilities.

Wireless Network Configurations

IN THIS CHAPTER

Wireless LAN Architecture

Most wireless LANs operate over unlicensed frequencies at near-ethernet speeds using carrier sense protocols to share a radio wave or infrared light medium. The majority of these devices are capable of transmitting information up to 1,000 feet between computers within an open environment, and their cost per user ranges from $100 to $500. In addition, most wireless LAN products offer Simple Network Management Protocol (SNMP) to support network management through the use of SNMP-based management platforms and applications. Figure 2.1 illustrates the concept of a wireless local area network interfacing with a wired network.

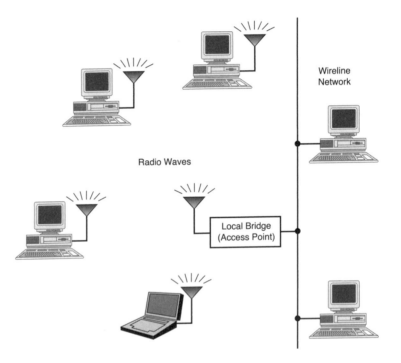

FIGURE 2.1

A wireless local area network provides connectivity over the airwaves within a local area, such as a building.

Wireless networks perform functions similar to their wired ethernet and token-ring counterparts. In general, networks perform the following functions to enable the transfer of information from source to destination:

1. The medium provides a bit pipe (a path for data to flow) for the transmission of data.
2. Medium access techniques facilitate the sharing of a common medium.

3. Synchronization and error control mechanisms ensure that each link transfers the data intact.

4. Routing mechanisms move the data from the originating source to the intended destination.

5. Connectivity software interfaces an appliance, such as a pen-based computer or bar code scanner, to application software hosted on a server.

Figure 2.2 illustrates the logical architecture of a wireless LAN.

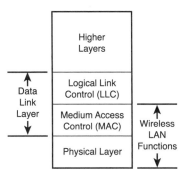

FIGURE 2.2

A wireless local area network provides functions related to the Medium Access Control (MAC) and Physical layers of a network's architecture.

Medium Access Control (MAC) Sublayer

Medium access control, which is a Data Link layer function in a radio-based wireless LAN, enables multiple appliances to share a common transmission medium via a carrier sense protocol similar to ethernet. This protocol enables a group of wireless computers to share the same frequency and space. A wireless LAN MAC provides reliable delivery of data over somewhat error-prone wireless media.

As an analogy, consider a room of people engaged in a single conversation in which each person can hear if someone speaks. This represents a fully connected bus topology where everyone communicates using the same frequency and space. To avoid having two people speak at the same time, you should wait until the other person has finished talking. Also, no one should speak unless the room is silent. This simple protocol ensures that only one person speaks at a time, offering a shared use of the communications medium. Wireless systems operate in a similar fashion, except the communications are by way of radio signals. Figure 2.3 illustrates the generic carrier sense protocol, commonly known as *Carrier Sense Multiple Access (CSMA)*.

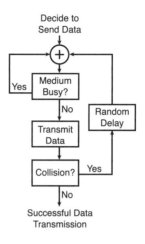

FIGURE 2.3

The operation of the carrier sense protocol works very similarly to a business meeting: You take turns talking when the room is quiet.

Wireless networks handle error control by having each station check incoming data for altered bits. If the destination station does not detect errors, it sends an acknowledgment back to the source station. If the station detects errors, the data link protocol ensures that the source station resends the packet. To continue the analogy, consider two people talking to each other outside. If one person is speaking and a disruption occurs, such as a plane flying overhead, the dialog might become distorted. As a result, the listener asks the speaker to repeat a phrase or two.

Because of propagation delays, it is possible for two wireless stations to sense that the medium is not busy, and both begin transmitting. This is similar to two people starting to talk at the same time. In that case, each person will generally stop talking, wait, then start talking again with hopes of avoiding another collision. Wireless LANs follow a similar process for mediating transmission collisions.

Physical Layer

The Physical layer provides for the transmission of bits through a communication channel by defining electrical, mechanical, and procedural specifications.

Modulation, which is a Physical layer function, is a process in which the radio transceiver prepares the digital signal within the network interface card (NIC) for transmission over the airwaves. *Spread spectrum* "spreads" a signal's power over a wider band of frequencies (see Figure 2.4), sacrificing bandwidth in order to gain signal-to-noise performance (referred to as *process gain*). This contradicts the desire to conserve frequency bandwidth, but the spreading process makes the data signal much less susceptible to electrical noise than conventional radio modulation techniques. Other transmission and electrical noise, typically narrow in bandwidth, will interfere with only a small portion of the spread spectrum signal, resulting in much less interference and fewer errors when the receiver demodulates the signal.

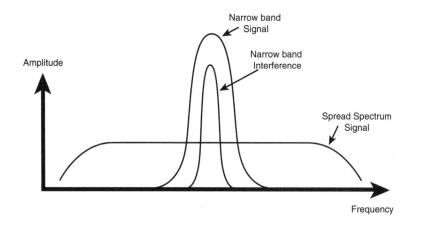

FIGURE 2.4
Because spread spectrum spreads the signal over a wider frequency range, common narrowband interference affects less of the spread spectrum signal than the narrowband signal.

Spread spectrum modulators commonly use one of two methods to spread the signal over a wider area: frequency hopping or direct sequence.

Frequency Hopping Spread Spectrum Radio

Frequency hopping works very much as its name implies. It modulates the data signal with a carrier signal that hops from frequency to frequency as a function of time over a wide band of frequencies (see Figure 2.5). An IEEE 802.11 frequency-hopping radio, for example, will hop the carrier frequency over the 2.4GHz frequency band between 2.4GHz and 2.483GHz.

The Advent of Frequency Hopping Spread Spectrum

Hedy Lamarr, who was a well-known film actress during the 1940s, conceived the idea of frequency hopping spread spectrum during the early part of the Second World War to keep the Germans from jamming the radios that guided U.S. torpedoes against German warships. (Lamarr was desperate to find a way she could help win the war against Germany. She was strongly opposed to the Nazis; in fact, she left her first husband for selling munitions to Hitler.)

Lamarr's idea was to transmit communications signals by randomly hopping from frequency to frequency to prevent the enemy from knowing what radio signal frequency to send for jamming purposes. It's amazing that she had no technical education but still thought of this very important communications concept.

Lamarr and film score composer George Antheil, who had extensive experience in synchronizing the sounds of music scores with motion pictures, set out to perfect the idea. One problem was how the torpedo's receiver was to know the frequency to listen to at specific times, because the idea was to send a random sequence of frequencies. Antheil was able to devise methods to keep a frequency-hopping receiver synchronized with the transmitter. His idea was to send signals to the torpedo using a long pattern of different frequencies that would appear to be random. The receiver, knowing the secret hopping pattern, would be able to tune to the correct frequency at the right time. This pseudo-random hopping sequence is what the frequency hopping version of 802.11 uses today.

Lamarr and Antheil sent details of their invention to the National Inventors Council. Charles Kettering, the director of the council, encouraged them to patent the idea. They filed the patent in 1941. Lamarr and Antheil then teamed with electrical engineers from MIT to provide the technical design. On August 11, 1942, Lamarr and Antheil received U.S. Patent Number 2,292,387 for their idea.

Because of the newness of the technology and clumsy mechanical nature of the initial design, spread spectrum was never used during World War II. The initial prototype used many moving parts to control the frequency of transmission and reception.

In the 1950s, Sylvania began experimenting with frequency hopping, using newly developed digital components in place of the initial mechanical system. By then, Lamarr and Antheil's patent had expired. Sylvania, under contract with the U.S. Navy, utilized spread spectrum for the first time on ships sent to blockade Cuba in 1962. In the mid-1980s, the U.S. military declassified spread spectrum technology, and commercial companies began to exploit it for consumer electronics. Of course, today the technology is a key modulation technique that the IEEE 802.11 standard specifies.

Lamarr and Antheil conceived an excellent modulation technique; however, they never received any compensation for their idea. Their main interest, expressed in a high degree of patriotism, was to help win the war against the Nazis. In March 1997, Lamarr and Antheil were honored with the Electronic Frontier Foundation's Pioneer Award at its San Francisco convention, the Computers, Freedom, and Privacy Conference.

A hopping code determines the frequencies the radio will transmit and in which order. To receive the signal properly, the receiver must be set to the same hopping code and listen to the incoming signal at the right time and correct frequency. FCC regulations require manufacturers to use 75 or more frequencies per transmission channel with a maximum *dwell time* (the time spent at a particular frequency during any single hop) of 400ms. If the radio encounters interference on one frequency, it will retransmit the signal on a subsequent hop on another frequency.

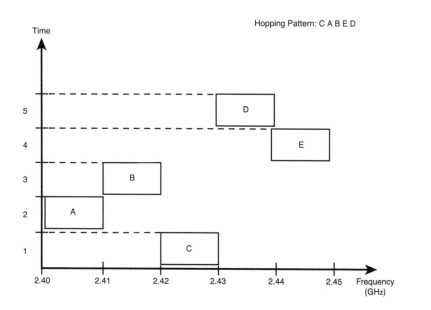

FIGURE 2.5

With frequency hopping spread spectrum, the carrier frequency changes periodically.

The frequency hopping technique reduces interference because an interfering signal from a narrowband system will affect the spread spectrum signal only if both are transmitting at the same frequency at the same time. Thus, the aggregate interference will be very low, resulting in few or no bit errors.

It is possible to have operating radios use spread spectrum within the same frequency band and not interfere, assuming they each use a different hopping pattern. While one radio is transmitting at one particular frequency, the other radio is using a different frequency. A set of hopping codes that never uses the same frequencies at the same time is considered *orthogonal*. The FCC's requirement for the number of different transmission frequencies allows frequency-hopping radios to have many non-interfering channels.

Direct Sequence Spread Spectrum Radio

Direct sequence spread spectrum combines a data signal at the sending station with a higher data rate bit sequence, which many refer to as a *chipping code* (also known as a *processing gain*). A high processing gain increases the signal's resistance to interference. The minimum linear processing gain that the FCC allows is 10, and most commercial products operate under 20. The IEEE 802.11 Working Group has set its minimum processing gain requirement at 11 chips.

> **NOTE**
>
> The first commercial use of direct sequence spread spectrum was developed by Equitorial Communications in 1980 for multiple access communications over synchronous satellite transponders.

Figure 2.6 shows an example of the operation of direct sequence spread spectrum. A chipping code is assigned to represent 1 and 0 data bits. As the data stream is transmitted, the corresponding code is actually sent. For example, the transmission of a data bit equal to 1 would result in the sequence 00010011100 being sent.

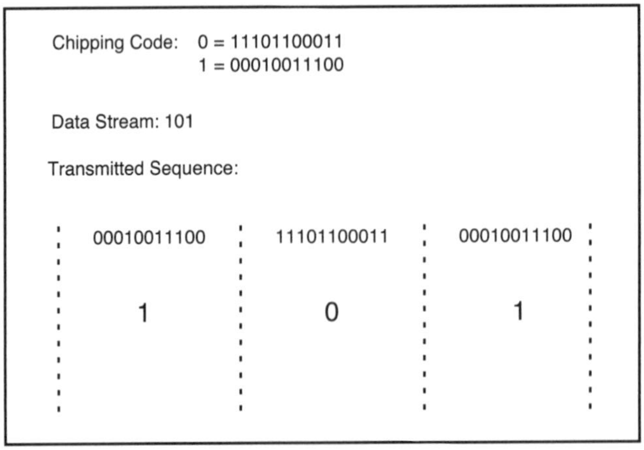

```
Chipping Code:   0 = 11101100011
                 1 = 00010011100

Data Stream: 101

Transmitted Sequence:


    00010011100   :   11101100011   :   00010011100


         1        :        0        :        1
```

FIGURE 2.6
Direct sequence spread spectrum sends a specific string of bits for each data bit sent.

In most cases, frequency hopping is the most cost-effective type of wireless LAN to deploy if the need for network bandwidth is 2Mbps or less. Direct sequence, having higher potential data rates, would be best for bandwidth-intensive applications.

ISM Radio Frequency Bands

In 1985, in an attempt to stimulate the production and use of wireless network products, the FCC modified Part 15 of the radio spectrum regulation, which governs unlicensed devices. The modification authorized wireless network products to operate in the industrial, scientific, and medical (ISM) bands. The ISM frequencies are shown in Figure 2.7.

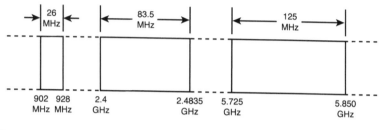

FIGURE 2.7

The industrial, scientific, and medical (ISM) frequency bands offer greater bandwidth at higher frequencies.

The FCC allows a user to operate a wireless product without obtaining an FCC license if the product meets certain requirements, such as operating under 1 watt of transmitter output power. This deregulation of the frequency spectrum eliminates the need for user organizations to perform costly and time-consuming frequency planning to coordinate radio installations that will avoid interference with existing radio systems. This is even more advantageous if you plan to move your equipment frequently, because you can avoid the paperwork involved in licensing the product again at the new location. As you can see, more bandwidth is available within the higher frequency bands, which will support higher data rates.

Implementing ISM Bands

All commercial companies can deploy wireless networks that operate within the ISM bands; however, be sure to coordinate the use of ISM frequencies with the company's frequency manager if one exists. This is especially important with hospitals, where medical instruments may be using ISM frequencies as well. This coordination will significantly reduce the possibility of interference.

Also be aware that the U.S. military manages frequencies by special non-FCC organizations. If you plan to operate a wireless network on a military base, you must first contact the base frequency manager and obtain a special operating license. If the radio LAN frequencies might interfere with radio equipment used on base, you probably will not be granted a license.

Many wireless LANs initially deployed in the United States operated at 902MHz, but this frequency is not available throughout the world. The 2.4GHz band is the only unlicensed band available worldwide. This band was approved in North and South America in the mid-1980s and was accepted in Europe and Asia in 1995. Companies first began developing products in the 902MHz band because manufacturing costs in that band were cheaper. The lack of availability of this band in some areas and the need for greater bandwidth, however, drove these companies to migrate many of their products to the 2.4GHz band. In addition, more and more wireless LAN manufacturers are now moving their products to the 5GHz band to take advantage of larger amounts of bandwidth and less potential interference with the vast number of devices operating in the 2.4GHz frequencies.

TIP

When operating radio-based wireless LAN devices, always follow these safety tips:

- Avoid touching the antenna when transmitting.
- Do not operate the transmitter near areas where unshielded blasting caps reside.
- Ensure that the antenna or a dummy load is connected to the radio before transmitting. Radio waves will reflect back into the radio if no load is connected, which could result in damaging the radio.

Narrowband Radio Modulation

Conventional radio systems, such as television and AM/FM radio, use *narrowband modulation*. These systems concentrate all their transmit power within a narrow range of frequencies, making efficient use of the radio spectrum in terms of frequency space. The idea behind most communications design is to conserve as much bandwidth as possible; therefore, most transmitted signals use a relatively narrow slice of the radio frequency spectrum.

Other systems using the same transmit frequency, however, will cause a great deal of interference because the noise source will corrupt most of the signal. To avoid interference, the FCC generally requires a user of a narrowband system to obtain an FCC license to coordinate the operation of radios properly. Narrowband products can have a strong advantage because the user can be fairly sure of operating without interference. If interference does occur, the FCC will generally resolve the matter. This makes narrowband modulation good for longer links traversing cities, where significant interference may result. The disadvantage is that the licensing process can take two or three months to complete. You must complete an application, usually with the help of a frequency consultant, and submit it to the FCC for approval. Thus, you can't be in a hurry to establish the wireless links. Plus, you will probably have to coordinate with the FCC when making changes to the wireless point-to-point network topology.

Infrared Light–Based Wireless LANs

Infrared light is an alternative to using radio waves for wireless LAN connectivity. The wavelength of infrared light is longer (lower in frequency) than the spectral colors, but much shorter (higher in frequency) than radio waves. Under most lighting conditions, infrared light is invisible to the naked eye. Infrared light LAN products operate around the 820 nanometer wavelength because air offers the least attenuation at that point in the infrared spectrum.

> **NOTE**
>
> Sir William Herschel discovered infrared light in 1800 when he separated sunlight into its component colors with a prism. He found that most of the heat in the beam fell in the spectral region where no visible light existed, just beyond the red.

In comparison to radio waves, infrared light offers higher degrees of security and performance. These LANs are more secure because infrared light does not propagate through opaque objects, such as walls, keeping the data signals contained within a room or building. Also, common noise sources such as microwave ovens and radio transmitters will not interfere with the light signal. In terms of performance, infrared light has a great deal of bandwidth, making it possible to operate at very high data rates. However, infrared light is not as suitable as radio waves for mobile applications because of its limited coverage.

You've probably been using a diffused infrared device for years—the television remote control, which enables you to operate your TV from a distance without the use of wires. When you press a button on the remote, a corresponding code modulates an infrared light signal that is transmitted to the TV. The TV receives the code and performs the applicable function. This is fairly simple, but infrared-based LANs are not much more complex. The main difference is that LANs use infrared light at slightly higher power levels and use communications protocols to transport data.

When using infrared light in a LAN, the ceiling can be a reflection point (see Figure 2.8). This technique uses carrier sense protocols to share access to the ceiling. Imagine, for example, that there is a room containing four people who can communicate only via flashlights. To send information, they can encode letters that spell words using a system such as Morse code. If someone wants to send information, he first looks at the ceiling to see if someone is currently transmitting (shining light onto the ceiling). If there is a transmission taking place, the person wanting to send the information waits until the other person stops sending the message. If no one is transmitting, the source person will point his flashlight at the ceiling and turn the light on and off, according to the code that represents the information being sent.

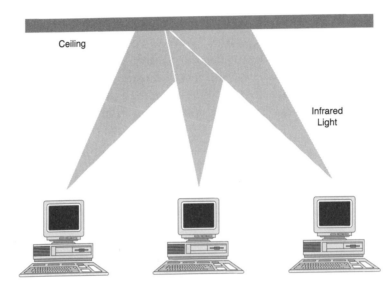

FIGURE 2.8

A diffused infrared-based wireless LAN system uses the ceiling as a reflection point.

To alert the destination person of an incoming message, the sender transmits the proper sequence of code words that represents the destination person's name. All people in the room will be constantly looking at the ceiling, waiting for light signals containing their addresses. If a person sees his name, he will pay attention to the rest of the transmission. Through this method, each person will be able to send and receive information.

> **NOTE**
>
> Because of geometry, diffused infrared light stations are limited in separation distance, typically 30 to 50 feet. The lower the ceiling, the smaller the range between stations. A ceiling height of 10 feet will limit the range to around 40 feet. To extend the operating range, you can use infrared access points to connect cells together via a wired backbone.
>
> Because they depend on ceilings and walls, diffused infrared LANs will not operate outdoors.

Carrier Current LANs

A quasi-wireless LAN technique, called *carrier currents*, is the use of power lines as a medium for the transport of data. Even though this type of LAN is not really wireless, it's worth mentioning because it doesn't require the installation of network cabling. In the next year or so, you should begin seeing products that implement this approach. This technique is very similar to using an analog modem to communicate over telephone wires. Designers of the telephone system did not plan to accommodate computer communications, but people use modems every day to communicate their data. The telephone system is capable of supporting analog signals with the range of 0KHz to 4KHz. A telephone modem converts the computer's digital waveform to an analog signal within this range and transmits to the computer you choose. The modem at the distant end receives the "telephone signal" and converts the data back into a digital signal that is understood by the computer.

Power line circuits within your home and office provide enough bandwidth to support 1Mbps to 2Mbps data signals. Utility companies and others designed these circuits to carry 60Hz alternating current, typically at 110 volts. It is possible, then, to have a *power line* modem that interfaces a computer to the power circuitry (see Figure 2.9). The interface acts much like a telephone modem and converts the digital data within your computer to an analog signal for transmission through the electrical wires.

The 110 volt alternating current in the circuit does not affect the signal (or vice versa) because the signals are at different frequencies. The interface has filters that will block the lower 60Hz frequency from being received.

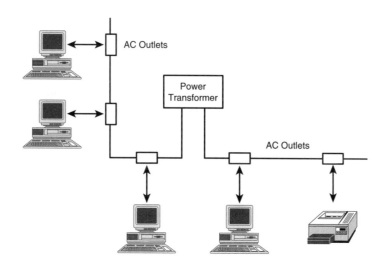

FIGURE 2.9

A carrier current LAN system provides network connectivity via the electrical wires.

> **NOTE**
>
> Several vendors have had home automation products on the market for decades that use carrier current signals. Radio Shack, for example, sells a master console that enables you to control various types of devices, such as coffee pots, lamps, heating systems, and so on, via carrier currents sent through the electrical power lines in the home. The master console and the appliances interface to the system via inexpensive modules that plug into a wall outlet and communicate to the master console.

The advantages of this technique are ease of installation and low-cost products. A disadvantage of the power line approach is that the presence of electrical transformers, designed to electrically couple signals at 60Hz, will block higher frequency data signals. Most homes and smaller facilities will not have this problem because usually only one side of the transformer is available; however, larger buildings, especially industrial centers, will have multiple electrical wire legs connected by transformers. The presence of transformers, therefore, will limit connectivity among sites.

Wireless LAN Components and Systems

The major components of a wireless LAN are a wireless NIC and a wireless local bridge, which is often referred to as an *access point*. The wireless NIC interfaces the appliance with the wireless network, and the access point interfaces the wireless network with a wired network. Most wireless NICs interface appliances to the wireless network by implementing a carrier sense access protocol and modulating the data signal with a spreading sequence.

End-User Appliances

As with any system, there needs to be a way for users to interface with applications and services. Whether the network is wireless or wired, an *end-user appliance* is an interface between the user and the network. Following are the classes of end-user appliances that are most effective for wireless networks:

- Desktop workstations
- Laptop computers
- Palmtop computers
- Handheld PCs
- Pen-based computers
- Personal digital assistants (PDAs)

- Handheld scanners and data collectors
- Handheld printers

> **NOTE**
>
> When evaluating appliances for use with a mobile application, be sure to consider the ergonomics of the unit. You certainly won't be able to realize any of the benefits of a wireless network if users don't use the system because of appliances that weigh too much or are difficult to use.

Network Software

A wireless network consists of software that resides on different parts of the network. A network operating system (NOS) such as Microsoft NT Server, hosted on a high-end PC, provides file, print, and application services. Many NOSs are server oriented, as shown in Figure 2.10, where the core application software and databases reside. In most cases, the appliances will interface via TCP/IP with application software or a database running on the NOS.

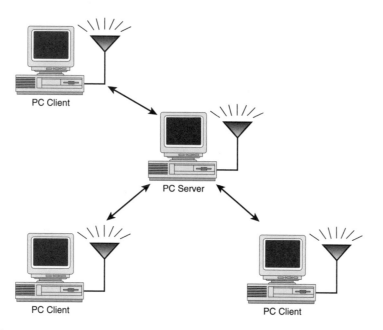

FIGURE 2.10

The server-based network operating system provides a centralized platform for applications and data storage for mobile users.

Client software, located on the end-user's appliance, directs the user's commands to the local appliance software or steers them out through the wireless network. The software residing on a wireless appliance is very similar to software that runs on a wired appliance. The main difference is that it is important to develop the wireless software to optimize the use of the wireless network's relatively small amount of bandwidth.

The software performing application functions can run on a server/host, the appliance, or a combination of both. In some cases, such as with applications running on an IBM mainframe, IBM AS/400, or a UNIX-based host, the wireless appliances may need to run terminal emulation. This makes the appliance act as a dumb terminal, simply interfacing the keyboard, screen, printer, and so on with the application running on the host. With client/server systems, the software on the appliance may perform part or all of the application's functionality and merely interface with a database located on a server, such as Microsoft NT Server.

> **NOTE**
>
> A wireless network appears to be transparent to application software and operating systems on the network. As a result, applications written for a wired network generally can run without changes over a wireless network.

In some cases, a gateway running middleware is necessary to provide an interface between the appliance and the application software running on the server. The appliances communicate with the host/server through the gateway. The gateway acts as a proxy for the various appliances. The advantages of using the gateway are as follows:

- **Better RF Throughput**   With the presence of a transport and application gateway, the appliances communicate with the gateway by using a lightweight protocol that is wireless friendly, unlike TCP/IP.

- **Reliability**   Since the gateway proxies all the appliances, any outages in communication due to the appliances roaming out of range are transparent to the host/server.

- **Longer Battery Life**   When the appliances are idle, the network software does not have to send out keep-alive packets periodically to keep the connection to the host/server open. This will be done by the gateway.

Wireless Network Interface Card

Computers process information in digital form, with low direct current (DC) voltages representing data ones and zeros. These signals are optimum for transmission within the computer, not for transporting data through wired or wireless media. A wireless network interface couples the digital signal from the end-user appliance to the wireless medium, which is air, to enable an efficient transfer of data between sender and receiver. This process includes the modulation and amplification of the digital signal to a form acceptable for propagation to the receiving location.

> **NOTE**
>
> *Modulation* is the process of translating the baseband digital signal used in the appliance to an analog form suitable for transmission through the air. This process is very similar to the common telephone modem, which converts a computer's digital data into an analog form within the 4KHz limitation of the telephone circuit. The wireless modulator translates the digital signal to a frequency that propagates well through the atmosphere. Of course, wireless networks employ modulation by using radio waves and infrared light.

The wireless network interface generally takes the shape of a wireless NIC or an external modem that facilitates the modulator and communications protocols. These components interface with the user appliance via a computer bus, such as ISA (Industry Standard Architecture) or PCMCIA (Personal Computer Memory Card International Association). The ISA bus comes standard in most desktop PCs. Many portable computers have PCMCIA slots that accept credit card–size NICs. PCMCIA specifies three interface sizes: Type I (3.3 millimeters), Type II (5.0 millimeters), and Type III (10.5 millimeters). Some companies also produce wireless components that connect to the computer via the RS-232 serial port and parallel port.

The interface between the user's appliance and NIC also includes a software driver that couples the client's application or NOS software to the card. The following driver standards are common:

- **NDIS (Network Driver Interface Specification)**   A driver used with Microsoft network operating systems.

- **ODI (Open Datalink Interface)**   A driver used with Novell network operating systems.

- **PDS (Packet Driver Specification)**   A generic DOS-based driver developed by FTP Software, Inc., for use with TCP/IP-based implementations.

> **NOTE**
>
> Be sure to investigate the existence of suitable drivers (NDIS, ODI, PACKET) for the wireless NIC and operating system, and fully test its functionality with your chosen appliance before making a large investment in wireless network hardware.

The most widely sold wireless LAN NICs today use radio waves as a medium between computers and peripherals. An advantage of radio waves over other forms of wireless connectivity is that they can interconnect users without line of sight and propagate through walls and other obstructions with fairly little attenuation, depending on the type of wall construction. Even though several walls might separate the user from the server or wireless bridge, users can maintain connections to the network. This supports true mobility. With radio-LAN products, a user with a portable computer can move freely through the facility while accessing data from a server or running an application.

A disadvantage of using radio waves, however, is that an organization must manage them along with other electromagnetic propagation. Medical equipment and industrial components may use the same radio frequencies as wireless LANs, which could cause interference. An organization must determine whether potential interference is present before installing a radio-based LAN. Because radio waves penetrate walls, security might also be a problem. Unauthorized people from outside the controlled areas could receive sensitive information; however, vendors often scramble the data signal to protect the information from being understood by inappropriate people. Refer to the section "Wireless LAN Implications," in Chapter 1, "Introduction to Wireless Networks," for more details on issues related to wireless LANs.

Wireless Local Bridges

Network bridges are an important part of any network: They connect multiple LANs at the MAC layer to produce a single logical network. The MAC layer, which provides medium access functions, is part of IEEE's architecture describing LANs. The functionality of the MAC Layer, along with the Logical Link Control (LLC), fits within the Data Link layer of ISO's OSI Reference Model. Chapter 3, "Overview of the IEEE 802.11 Standard," describes how the LLC works. Bridges interface LANs together, such as ethernet to ethernet or ethernet to token ring, and also provide a filtering of packets based on their MAC layer address. This enables an organization to create segments within an enterprise network.

If a networked station sends a packet to another station located on the same segment, the bridge will not forward the packet to other segments or the enterprise backbone. If the packet's destination is on a different segment, however, the bridge will allow the packet to pass through to the destination segment. Thus, bridges ensure that packets do not wander into parts of the network where they are not needed. This process, known as *segmentation*, makes better use of network bandwidth and increases overall performance.

There are two types of bridges:

- **Local bridges**   These connect LANs within close proximity.
- **Remote bridges**   These connect sites that are separated by distances greater than the LAN protocols can support.

Figure 2.11 illustrates the differences between local and remote network bridges. Traditionally, organizations have used leased digital circuits, such as T1 and 56Kbps, to facilitate the connections between a pair of remote bridges.

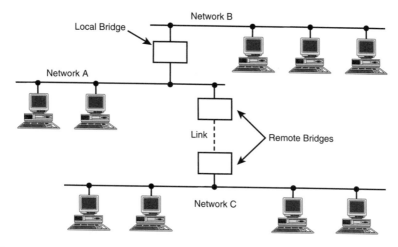

FIGURE 2.11

Local bridges connect LANs within a local area, whereas remote bridges connect LANs over a wider area.

Most companies that develop wireless LAN NICs also sell a wireless local bridge referred to as an *access point* that makes available connections to wired network-based servers and enables multiple wireless cell configurations. The filtering process of a local bridge (whether it is a wireless or wired type) is critical in maintaining a network configuration that minimizes unnecessary data traffic. When the bridge receives a packet, it creates a record containing the MAC address (which differentiates the bridge from other network devices) and the physical port it receives the frame on in a dynamic table. Wireless bridges, however, will forward all broadcast frames.

Antenna

The antenna radiates the modulated signal through the air so that the destination can receive it. Antennas come in many shapes and sizes and have the following specific electrical characteristics:

- Propagation pattern
- Gain
- Transmit power
- Bandwidth

The *propagation pattern* of an antenna defines its coverage. A truly omnidirectional antenna transmits its power in all directions, whereas a directional antenna concentrates most of its power in one direction. Figure 2.12 illustrates the differences.

A directional antenna has more gain (degree of amplification) than the omnidirectional type and is capable of propagating the modulated signal farther because it focuses the power in a single direction. The amount of gain depends on the directivity of the antenna. An omnidirectional antenna has a gain equal to one; that is, it doesn't focus the power in any particular direction. Omnidirectional antennas are best for indoor wireless networks because of relatively shorter-range requirements and less susceptibility to outward interference.

Directional antennas will best satisfy a need for interconnecting buildings within metropolitan areas because of greater range and the desire to minimize interference with other systems.

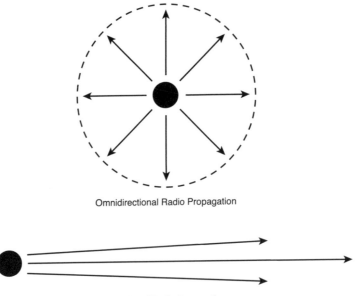

Omnidirectional Radio Propagation

Directional Radio Propagation

FIGURE 2.12

An omnidirectional antenna broadcasts radio waves in all directions, whereas a directional antenna focuses the power in a particular direction.

The combination of transmit power and gain of an antenna defines the distance the signal will propagate. Long-distance transmissions require higher power and directive radiation patterns, whereas shorter-distance transmissions can get by with less power and gain. With wireless networks, the transmission power is relatively low, typically one watt or less.

> **NOTE**
>
> Consider the following types of antennas when developing wireless LAN products:
>
> - **Snap-on antenna** Connects directly to the radio card and provides relatively low gain via an omnidirectional radio propagation pattern. This relatively small antenna is better for highly mobile applications when a larger antenna is impractical.
> - **Dipole antenna** Sits on a desk or table and connects to the radio card via a short antenna cable. This approach provides relatively low gain. This antenna is best for portable applications.
> - **High-gain antenna** Attaches to a wall or antenna pole/tower and connects to the radio card or access point via a relatively long antenna cable. This approach provides relatively high gain and is best for access points and permanent stations.

Bandwidth is the effective part of the frequency spectrum that the signal propagates. For example, the telephone system operates in a bandwidth roughly from 0KHz to 4KHz. This is enough bandwidth to accommodate most of the frequency components within our voices. Radio wave systems have more bandwidths located at much higher frequencies. Data rates and bandwidth are directly proportional: The higher the data rate, the more bandwidth you'll need.

> **NOTE**
>
> If you're considering integrating a radio NIC into a particular PCMCIA-based appliance such as a handheld data collector, you may have to redesign the antenna mounting hardware to accommodate the construction of the appliance.

Some companies within the wireless LAN industry are developing what's referred to as a "smart antenna" technology. A smart antenna makes it possible to electronically and automatically concentrate transmitted signal power in directions where end users will be operating the wireless LAN (not in directions that end up bouncing off walls and other obstacles). This technology extends the range of a wireless LAN and reduces the number of access points needed.

The Communications Channel

All information systems employ a communications channel along which information flows from source to destination. Ethernet networks may use twisted-pair or coaxial cable. Wireless networks use air as the medium. At the earth's surface, where most wireless networks operate, pure air contains gases such as nitrogen and oxygen. This atmosphere provides an effective medium for the propagation of radio waves and infrared light.

Rain, fog, and snow increase the amount of water in the air and can cause significant attenuation to the propagation of modulated wireless signals. Smog clutters the air, adding attenuation to the communications channel as well. In addition, leaves on trees will block transmissions in the spring and summer. *Attenuation* is a decrease in the amplitude of the signal, and it limits the operating range of the system. The ways to combat attenuation is to either increase the transmission power of the wireless devices, which in most cases is limited by the FCC, or incorporate special amplifiers called *repeaters* that receive attenuated signals, revamp them, and transmit downline to the end station or next repeater.

Peer-to-Peer Wireless LANs

For small single-floor offices or stores, a peer-to-peer wireless LAN may suffice. Peer-to-peer wireless LANs require wireless NICs only in the devices connected to the network, as shown in Figure 2.13. Access points are not necessary unless users will need connections to wired network-based resources such as servers.

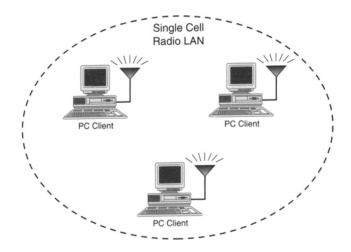

FIGURE 2.13

A single-cell wireless LAN provides connectivity within radio range, and no access point is required unless there is a need to interface with a wired network.

The area covered by stations within a peer-to-peer network is called a *Basic Service Area (BSA)*, which covers approximately 75 to 300 feet between all units in a typical office environment, depending on data rates. A single radio-based wireless LAN segment, such as the BSA, can support 6–25 users and still keep network access delays at an acceptable level. These networks require no administration or preconfiguration.

Case Study 2.1:

Wireless Bar Code System

A manufacturer in North America is a leading provider of bar code printers and supplies. As part of the company's goal to streamline processes within its manufacturing plant and warehouse, a process improvement team applied the use of mobile handheld bar code scanning and printing devices with the support of a wireless LAN within its Central Distribution Center (CDC).

Before implementing the system, the CDC was experiencing inefficiencies because clerks needed to walk back and forth between stacks of finished goods and a desktop terminal used to determine a warehouse storage location for the items. The clerks would collect information from the finished goods by writing it down on a piece of paper, then walk to the terminal to query the company's warehouse management system for a recommended storage location. The clerk would write this location information on a large label, walk back to the product, and affix the label to the product's container. Later, a forklift operator would come by and place the container in the correct location on the warehouse floor. The process of walking back and forth between the products and the terminal made inefficient use of the clerk's time, which slowed the movement of products through the plant.

The solution to this problem consists of Monarch Marking System's DOS-based Pathfinder Ultra RF handheld bar code scanner and printer, equipped with an Aironet (now Cisco) 2.4GHz frequency hopping radio. Only one radio cell was necessary to cover the area used to stage the finished goods. An Aironet 2.4GHz access point was needed, though, to provide an interface for the existing ethernet network, which led to the mainframe computer running the warehouse management system. With this collection of components, the clerk can now scan the finished product's bar code, which is used to query the warehouse management system for a valid put-away location, then print a label indicating the applicable location information.

Through the use of the scan, print, and apply function, the solution eliminates the need to walk back and forth to the terminal, increasing productivity by 50%. In addition, the solution provides significant gains in accuracy through the elimination of human error.

Multiple Cell Wireless LANs

If an organization requires greater range than the limitations of a single cell, you can use a set of access points and a wired network backbone to create a multiple-cell configuration (see Figure 2.14). Such a configuration can cover larger multiple-floor buildings, warehouses, and hospitals. In this environment, a handheld PC or data collector with a wireless NIC can roam within the coverage area while maintaining a live connection to the corporate network.

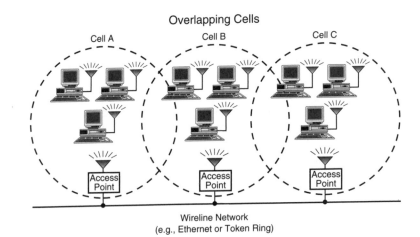

FIGURE 2.14

A multiple-cell wireless LAN provides continuous network connectivity when the area exceeds the range of a single-cell wireless LAN.

Designers can configure multiple cell wireless LANs to satisfy different connectivity requirements. For example, you could configure cells A, B, and C (refer to Figure 2.14) identically to enable users to roam anywhere within range of any access point to maintain seamless connections throughout a facility. If you have various functional groups that you want to keep separate, then you could set up cell A with one set of parameters and establish cells B and C with common parameters. This would be of benefit, for example, if cell A covered the area of manufacturing and cells B and C covered the area of the warehouse.

The ideal wireless LAN configuration for your organization depends primarily on user requirements and geography. If you have a relatively small group that requires wireless connectivity within the immediate area, then a single cell may do the job. If users are spread throughout the entire facility, however, then you might need a multiple-cell configuration. In either case, bridges may be necessary to support user access to resources located on the wired infrastructure.

Wireless Metropolitan Area Networks

Organizations often have requirements for communication between facilities in a semi-local area, such as a city block or metropolitan area. A hospital, for example, might consist of several buildings within the same general area, separated by streets and rivers. A utility company also might have multiple service centers and office buildings within a metropolitan area.

Traditionally, companies use physical media—such as buried metallic wire, optical fiber, or leased 56Kbps or T1 circuits—to provide necessary connections. These forms of media, however, do not satisfy needs for mobile computing. In addition, the physical approach might require a great deal of installation time and can result in expensive monthly service fees. A cable installation between sites several thousand feet apart can cost thousands of dollars or more, and leasing fees can easily be hundreds of dollars per month. In some cases, leased communications lines might not even be available.

Radio-Based Wireless Point-to-Point Network

Wireless point-to-point networks (often called *wireless metropolitan area networks*) use technologies very similar to wireless LANs. Therefore, this section concentrates on technological aspects differing from wireless LANs.

A radio-based wireless point-to-point network (see Figure 2.15) is currently the most common method for providing connectivity within a metropolitan area. These products have highly directional antennas to focus the signal power in a narrow beam, maximizing the transmission distance. As a result, spread spectrum products operating under one watt of power can reach single-hop transmission distances of 30 miles. The actual transmission distance of a particular product, though, depends on environmental conditions and terrain. Rain, for example, causes resistance to the propagation of radio signals, decreasing the effective range. A mountainous area will also hamper the transmission range of the signals.

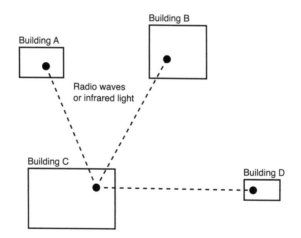

FIGURE 2.15

A radio-based wireless point-to-point network is a flexible way of connecting buildings that are spread throughout a city.

Radio-based wireless point-to-point network data rates are 11Mbps for the shorter-range products operating over two- to three-mile links. Applicable products operate over a 30-mile link, but they will transmit at much lower data rates to obtain the longer range. In addition, these products use either spread spectrum or narrowband modulation.

Case Study 2.2:

Cost Savings with a Wireless Point-to-Point Network

A wireless point-to-point network results in tangible savings rather quickly. A manufacturer in Texas, for example, installed this type of system between its existing plant and a new plant under construction about 12 miles away. The alternative was to install and lease a digital line between the facilities. The company recovered all the installation costs in less than two years and is now gaining positive returns on its investment. Many other companies are also realizing these types of benefits.

Laser-Based Wireless Point-To-Point Networks

Another class of wireless point-to-point networks uses laser light as a carrier for data transmission. A laser emits coherent light at a precise wavelength in a narrow beam. Most laser point-to-point networks use lasers that produce infrared light.

As with other wireless techniques, a laser modem in this type of system modulates the data with a light signal to produce a light beam capable of transmitting data. With light, these data rates can be extremely high. Most laser links can easily handle ethernet (10Mbps), 4–16Mbps token ring, and higher data rates. Figure 2.16 illustrates a laser point-to-point network.

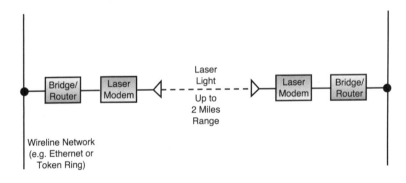

FIGURE 2.16

A laser-based wireless point-to-point network provides very secure connections between ethernet or token ring networks separated by up to two miles.

To maintain safe operation, a laser link typically has a range of less than a mile. These devices comply with the Center for Devices and Radiological Health standards, and most operate at Class III, which can cause eye damage under some circumstances. Much longer distances are possible, but you would have to increase the power to a level that would damage buildings and injure living things.

Weather is also an influence on the transmission distance of laser systems. A nice, clear day with very little smog will support the one-mile operating distance. Snow, rain, fog, smog, and dust cause attenuation, which could limit the effective range to a half mile or less. A fairly heavy rain shower (3–4 inches per hour), for example, will introduce approximately 6dB of attenuation per kilometer. As a result, you need to plan the link according to potential changes in weather.

Why use laser-based point-to-point network technology over radio types? One reason is the need for high-speed data transmission. A laser point-to-point system will sustain 20Mbps and higher data rates, which may be necessary for supporting transfer CAD (Computer Assisted Drawing) files and X-ray images. Also, you do not have to obtain an FCC license. The FCC doesn't manage frequencies above 300GHz; therefore, you can set up a laser system as quickly as you can set up a license-free spread spectrum radio system.

When using a laser, very few other systems can cause interference. Even at high microwave frequencies, radio signals are far from the spectral location of laser light, which eliminates the possibility of interference from these systems. Also, an interfering laser beam is unlikely because it would have to be pointed directly at your receiving site. It is possible that someone might do this purposely to jam your system, but otherwise it won't occur.

> **TIP**
>
> Sunlight consists of approximately 60% infrared light and can cause interference. The rising or setting sun might emit rays of light at an angle that the laser transducers can receive, causing interference in the early morning and late afternoon. Therefore, an organization should avoid placing laser links with an east-west orientation.
>
> Generally, laser-based point-to-point networks are highly resistant to interference. Thus, laser links might be the best solution in a city full of radio-based devices, especially for applications where you must minimize downtime. Be careful, though, to plan the installation of laser systems in cities with the assumption that someone may decide to erect a high rise building directly in the laser's path.

To accommodate a line-of-sight path between source and destination, the best place to install the laser link is on top of a building or tower. This avoids objects blocking the beam, which can cause a disruption of operation. Birds are generally not a problem because they can see infrared light and will usually avoid the beam. A bird flying through the beam, however, will cause a momentary interruption. If this occurs, higher-level protocols, such as ethernet or token ring, will trigger a retransmission of the data. The infrared beam will not harm the bird.

Laser-based systems offer more privacy than radio links. Someone wanting to receive the laser data signal would have to place himself directly in the beam's path (see Figure 2.17). Also, the eavesdropper would have to capture the light to obtain the data, significantly attenuating or completely disrupting the signal at the true destination. This means he would have to put himself next to the laser modem at either end of the link by standing on top of the building or climbing to the top of a tower. Physical security, such as fences and guards, can eliminate this type of sabotage.

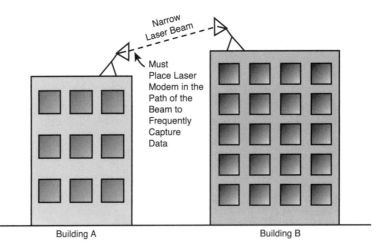

FIGURE 2.17
It is very difficult to capture data from a laser-based wireless point-to-point network.

Radio-Based Wireless Point-to-Multipoint Networks

Many service companies are in the process of implementing wireless point-to-multipoint networks to support fixed location and mobile users with needs for accessing the Internet. Figure 2.18 illustrates this configuration. In some cases, these companies are using IEEE 802.11 or proprietary technologies as the basis for these implementations.

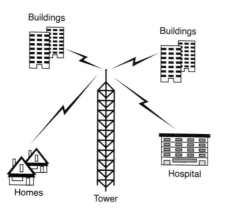

FIGURE 2.18

Point-to-multipoint wireless networks offer wider coverage from a single point.

Two emerging wireless MAN technologies are MMDS (Multichannel Multipoint Distribution Service) and LMDS (Local Multipoint Distribution Service). MMDS and LMDS primarily support fixed broadband wireless access to the Internet. With MMDS, a transmitting tower placed at a high elevation can reach customers with receiving dishes on their buildings within a 35-mile radius. In some cases, repeaters may extend the range into remote areas. MMDS is designed to operate in the 2.1 to 2.7GHz radio frequencies, at transmission power of 1 to 100 watts, with data rates up to 10Mbps with a 35-mile range. MMDS doesn't require line-of-sight.

MMDS is likely to prevail as the preferred choice for fixed wireless broadband connectivity in North America. Network service providers are rapidly deploying MMDS technology throughout the U.S. to reach local customers without negotiating access agreements with regional Bell operating companies. The advantage to the customer of using MMDS service is that the service provider will maintain the equipment and connections. Initial capital outlay is minimal, and the customer pays only a monthly service fee.

An LMDS system consists of a series of cells defined by individual base stations connected to a central control point. An LMDS is designed to operate at 24, 28, 31, 38, and 40GHz radio frequencies, at transmission power of 1 to 100 watts, with data rates up to 155Mbps with a 2-mile range. LMDS transmissions are strictly line-of-sight. For this reason, carriers are apt to target business districts where rooftop mounting of subscriber dishes is permissible. Companies will likely subscribe to LMDS services for virtual private networks, packet or ATM telephony, and streaming video (including video broadcasting).

2

WIRELESS NETWORK CONFIGURATIONS

Overview of the IEEE 802.11 Standard

IN THIS CHAPTER

The Importance of Standards

Vendors and some end users initially expected markets to dive head first into implementing wireless networks. Markets did not respond as predicted, and flat sales growth of wireless networking components prevailed through most of the 1990s. Relatively low data rates, high prices, and especially the lack of standards kept many end users from purchasing the wire-free forms of media.

For those having applications suitable for lower data rates and enough cost savings to warrant purchasing wireless connections, the only choice before 1998 was to install proprietary hardware to satisfy requirements. As a result, some organizations today still have proprietary wireless networks for which you have to replace both hardware and software to be compliant with the IEEE 802.11 standard. In response to lacking standards, the Institute for Electrical and Electronic Engineers (IEEE) developed the first internationally recognized wireless LAN standard: IEEE 802.11.

Types of Standards

There are two main types of standards: official and public. An *official standard* is published and known to the public, but it is controlled by an official standards organization, such as IEEE. Government or industry consortiums normally sponsor official standards groups. Official standards organizations generally ensure coordination at both the international and domestic level.

A *public standard* is similar to an official standard, except it is controlled by a private organization, such as the Wireless LAN Interoperability Forum. Public standards, often called *de facto standards*, are common practices that have not been produced or accepted by an official standards organization. These standards, such as TCP/IP, are the result of widespread proliferation. In some cases, public standards that proliferate, such as the original Ethernet, eventually pass through standards organizations and become official standards.

Companies should strive to adopt standards and recommended products within their organizations for all aspects of information systems. What type of standards should you use? For most cases, focus on the use of an official standard if one is available and proliferating. This will help ensure widespread acceptance and longevity of your wireless network implementation. If no official standard is suitable, a public standard would be a good choice. In fact, a public standard can often respond faster to changes in market needs because it usually has less organizational overhead for making changes. Be sure to avoid non-standard or proprietary system components, unless there are no suitable standards available.

> ## Case Study 3.1:
>
> ## 802.11 Versus Proprietary Standards
>
> A large retail chain based in Sacramento, California, had requirements to implement a wireless network to provide mobility within its 10 warehouses located all over the U.S. The application called for clerks within the warehouse to use new handheld wireless data collectors that perform inventory management functions.
>
> The company, already having one vendor's data collection devices (we'll call these brand X), decided to use that vendor's brand Y proprietary wireless data collectors and its proprietary wireless network (the vendor didn't offer an 802.11-compliant solution). This decision eliminated the need to work with additional vendors for the new handheld devices and the wireless network.
>
> A year passed after the installation, and enhancement requirements began to pour in for additional mobile appliances that were not available from the brand X vendor. This forced the company to consider the purchase of new brand Z appliances from a different vendor. The problem, though, was that the brand Z appliances, which were 802.11-compliant, didn't interoperate with the installed proprietary brand Y wireless network. Because of the cost associated with replacing its network with one that was 802.11-compliant (the brand Y wireless network had no upgrade path to 802.11), the company couldn't implement the new enhancement cost effectively.
>
> The company could have eliminated the problem of not being able to implement the new enhancement if it would have implemented the initial system with 802.11-compliant network components because most vendors offer products that are compatible with 802.11, but not all the proprietary networks. The result would have been the ability to consider multiple vendors for a wider selection of appliances.

3

OVERVIEW OF THE
IEEE 802.11
STANDARD

Institute for Electrical and Electronic Engineers (IEEE)

The IEEE is a non-profit professional organization founded by a handful of engineers in 1884 for the purpose of consolidating ideas dealing with electrotechnology. The IEEE plays a significant role in publishing technical works, sponsoring conferences and seminars, accreditation, and standards development. With regard to LANs, the IEEE has produced some very popular and widely used standards. For example, the majority of LANs in the world use network interface cards based on the IEEE 802.3 (ethernet) and IEEE 802.5 (token ring) standards.

Before someone can develop an IEEE standard, he must submit a Project Authorization Request (PAR) to the IEEE Standards Board. If the board approves the PAR, IEEE establishes a working group to develop the standard. Members of the working groups serve voluntarily and without compensation, and they are not necessarily members of the institute. The working group begins by writing a draft standard and then submits the draft to a balloting group of selected IEEE members for review and approval. The ballot group consists of the standard's developers, potential users, and other people having a general interest.

Before publication, the IEEE Standards Board performs a review of the Final Draft Standard and then considers approval of the standard. The resulting standard represents a consensus of broad expertise from within IEEE and other related organizations. All IEEE standards are reviewed at least once every five years for revision or reaffirmation.

> **NOTE**
>
> In May 1991, a group led by Victor Hayes submitted a Project Authorization Request (PAR) to IEEE to initiate the 802.11 working group. Hayes became chairman of the working group and led the standards effort to its completion in June 1997.

Benefits of the 802.11 Standard

The benefits of using standards such as those published by IEEE are great. The following sections explain the benefits of complying with standards, especially IEEE 802.11.

Appliance Interoperability

Compliance with the IEEE 802.11 standard makes possible interoperability between multiple-vendor appliances and the chosen wireless network type. This means you can purchase an 802.11-compliant scanner from Symbol and a Pathfinder Ultra handheld scanner/printer from Monarch Marking Systems and they will both interoperate within an equivalent 802.11 wireless network, assuming 802.11 configuration parameters are set equally in both devices. Standard compliance increases price competition and enables companies to develop wireless LAN components with lower research and development costs. This enables a greater number of smaller companies to develop wireless components.

As shown in Figure 3.1, appliance interoperability prevents dependence on a single vendor for appliances. Without a standard, for example, a company having a non-standard proprietary network would be dependent on purchasing only appliances that operate on that particular network. With an 802.11-compliant wireless network, you can use any equivalent 802.11-compliant appliance. Because most vendors have migrated their products to 802.11, you have a much greater selection of appliances for 802.11 standard networks.

Fast Product Development

The 802.11 standard is a well-tested blueprint that developers can use to implement wireless devices. The use of standards decreases the learning curve required to understand specific technologies because the standard-forming group has already invested the time to smooth out any wrinkles in the implementation of the applicable technology. This leads to the development of products in much less time.

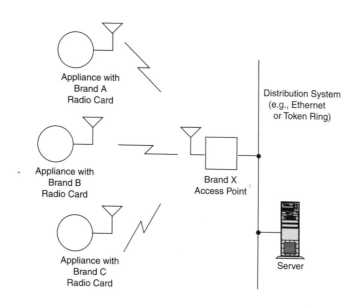

FIGURE 3.1

Appliance interoperability ensures that multiple-vendor appliances will communicate over equivalent wireless networks.

Stable Future Migration

Compliance with standards helps protect investments and avoids legacy systems that must be completely replaced in the future as those proprietary products become obsolete. The evolution of wireless LANs should occur in a fashion similar to 802.3, Ethernet. Initially, Ethernet began as a 10Mbps standard using coaxial cable media. The IEEE 802.3 working group enhanced the standard over the years by adding twisted-pair, optical fiber cabling, and 100Mbps and 1000Mbps data rates.

Just as IEEE 802.3 did, the 802.11 working group recognizes the investments organizations make in network infrastructure and the importance in providing migration paths that maximize the installed base of hardware. As a result, 802.11 will certainly ensure stable migration from existing wireless LANs as higher-performance wireless networking technologies become available.

Price Reductions

High costs have always plagued the wireless LAN industry; however, prices have dropped significantly as more vendors and end users comply with 802.11. One of the reasons for lower prices is that vendors no longer need to develop and support lower-quantity proprietary subcomponents, cutting-edge design, manufacturing, and support costs. Ethernet went through a similar lowering of prices as more and more companies began complying with the 802.3 standard.

Avoiding Silos

Over the past couple of decades, MIS organizations have had a difficult time maintaining control of network implementations. The introduction of PCs, LANs, and visual-based development tools has made it much easier for non-MIS organizations, such as finance and manufacturing departments, to deploy their own applications. One part of the company, for example, may purchase a wireless network from one vendor, then another part of the company may buy a different wireless network. As a result, *silos*—non-interoperable systems—appear within the company, making it very difficult for MIS personnel to plan and support compatible systems. Some people refer to these silos as *stovepipes*.

Acquisitions bring dissimilar systems together as well. One company with a proprietary system may purchase another having a different proprietary system, resulting in non-interoperability. Figure 3.2 illustrates the features of standards that minimize the occurrence of silos.

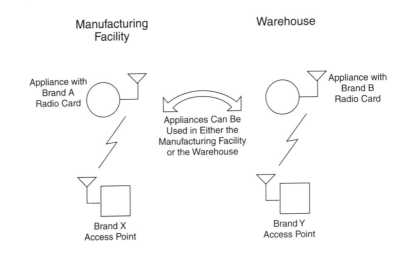

FIGURE 3.2
Compliance with the IEEE 802.11 standard can minimize the implementation of silos.

Case Study 3.2:

Problems with Mixed Standards

A company located in Barcelona, Spain, specializes in the resale of women's clothes. This company, having a MIS group without much control over the implementation of distributed networks in major parts of the company, has projects underway to implement wireless networks for an inventory application and a price-marking application.

Non-MIS project managers located in different parts of the company lead these projects. They have little desire to coordinate their projects with MIS because of past difficulties. As a result, both project managers end up implementing non-compatible proprietary wireless networks to satisfy their networking requirements.

The project managers install both systems: one that covers the sales floor space of their 300 stores (for price marking) and one that encompasses 10 warehouses (for doing inventory functions). Even though the systems are not compatible, all is fine for the users operating the autonomous systems.

The problems with this system architecture, though, are the difficulty in providing operational support and inflexibility. The company must maintain purchasing and warranty contracts with two different wireless network vendors, service personnel will need to acquire and maintain an understanding of the operation of two networks, and the company will not be able to share appliances and wireless network components between the warehouses and the stores.

As a result, the silos in this case make the networks more expensive to support and limit their flexibility in meeting future needs. The implementation of standard 802.11-compliant networks would have avoided these problems.

The IEEE 802 LAN Standards Family

The IEEE 802 Local and Metropolitan Area Network Standards Committee is a major working group charted by IEEE to create, maintain, and encourage the use of IEEE and equivalent IEC/ISO standards. The IEEE formed the committee in February 1980, and this committee meets as a plenary body at least three times per year. The IEEE 802 committee produces the series of standards known as IEEE 802.x, and the JTC 1 series of equivalent standards is known as ISO 8802-nnn.

IEEE 802 includes a family of standards, as depicted in Figure 3.3. The MAC and Physical layers of the 802 standard were organized into a separate set of standards from the LLC because of the interdependence between medium access control, medium, and topology.

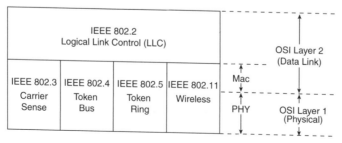

FIGURE 3.3

The IEEE 802 family of standards falls within the scope of layers 1 and 2 of the OSI Reference Model.

NOTE

Visit the IEEE 802 LAN/MAN Standards Committee Web site at
http://www.manta.ieee.org/groups/802/ for more information on 802 LAN standards.

IEEE 802.2 LLC Overview

The LLC is the highest layer of the IEEE 802 Reference Model and provides functions similar to the traditional data link control protocol: HDLC (High-Level Data Link Control). ISO/IEC 8802-2 (ANSI/IEEE Standard 802.2), dated May 7, 1998, specifies the LLC. The purpose of the LLC is to exchange data between end users across a LAN using an 802-based MAC controlled link. The LLC provides addressing and data link control, and it is independent of the topology, transmission medium, and medium access control technique chosen.

Higher layers, such as TCP/IP, pass user data down to the LLC expecting error-free transmission across the network. The LLC in turn appends a control header, creating an LLC protocol data unit (PDU). The LLC uses the control information in the operation of the LLC protocol (see Figure 3.4). Before transmission, the LLC PDU is handed down through the MAC service access point (SAP) to the MAC layer, which appends control information at the beginning and end of the packet, forming a MAC frame. The control information in the frame is needed for the operation of the MAC protocol.

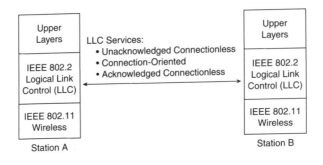

FIGURE 3.4

The LLC provides end-to-end link control over an 802.11-based wireless LAN.

IEEE 802.2 LLC Services

The LLC provides the following three services for a Network Layer protocol:

- Unacknowledged connectionless service
- Connection-oriented service
- Acknowledged connectionless service

These services apply to the communication between peer LLC layers—that is, one located on the source station and one located on the destination station. Typically, vendors will provide these services as options that the customer can select when purchasing the equipment.

All three LLC protocols employ the same PDU format that consists of four fields (see Figure 3.5). The Destination Service Access Point (DSAP) and Source Service Access Point (SSAP) fields each contain 7-bit addresses that specify the destination and source stations of the peer LLCs. One bit of the DSAP indicates whether the PDU is intended for an individual or group station(s). One bit of the SSAP indicates whether it is a command or response PDU. The format of the LLC Control field is identical to that of HDLC, using extended (7-bit) sequence numbers. The Data field contains the information from higher-layer protocols that the LLC is transporting to the destination.

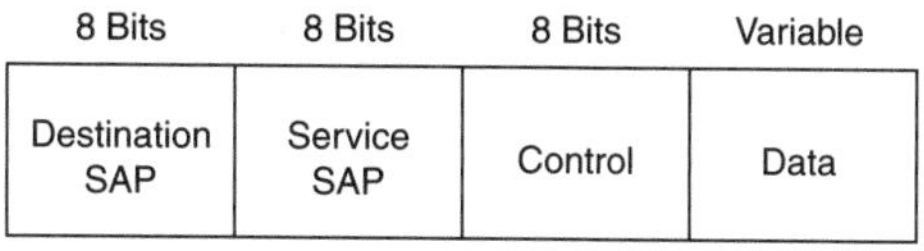

8 Bits	8 Bits	8 Bits	Variable
Destination SAP	Service SAP	Control	Data

FIGURE 3.5

The LLC PDU consists of data fields that provide the LLC functionality.

The Control field has bits that indicate whether the frame is one of the following types:

- **Information**   Used to carry user data.
- **Supervisory**   Used for flow control and error control.
- **Unnumbered**   Various protocol control PDUs.

Unacknowledged Connectionless Service

The *unacknowledged connectionless service* is a datagram-style service that does not involve any error-control or flow-control mechanisms. This service does not involve the establishment of a data link layer connection (such as between peer LLCs). This service supports individual, multicast, and broadcast addressing. This service simply sends and receives LLC PDUs with no acknowledgement of delivery. Because the delivery of data is not guaranteed, a higher layer, such as TCP, must deal with reliability issues.

The unacknowledged connectionless service offers advantages in the following situations:

- If higher layers of the protocol stack provide the necessary reliability and flow-control mechanisms, then it would be inefficient to duplicate them in the LLC. In this case, the unacknowledged connectionless service would be appropriate. TCP and the ISO transport protocol, for example, already provide the mechanisms necessary for reliable delivery.

- It is not always necessary to provide feedback pertaining to successful delivery of information. The overhead of connection establishment and maintenance can be inefficient for applications involving the periodic sampling of data sources, such as monitoring sensors. The unacknowledged connectionless service would best satisfy these requirements.

Case Study 3.3:

Using Unacknowledged Connectionless Service to Minimize Overhead

The executive office building of a high-rent advertising agency in Southern California has 20 sensors to monitor temperatures throughout its building as an input to the heating and air conditioning system. These sensors send short information packets every minute to an application on a centralized server that updates a temperature table in a database. The heating and air conditioning system uses this information to control the temperature in different parts of the building.

For this application, the server does not need to acknowledge the receipt of every sensor transmission because the information updates are not critical. The system can maintain a comfortable temperature throughout the building even if the system misses a temperature update from time to time.

Additionally, it is not feasible to require the sensors to establish connections with the server to send the short information packets. As a result, designers of the system chose to use the LLC unacknowledged connectionless service to minimize overhead on the network, making the limited wireless network bandwidth available to other applications.

Connection-Oriented Service

The *connection-oriented service* establishes a logical connection that provides flow control and error control between two stations needing to exchange data. This service does involve the establishment of a connection between peer LLCs by performing connection establishment, data transfer, and connection termination functions. The service can connect only two stations; therefore, it does not support multicast or broadcast modes. The connection-oriented service offers advantages mainly if higher layers of the protocol stack do not provide the necessary reliability and flow-control mechanisms, which is generally the case with terminal controllers.

Flow control is a protocol feature that ensures that a transmitting station does not overwhelm a receiving station with data. With flow control, each station allocates a finite amount of memory and buffer resources to store sent and received PDUs.

Networks, especially wireless networks, suffer from induced noise in the links between network stations that can cause transmission errors. If the noise is high enough in amplitude, it causes errors in digital transmission in the form of altered bits. This will lead to inaccuracy of the transmitted data, and the receiving network device may misinterpret the meaning of the information.

The noise that causes most problems with networks is usually Gaussian and impulse noise. Theoretically, the amplitude of Gaussian noise is uniform across the frequency spectrum, and it normally triggers random single-bit independent errors. Impulse noise, the most disastrous, is characterized by long quiet intervals of time followed by high amplitude bursts. This noise results from lightning and switching transients. Impulse noise is responsible for most errors in digital communication systems and generally provokes errors to occur in bursts.

To guard against transmission errors, the connection-oriented and acknowledged-connectionless LLCs use error control mechanisms that detect and correct errors that occur in the transmission of PDUs. The LLC ARQ mechanism recognizes the possibility of the following two types of errors:

- **Lost PDU**   A PDU fails to arrive at the other end or is damaged beyond recognition.
- **Damaged PDU**   A PDU has arrived, but some bits are altered.

When a frame arrives at a receiving station, the station checks whether there are any errors present by using a *Cyclic Redundancy Check (CRC)* error detection algorithm. In general, the receiving station will send back a positive or negative acknowledgement, depending on the outcome of the error detection process. In case the acknowledgement is lost in route to the sending station, the sending station will retransmit the frame after a certain period of time. This process is often referred to as *Automatic Repeat Request (ARQ)*.

Overall, ARQ is best for the correction of burst errors because this type of impairment occurs in a small percentage of frames, thus not invoking many retransmissions. Because of the feedback inherent in ARQ protocols, the transmission links must accommodate half-duplex or full-duplex transmissions. If only simplex links are available because of feasibility, then it is impossible to use the ARQ technique because the receiver would not be able to notify the transmitter of bad data frames.

NOTE

When single-bit errors predominate or when only a simplex link is available, forward error correction (FEC) can provide error correction. FEC algorithms provide enough redundancy in data transmissions to enable the receiving station to correct errors without needing the sending station to retransmit the data.

FEC is effective for correcting single-bit errors, but it creates a great deal of overhead in the transmissions to protect against multiple errors, such as burst errors. The IEEE LLC, though, specifies only the use of ARQ-based protocols for controlling errors.

The following are two approaches for retransmitting unsatisfactory blocks of data using ARQ:

- **Continuous ARQ** With this type of ARQ, often called a *sliding window protocol,* the sending station transmits frames continuously until the receiving station detects an error. The sending station is usually capable of transmitting a specific number of frames and maintains a table indicating which frames have been sent.

  The system implementor can set the number of frames sent before stopping via configuration parameters of the network device. If a receiver detects a bad frame, it will send a negative acknowledgement back to the sending station requesting that the bad frame be sent again. When the transmitting station gets the signal to retransmit the frame, several subsequent frames may have already been sent (due to propagation delays between the sender and receiver); therefore, the transmitter must go back and retransmit the bad data frame.

  There are a couple of ways the transmitting station can send frames again using continuous ARQ. One method is for the source to retrieve the bad frame from the transmit buffer and send it and all frames following it. This is called the *go-back-n technique.* A problem is that when n (the number of frames the transmitter sent after the bad frame plus one) becomes large, the method becomes inefficient. This is because the retransmission of just one frame means that a large number of possibly good frames will also be resent, thus decreasing throughput.

  The go-back-n technique is useful in applications for which receiver buffer space is limited because all that is needed is a receiver window size of one (assuming frames are to be delivered in order). When the receive node rejects a bad frame (sends a negative acknowledgment), it does not need to buffer any subsequent frames for possible reordering while it is waiting for the retransmission, because all subsequent frames will also be sent.

  An alternative to the continuous go-back-n technique is a method that selectively retransmits only the bad frame, then resumes normal transmission at the point just before getting the notification of a bad frame. This approach is called *selective repeat.* It is obviously better than continuous go-back-n in terms of throughput because only the bad frame needs retransmission. With this technique, however, the receiver must be capable of storing a number of frames if they are to be processed in order. The receiver needs to buffer data that has been received after a bad frame was requested for retransmission since only the damaged frame will be sent again.

- **Stop-and-wait ARQ** With this method, the sending station transmits a frame, then stops and waits for some type of acknowledgment from the receiver on whether a particular frame was acceptable or not. If the receiving station sends a negative acknowledgment, the frame will be sent again. The transmitter will send the next frame only after it receives a positive acknowledgment from the receiver.

An advantage of stop-and-wait ARQ is that it does not require much buffer space at the sending or receiving station. The sending station needs to store only the current transmitted frame. However, stop-and-wait ARQ becomes inefficient as the propagation delay between source and destination becomes large. For example, data sent on satellite links normally experiences a round-trip delay of several hundred milliseconds; therefore, long block lengths are necessary to maintain a reasonably effective data rate. The trouble is that with longer frames, the probability of an error occurring in a particular block is greater. Thus, retransmission will occur often, and the resulting throughput will be lower.

Case Study 3.4:

Using Automatic Repeat Request (ARQ) to Reduce Errors

A mobile home manufacturer in Florida uses robots on the assembly line to perform welding. Designers of the robot control system had to decide to use ARQ or FEC for controlling transmission errors between the server and the robots. The company experiences a great deal of impulse noise from arc welders and other heavy machinery.

In the midst of this somewhat hostile environment, the robots require error-free information updates to ensure they function correctly. Designers of the system quickly ruled out the use of FEC because of the likely presence of burst errors due to impulse noise. ARQ, with its capability to detect and correct frames having lots of bit errors, was obviously the best choice.

Acknowledged Connectionless Service

As with the The unacknowledged connectionless service, the *acknowledged connectionless service* does not involve the establishment of a logical connection with the distant station. But the receiving stations with the acknowledged version do confirm successful delivery of datagrams. Flow and error control is handled through use of the stop-and-wait ARQ method.

The acknowledged connectionless service is useful in several applications. The connection-oriented service must maintain a table for each active connection for tracking the status of the connection. If the application calls for guaranteed delivery, but there is a large number of destinations needing to receive the data, then the connection-oriented service may be impractical because of the large number of tables required. Examples that fit this scenario include process control and automated factory environments that require a central site to communicate with a large number of processors and programmable controllers. In addition, the handling of important and time-critical alarm or emergency control signals in a factory would also fit this case. In all these examples, the sending station needs an acknowledgment to ensure successful delivery of the data; however, an urgent transmission cannot wait for a connection to be established.

> **NOTE**
>
> A company having a requirement to send information to multiple devices needing positive acknowledgement of the data transfer can use the acknowledged connectionless LLC service. For example, a marina may find it beneficial to control the power to different parts of the boat dock via a wireless network. Of course, the expense of a wireless network may not be justifiable for this application alone.
>
> Other applications, such as supporting data transfers back and forth to the cash register at the gas pump and the use of data collection equipment for inventorying rental equipment, can share the wireless network to make a more positive business case. For shutting off the power on the boat dock, the application would need to send a message to the multiple power controllers, and then expect an acknowledgement to ensure the controller receives the notification and that the power is shut off. For this case, the connectionless transfer, versus connection-oriented, makes more sense because it wouldn't be feasible to make connections to the controllers to support such a short message.

LLC/MAC Layer Service Primitives

Layers within the 802 architecture communicate with each other via service primitives having the following forms:

- **Request** A layer uses this type of primitive to request that another layer perform a specific service.

- **Confirm** A layer uses this type of primitive to convey the results of a previous service request primitive.

- **Indication** A layer uses this type of primitive to indicate to another layer that a significant event has occurred. This primitive could result from a service request or from some internally generated event.

- **Response** A layer uses this type of primitive to complete a procedure initiated by an indication primitive.

These primitives are an abstract way of defining the protocol, and they do not imply a specific physical implementation method. Each layer within the 802 model uses specific primitives. The LLC layer communicates with its associated MAC layer through the following specific set of service primitives:

- **MA-UNITDATA.request** The LLC layer sends this primitive to the MAC layer to request the transfer of a data frame from a local LLC entity to a specific peer LLC entity or group of peer entities on different stations. The data frame could be an information frame containing data from a higher layer or a control frame (such as a supervisory or unnumbered frame) that the LLC generates internally to communicate with its peer LLC.

- **MA-UNITDATA.indication**   The MAC layer sends this primitive to the LLC layer to transfer a data frame from the MAC layer to the LLC. This occurs only if the MAC has found that a frame it receives from the Physical layer is valid and has no errors and the destination address indicates the correct MAC address of the station.

- **MA-UNITDATA-STATUS.indication**   The MAC layer sends this primitive to the LLC layer to provide status information about the service provided for a previous MA-UNITDATA.request primitive.

Introduction to the IEEE 802.11 Standard

The initial 802.11 PAR states that "...the scope of the proposed [wireless LAN] standard is to develop a specification for wireless connectivity for fixed, portable, and moving stations within a local area." The PAR further says that "...the purpose of the standard is to provide wireless connectivity to automatic machinery and equipment or stations that require rapid deployment, which may be portable, handheld, or which may be mounted on moving vehicles within a local area."

The resulting standard, which is officially called "IEEE Standard for Wireless LAN Medium Access (MAC) and Physical Layer (PHY) Specifications," defines over-the-air protocols necessary to support networking in a local area. As with other IEEE 802–based standards (such as 802.3 and 802.5), the primary service of the 802.11 standard is to deliver MSDUs (MAC Service Data Units) between peer LLCs. Typically, a radio card and access point provide functions of the 802.11 standard.

> **NOTE**
>
> To order a copy of the IEEE 802.11 standard, contact the IEEE 802 Document Order Service at 800-678-4333. You can also order the standard via IEEE's Web site at www.ieee.org.

The 802.11 standard provides MAC and PHY (Physical Layer) functionality for wireless connectivity of fixed, portable, and moving stations moving at pedestrian and vehicular speeds within a local area. Specific features of the 802.11 standard include the following:

- Support of asynchronous and time-bounded delivery service.

- Continuity of service within extended areas via a distribution system, such as ethernet.

- Accommodation of transmission rates of 1Mbps and 2Mbps (802.11a and 802.11b extensions offer higher data rates than the base standard).

3

OVERVIEW OF THE
IEEE 802.11
STANDARD

- Support of most market applications.
- Multicast (including broadcast) services.
- Network management services.
- Registration and authentication services.

Target environments for use of the standard include the following:

- Inside buildings, such as offices, banks, shops, malls, hospitals, manufacturing plants, and residences
- Outdoor areas, such as parking lots, campuses, building complexes, and outdoor plants

The 802.11 standard takes into account the following significant differences between wireless and wired LANs:

- **Power management**   Because most wireless LAN NICs are available in PCMCIA Type II format, obviously you can outfit portable and mobile handheld computing equipment with wireless LAN connectivity. The problem, though, is that these devices must rely on batteries to power the electronics within them. The addition of a wireless LAN NIC to a portable computer can drain batteries quickly.

  The 802.11 working group struggled with finding solutions to conserve battery power; however, they found techniques enabling wireless NICs to switch to lower-power standby modes periodically when not transmitting, reducing the drain on the battery. The MAC layer implements power management functions by putting the radio to sleep (lowering the power drain) when no transmission activity occurs for some specific or user-definable time period. The problem, though, is that a sleeping station can miss critical data transmissions. The 802.11 standard solves this problem by incorporating buffers to queue messages. The standard calls for sleeping stations to awaken periodically and retrieve any applicable messages.

- **Bandwidth**   The ISM spread spectrum bands do not offer a great deal of bandwidth, keeping data rates lower than desired for some applications. The 802.11 working group, however, dealt with methods to compress data, making the best use of available bandwidth.

- **Security**   Wireless LANs transmit signals over much larger areas than do those using wired media, such as twisted-pair, coaxial cable, and optical fiber. In terms of privacy, therefore, a wireless LAN has a much larger area to protect. To employ security, the 802.11 group coordinated its work with the IEEE 802.10 standards committee responsible for developing security mechanisms for all 802-series LANs.

- **Addressing**   The topology of a wireless network is dynamic; therefore, the destination address does not always correspond to the destination's location. This raises a problem when routing packets through the network to the intended destination. Thus, you may need to use a TCP/IP-based protocol such as MobileIP to accommodate mobile stations.

IEEE 802.11 Topology

The IEEE 802.11 topology consists of components interacting to provide a wireless LAN that enables station mobility transparent to higher protocol layers, such as the LLC. A *station* is any device that contains functionality of the 802.11 protocol (in other words, the MAC layer, the PHY layer, and an interface to a wireless medium). The functions of the 802.11 standard reside physically in a radio NIC, the software interface that drives the NIC, and the access point. The 802.11 standard supports the following two topologies:

- Independent Basic Service Set (IBSS) networks
- Extended Service Set (ESS) networks

These networks use a basic building block the 802.11 standard refers to as a BSS, providing a coverage area whereby stations of the BSS remain fully connected. A station is free to move within the BSS, but it can no longer communicate directly with other stations if it leaves the BSS.

NOTE

Harris Semiconductor (now Intersil) was the first company to offer a complete radio chipset (called PRISM) for direct sequence spread spectrum that is fully compliant with IEEE 802.11. The PRISM chip set includes six integrated microcircuits that handle all signal processing requirements of 802.11.

Independent BSS (IBSS) Networks

An IBSS is a standalone BSS that has no backbone infrastructure and consists of at least two wireless stations (see Figure 3.6). This type of network is often referred to as an *ad hoc network* because it can be constructed quickly without much planning. The ad hoc wireless network will satisfy most needs of users occupying a smaller area, such as a single room, sales floor, or hospital wing.

Extended Service Set (ESS) Networks

For requirements exceeding the range limitations of an independent BSS, 802.11 defines an Extended Service Set (ESS) LAN, as illustrated in Figure 3.7. This type of configuration satisfies the needs of large coverage networks of arbitrary size and complexity.

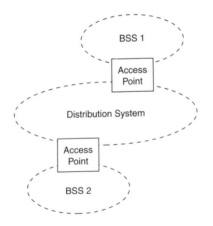

FIGURE 3.6

An independent BSS (IBSS) is the most basic type of 802.11 wireless LAN.

FIGURE 3.7

An Extended Service Set (ESS) 802.11 wireless LAN consists of multiple cells interconnected by access points and a distribution system, such as ethernet.

The 802.11 standard recognizes the following mobility types:

- **No-transition**   This type of mobility refers to stations that do not move and those that are moving within a local BSS.
- **BSS-transition**   This type of mobility refers to stations that move from one BSS in one ESS to another BSS within the same ESS.
- **ESS-transition**   This type of mobility refers to stations that move from a BSS in one ESS to a BSS in a different ESS.

The 802.11 standard clearly supports the no-transition and BSS-transition mobility types. The standard, though, does not guarantee that a connection will continue when making an ESS-transition.

The 802.11 standard defines the *distribution system* as an element that interconnects BSSs within the ESS via access points. The distribution system supports the 802.11 mobility types by providing logical services necessary to handle address-to-destination mapping and seamless integration of multiple BSSs. An *access point* is an addressable station providing an interface to the distribution system for stations located within various BSSs. The independent BSS and ESS networks are transparent to the LLC layer.

Within the ESS, the 802.11 standard accommodates the following physical configuration of BSSs:

- **BSSs partially overlap**   This type of configuration provides contiguous coverage within a defined area, which is best if the application cannot tolerate a disruption of network service.

- **BSSs are physically disjointed**   For this case, the configuration does not provide contiguous coverage. The 802.11 standard does not specify a limit to the distance between BSSs.

- **BSSs are physically collocated**   This may be necessary to provide a redundant or higher-performing network.

The 802.11 standard does not constrain the composition of the distribution system; therefore, it may be 802 compliant or some non-standard network. If data frames need transmission to and from a non-IEEE 802.11 LAN, then these frames, as defined by the 802.11 standard, enter and exit through a logical point called a *portal*. The portal provides logical integration between existing wired LANs and 802.11 LANs. When the distribution system is constructed with 802-type components, such as 802.3 (ethernet) or 802.5 (token ring), then the portal and the access point become one and the same.

3

OVERVIEW OF THE
IEEE 802.11
STANDARD

NOTE

Before deeming their devices as 802.11 compliant, manufacturers should follow the protocol implementation compliance procedures that the 802.11 standard specifies in its appendix. The procedures state that the vendor shall complete a Protocol Implementation Conformance Statement (PICS) pro forma. The structure of the PICS pro forma mainly includes a list of questions that the vendor responds to with yes or no answers, indicating adherence to mandatory and optional portions of the standard.

For Wi-Fi certification, refer to the test matrix document located at http://www.wi-fi.com/downloads/test_matrix.PDF.

IEEE 802.11 Logical Architecture

A topology provides a means of explaining necessary physical components of a network, but the *logical architecture* defines the network's operation. As Figure 3.8 illustrates, the logical architecture of the 802.11 standard that applies to each station consists of a single MAC and one of multiple PHYs.

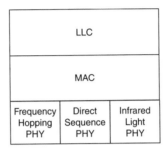

FIGURE 3.8

A single 802.11 MAC layer supports three separate PHYs: frequency hopping spread spectrum, direct sequence spread spectrum, and infrared light.

IEEE 802.11 MAC Layer

The goal of the MAC layer is to provide access control functions (such as addressing, access coordination, frame check sequence generation and checking, and LLC PDU delimiting) for shared-medium PHYs in support of the LLC layer. The MAC layer performs the addressing and recognition of frames in support of the LLC. The 802.11 standard uses CSMA/CA (carrier sense multiple access with collision avoidance), and standard ethernet uses CSMA/CD (carrier sense multiple access with collision detection). It is not possible to both transmit and receive on the same channel using radio transceivers; therefore, an 802.11 wireless LAN takes measures only to avoid collisions, not detect them.

IEEE 802.11 Physical Layers

The 802.11 standard specifies several Physical layers. The initial standard approved in 1997 included frequency hopping and direct sequence spread spectrum, delivering data rates of 1 and 2Mbps in the 2.4GHz band. This initial release also defined an infrared Physical layer operating at 1 and 2Mbps via passive ceiling reflection. The current 802.11 standard, released in December 1999, added an 11Mbps, high-rate version direct sequence standard commonly referred to as IEEE 802.11b. In addition, the current standard defines a Physical layer using OFDM (orthogonal frequency division multiplexing) to deliver data rates of up to 54Mbps in the 5GHz frequency band. Refer to Chapter 5, "IEEE 802.11 Physical (PHY) Layer," for more details on these standards.

As with the IEEE 802.3 standard, the 802.11 working group is considering additional PHYs as applicable technologies become available.

IEEE 802.11 Services

The 802.11 standard defines services that provide the functions that the LLC layer requires for sending MAC Service Data Units (MSDUs) between two entities on the network. These services, which the MAC layer implements, fall into two categories:

- **Station Services**   These include Authentication, Deauthentication, Privacy, and MSDU delivery.
- **Distribution System Services**   These include Association, Disassociation, Distribution, Integration, and Reassociation.

The following sections define the station and distribution system services.

Station Services

The 802.11 standard defines services for providing functions among stations. A station may be within any wireless element on the network, such as a handheld PC or handheld scanner. In addition, all access points implement station services. To provide necessary functionality, these stations need to send and receive MSDUs and implement adequate levels of security.

Authentication

Because wireless LANs have limited physical security to prevent unauthorized access, 802.11 defines authentication services to control LAN access to a level equal to a wired link. Every 802.11 station, whether part of an independent BSS or an ESS network, must use the authentication service prior to establishing a connection (referred to as an *association* in 802.11 terms) with another station with which it will communicate. Stations performing authentication send a unicast management authentication frame to the corresponding station.

The IEEE 802.11 standard defines the following two authentication services:

- **Open system authentication**   This is the 802.11 default authentication method. It is a very simple two-step process. First the station wanting to authenticate with another station sends an authentication management frame containing the sending station's identity. The receiving station then sends back a frame indicating whether it recognizes the identity of the authenticating station.
- **Shared key authentication**   This type of authentication assumes that each station has received a secret shared key through a secure channel independent from the 802.11 network. Stations authenticate through shared knowledge of the secret key. Use of shared key authentication requires implementation of the Wired Equivalent Privacy algorithm (WEP).

Deauthentication

When a station wants to disassociate from another station, it invokes the *deauthentication* service. Deauthentication is a notification and cannot be refused. A station performs deauthentication by sending an authentication management frame (or group of frames to multiple stations) to advise of the termination of authentication.

Privacy

With a wireless network, all stations and other devices can hear data traffic taking place within range on the network, seriously affecting the security level of a wireless link. IEEE 802.11 counters this problem by offering a privacy service option that raises the security level of the 802.11 network to that of a wired network.

The privacy service, applying to all data frames and some authentication management frames, is based on the 802.11 Wired Equivalent Privacy (WEP) algorithm that significantly reduces risks if someone eavesdrops on the network. This algorithm performs encryption of messages, as shown in Figure 3.9. With WEP, all stations initially start unencrypted. Refer to the section "Private Frame Transmissions," in Chapter 4, "IEEE 802.11 Medium Access Control (MAC) Layer," for a description of how WEP works.

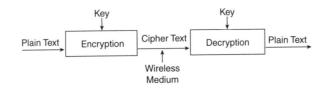

FIGURE 3.9
The Wired Equivalent Privacy (WEP) algorithm produces ciphertext, keeping eavesdroppers from listening in on data transmissions.

> **NOTE**
>
> The WEP protects RF data transmissions using a 64-bit seed key and the RC4 encryption algorithm. When enabled, WEC protects only the data packet information. Physical layer headers are left unencrypted so that all stations can properly receive control information for managing the network. Some companies today are offering 128-bit encryption.

Distribution System Services

Distribution system services, as defined by 802.11, provide functionality across a distribution system. Access points provide distribution system services. The following sections provide an overview of the services that distribution systems need to provide proper transfer of MSDUs.

Association

Each station must initially invoke the association service with an access point before it can send information through a distribution system. The association maps a station to the distribution system via an access point. Each station can associate with only a single access point, but each access point can associate with multiple stations. Association is also a first step to providing the capability for a station to be mobile between BSSs.

Disassociation

A station or access point may invoke the disassociation service to terminate an existing association. This service is a notification; therefore, neither party may refuse termination. Stations should disassociate when leaving the network. An access point, for example, may disassociate all its stations if being removed for maintenance.

Distribution

A station uses the distribution service every time it sends MAC frames across a distribution system. The 802.11 standard does not specify how the distribution system delivers the data. The distribution service provides the distribution system with only enough information to determine the proper destination BSS.

Integration

The integration service enables the delivery of MAC frames through a portal between a distribution system and a non-802.11 LAN. The integration function performs all required media or address space translations. The details of an integration function depend on the distribution system implementation and are beyond the scope of the 802.11 standard.

Reassociation

The reassociation service enables a station to change its current state of association. Reassociation provides additional functionality to support BSS-transition mobility for associated stations. The reassociation service enables a station to change its association from one access point to another. This keeps the distribution system informed of the current mapping between access point and station as the station moves from one BSS to another within an ESS. Reassociation also enables changing association attributes of an established association while the station remains associated with the same access point. The mobile station always initiates the reassociation service.

NOTE

IEEE 802.11 allows a client to roam among multiple access points that may be operating on the same or separate channels. To support the roaming function, each access point typically transmits a beacon signal every 100ms. Roaming stations use the beacon to gauge the strength of their existing access point connection. If the station senses a weak signal, the roaming station can implement the reassociation service to connect to an access point emitting a stronger signal.

Case Study 3.5: Using Reassociation for Improved Signal Transmission

A grocery store in Gulf Port, Mississippi, has a bar code–based shelf inventory system that helps the owners of the store keep track of what to stock, order, and so on. Several of the store clerks use handheld scanners during the store's closed hours to perform inventory functions. The store has a multiple-cell 802.11-compliant wireless LAN (ESS) consisting of access points A and B interconnected by an ethernet network. These two access points are sufficient to cover the store's entire floor space and backroom.

In the frozen meat section at one end of the store, a clerk using a handheld device may associate with access point A. As he walks with the device to the beer and wine section on the other end of the store, the mobile scanner (that is, the 802.11 station within the scanner) will begin sensing a signal from access point B. As the signal from B becomes stronger, the station will then reassociate with access point B, offering a much better signal for transmitting MSDUs.

NOTE

The 802.11 standard specifies the following optional MAC functions:

- **Point Coordination Function (PCF)**   Implemented in the access point and (in addition to the mandatory DCF) provides delivery of time-bounded data via synchronous communications using station-polling mechanisms.
- **Contention-Free Pollable**   Implemented in an independent station to enable time-bounded data transfers defined in the PCF.
- **Wired Equivalent Privacy (WEP)**   Provides frame transmission privacy similar to a wired network by generating secret shared encryption keys for source and destination stations.
- **Multiple Outstanding MSDUs**   An option that restricts the number of outstanding MSDUs to one in order to avoid reordering or unnecessarily discarding MSDUs between two LLCs.

> **NOTE**
>
> When two peer LLCs communicate over a network through the MAC and PHY layers, the capability to transmit multiple MSDUs (packets) and the presence of finite propagation delay make it possible for stations to reorder or unnecessarily discard the MSDUs. This problem becomes more significant as propagation delay or data rate increases because of the capability to have a greater number of outstanding MSDUs. Because of the higher potential data rates of 802.11a and the high potential for outdoor implementations, companies are likely to need the multiple outstanding MSDU option in 802.11 MAC software.

> **NOTE**
>
> Most end users of 802.11 and 802.11b radio cards and access points choose not to implement WEP. However, the transmission of unprotected data outdoors offers a greater risk than within a closed facility such as an office building. It is very likely that the high demand today for implementing wireless metropolitan networks will drive a significant need for information security mechanisms.

Station States and Corresponding Frame Types

The state existing between a source and destination station (see Figure 3.10) governs which IEEE 802.11 frame types the two stations can exchange.

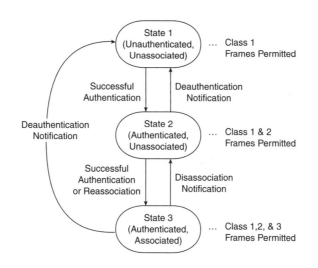

FIGURE 3.10

The operation of a station depends on its particular state.

The following types of functions can occur within each class of frame:

Class 1 Frames

- Control frames

  Request to send (RTS)

  Clear to send (CTS)

  Acknowledgment (ACK)

  Contention-free (CF)

- Management frames

  Probe request/response

  Beacon

  Authentication

  Deauthentication

  Announcement traffic indication message (ATIM)

- Data frames

Class 2 Frames

- Management Frames

  Association request/response

  Reassociation request/response

  Disassociation

Class 3 Frames

- Data frames

  Management frames

  Deauthentication

  Control frames

  Power Save Poll

To keep track of station state, each station maintains the following two state variables:

- **Authentication state**   Has values of unauthenticated and authenticated.
- **Association state**   Has values of unassociated and associated.

> **NOTE**
>
> The IEEE 802.11e working group is in the process of enhancing the 802.11 MAC to support QoS (quality of service) requirements. This effort is also providing improvements to 802.11 security and efficiency.

> **NOTE**
>
> Keep up to date on the IEEE 802.11 working group activities by periodically visiting its Web site at http://www.manta.ieee.org/groups/802/11/index.html.

As mentioned in this chapter, the 802.11 wireless LAN standard certainly has benefits that an organization should consider when selecting components that provide LAN mobility. IEEE 802 is a solid family of standards that will provide much greater multiple-level interoperability than proprietary systems. The 802.11 standard has the backing of IEEE, having an excellent track record of developing long-lasting standards, such as IEEE 802.3 (ethernet) and IEEE 802.5 (token ring).

Chapters 4 and 5 cover the details of the 802.11 standards.

Inside IEEE 802.11

IN THIS PART

IEEE 802.11 Medium Access Control (MAC) Layer

IN THIS CHAPTER

IEEE 802.11 MAC Layer Operations

Each station and access point on an 802.11 wireless LAN implements the MAC layer service, which provides the capability for peer LLC entities to exchange MAC service data units (MSDUs) between MAC service access points (SAPs). The MSDUs carry LLC-based frames that facilitate functions of the Logical Link Control (LLC) layer. Overall, MAC services encompass the transmission of MSDUs by sharing a wireless radio wave or infrared light medium.

The MAC layer provides these primary operations:

- Accessing the wireless medium
- Joining a network
- Providing authentication and privacy

The succeeding sections describe these operations.

> **NOTE**
>
> The ISO/IEC 8802-11 (ANSI/IEEE standard 802.11), dated August 20, 1999, defines the 802.11 MAC in clauses 6, 7, 8, 9, and 10.
>
> The 802.11 MAC sublayer was designed to be common among different 802.11 PHYs, such as 802.11 direct sequence, 802.11 frequency hopping, 802.11a, and 802.11b. However, the MAC communicates with specific PHYs using service access point primitives having different parameters. For example, the 802.11a MAC includes parameters specifying more data rates than the 802.11b MAC. This must be taken into consideration when designing the MAC software.

Accessing the Wireless Medium

Before transmitting a frame, the MAC coordination must first gain access to the network using one of the following modes:

- **Carrier-sense multiple access with collision avoidance (CSMA/CA)**   A contention-based protocol similar to IEEE 802.3 ethernet. The 802.11 specification refers to this mode as the *distributed coordination function (DCF)*.

- **Priority-based access**   A contention-free access protocol usable on infrastructure network configurations containing a controller called a point coordinator with the access points. The 802.11 specification refers to this mode as the *point coordination function (PCF)*.

Both the distributed and the point coordination functions can operate concurrently with the same BSS to provide alternating contention and contention-free periods. The following sections describe each of these MAC operational modes.

Distributed Coordination Function

The mandatory distributed coordination function is the primary access protocol for the automatic sharing of the wireless medium between stations and access points having compatible PHYs. Similar to the MAC coordination of the 802.3 ethernet wired line standard, 802.11 networks use a carrier-sense multiple access/collision avoidance (CSMA/CA) protocol for sharing the wireless medium.

Carrier Sense Mechanism

A combination of both physical and virtual carrier sense mechanisms enables the MAC coordination to determine whether the medium is busy or idle (see Figure 4.1). Each of the PHY layers provides a physical means of sensing the channel. The result of the physical channel assessment from the PHY coordination is sent to the MAC coordination as part of the information in deciding the status of the channel.

The MAC coordination carries out the virtual carrier sense protocol based on reservation information found in the Duration field of all frames. This information announces (to all other stations) a station's impending use of the medium. The MAC coordination will monitor the Duration field in all MAC frames and place this information in the station's NAV (network allocation vector) if the value is greater than the current NAV value. The NAV operates like a timer, starting with a value equal to the Duration field value of the last frame transmission sensed on the medium and counting down to zero. Once the NAV reaches zero, the station can transmit if the PHY coordination indicates a clear channel.

The physical channel assessment and NAV contents provide sufficient information for the MAC to decide the status of the channel. As an example, the PHY may determine there are no transmissions taking place on the medium, but the NAV may indicate that a previous frame transmission had a value in the applicable Duration field that disables transmissions for a specific time period. In that case, the MAC would hold off transmission of any frames until the Duration time period expires. If the channel is busy, the MAC protocol implements a backoff algorithm.

The CSMA/CA protocol avoids the probability of collisions among stations sharing the medium by using a random backoff time if the station's physical or logical sensing mechanism indicates a busy medium. The period of time immediately following a busy medium is when the highest probability of collisions occurs, especially under high utilization. The reason for this is that many stations may be waiting for the medium to become idle and will attempt to transmit at the same time. Once the medium is idle, a random backoff time defers a station from transmitting a frame, minimizing the chance that stations will collide.

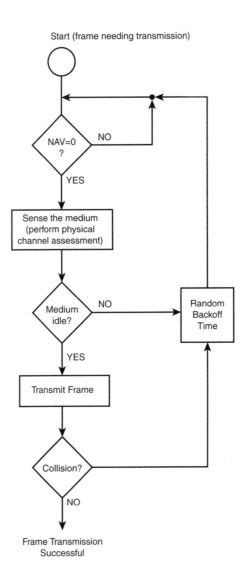

FIGURE 4.1

This flowchart illustrates the operation of the CSMA/CA contention-based 802.11 distributed coordination function (DCF) medium access protocol.

The MAC coordination calculates the random backoff time using the following formula:

```
Backoff Time = Random() * aSlotTime
```

Random() is a pseudo-random integer drawn from a uniform distribution over the interval [0,CW], in which CW (collision window) is an integer within the range of values of the MIB (management information base) attributes aCWmin and aCWmax. The random number drawn from this interval should be statistically independent among stations. aSlotTime equals a constant value found in the station's MIB.

NOTE

The MAC layer includes a *management information base (MIB)* that stores parameters the MAC protocol needs to operate. Refer to the 802.11 standard for a complete description of these parameters. Most access points require you to supply an alphanumeric name if accessing configuration parameters via the network.

The MAC layer has access to the MIB via the following MAC sublayer management entity (MLME) primitives:

- **MLME-GET.request**   Requests the value of a specific MIB attribute.
- **MLME-GET.confirm**   Returns the value of the applicable MIB attribute value that corresponds to a MLME-GET.request.
- **MLME-SET.request**   Requests that the MIB set a specific MIB attribute to a particular value.
- **MLME-SET.confirm**   Returns the status of the MLME-SET.request.

Figure 4.2 illustrates the value of CW as the station goes through successive retransmissions. The reason CW increases exponentially is to minimize collisions and maximize throughput for both low and high network utilization.

Under low utilization, stations are not forced to wait very long before transmitting their frame. On the first or second attempt, a station will make a successful transmission within a short period of time. If the utilization of the network is high, the protocol holds stations back for longer period of times to avoid the probability of multiple ones transmitting at the same time.

Under high utilization, the value of CW increases to relatively high values after successive retransmissions, providing substantial transmission spacing between stations needing to transmit. This mechanism does a good job of avoiding collisions; however, stations on networks with high utilization will experience substantial delays while waiting to transmit frames.

Error Recovery Mechanisms

Because of transmission impairments, such as interference and collisions, bit errors can disrupt the sequencing of frames. For example, station A may send an RTS (Request to Send) frame and never receive the corresponding CTS (Clear to Send). Or, station A may send a data frame and never receive an acknowledgement. Because of these problems, the MAC coordination performs error recovery mechanisms.

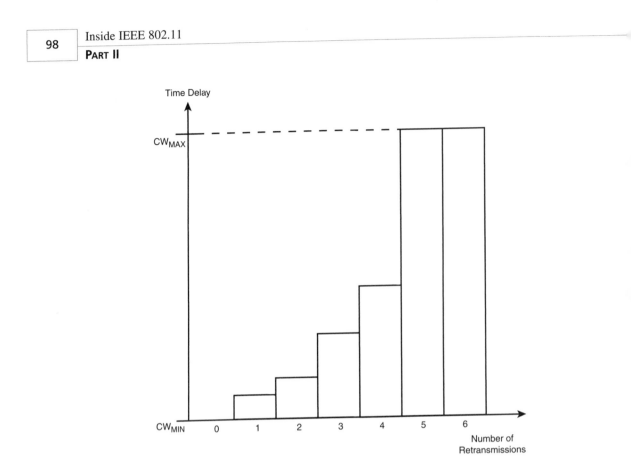

FIGURE 4.2
The backoff time increases exponentially between the minimum and maximum values of CW.

Stations initiating the exchange of frames have the responsibility of error recovery. This generally involves the retransmission of frames after a period of time if no response is heard from the destination station. This process, commonly referred to as *automatic repeat-request (ARQ)*, takes into account that bit errors could have made the ACK frame unrecognizable.

To regulate the number of retransmissions, the MAC coordination differentiates between short and long frames. For short frames (frames with length less than the MIB attribute aRTSThreshold), retransmissions continue until the number of attempts reaches the MIB value aShortRetryLimit. The MAC coordination retransmits long frames similarly based on the MIB value aLongRetrylimit. After exceeding the retry limit, the station discards the frame.

Access Spacing

The 802.11 specification defines several standard spacing intervals (defined in the MIB) that defer a station's access to the medium and provides various levels of priority. Figure 4.3 illustrates these intervals. Each interval defines the time between the end of the last symbol of the previous frame to the beginning of the first symbol of the next frame.

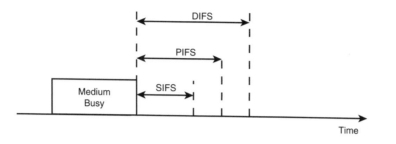

FIGURE 4.3

The interframe space (IFS) illustrates the spacing between different aspects of the MAC access protocol.

The following describes each of the interframe space (IFS) intervals:

- **Short IFS (SIFS)**   The SIFS is the shortest of the interframe spaces, providing the highest priority level by allowing some frames to access the medium before others. The following frames use the SIFS interval:
    - ACK (Acknowledgement) frame
    - CTS (Clear to Send) frame
    - The second or subsequent MSDU of a fragment burst

    These frames require expedient access to the network to minimize frame retransmissions.

- **PCF IFS (PIFS)**   The PIFS is the interval that stations operating under the point coordination function use to gain access to the medium. This provides priority over frames sent by the distributed coordination function. These stations can transmit contention-free traffic if they sense the medium is idle. This interval gives point coordination function–based stations a higher priority of access than DCF-based (CSMA) stations for transmitting frames.

- **DCF IFS (DIFS)**   All stations operating according to the distributed coordination function use the DIFS interval for transmitting data frames and management frames. This spacing makes the transmission of these frames lower priority than PCF-based transmissions.

- **Extended IFS (EIFS)**   All DCF-based stations use the EIFS interval—which goes beyond the time of a DIFS interval—as a waiting period when a frame transmission results in a bad reception of the frame due to an incorrect FCS value. This interval provides enough time for the receiving station to send an ACK frame.

Point Coordination Function (PCF)

The optional priority-based point coordination function provides contention-free frame transfer for processing time-critical information transfers. With this operating mode, a point coordinator resides in the access point to control the transmission of frames from stations. All stations obey the point coordinator by setting their NAV value at the beginning of each contention-free period. Stations optionally can respond to a contention-free poll (CF Poll frame), though.

At the beginning of the contention-free period, the point coordinator has an opportunity to gain control of the medium. The point coordinator follows the PIFS interval as a basis for accessing the medium; therefore, it may be able to maintain control during the contention-free period by waiting a shorter time between transmissions than stations operating under the distributed coordination function.

The point coordinator senses the medium at the beginning of each contention-free period. If the medium is idle after the PIFS interval, the point coordinator sends a beacon frame that includes the CF Parameter Set element. When stations receive the beacon, they update their NAV with the CFPMaxDuration value found in the CF Parameter Set. This value communicates the length of the contention-free period to all stations and prevents stations from taking control of the medium until the end of the contention-free period.

After sending the beacon frame, the point coordinator then transmits one of the following frames after waiting at least one SIFS interval:

- **Data frame**   This frame is directed from the access point's point coordinator to a particular station. If the point coordinator does not receive an ACK frame from the recipient, the point coordinator can retransmit the unacknowledged frame during the contention-free period after the PIFS interval. A point coordinator can send individual, broadcast, and multicast frames to all stations, including stations in Power Save mode that are pollable.

- **CF Poll frame**   The point coordinator sends this frame to a particular station, granting the station permission to transmit a single frame to any destination. If the polled station has no frame to send, it must send a Null data frame. If the sending station does not receive any frame acknowledgement, it cannot retransmit the frame unless the point coordinator polls it again. If the receiving station of the contention-free transmission is not CF Pollable, it acknowledges the reception of the frame using distributed coordination function rules.

- **Data+CF Poll frame**   In this case, the point coordinator sends a data frame to a station and polls that same station for sending a contention-free frame. This is a form of piggybacking that reduces overhead on the network.

- **CF End frame**   This frame is sent to identify the end of the contention period, which occurs when one of the following happens:

    - The CFPDurRemaining time expires.

    - The point coordinator has no further frames to transmit and no stations to poll.

Stations have an option of being *pollable*. A station can indicate its desire for polling using the CF Pollable subfield within the Capability Information field of an association request frame. A station can change its pollability by issuing a reassociation request frame. The point coordinator maintains a polling list of eligible stations that may receive a poll during the contention-free period. The point coordinator will send at least one CF poll if entries exist in the polling list in order by ascending AID value. When associating with an access point, a station may request to be on the polling list via the Capability Information field.

The point coordination function does not routinely operate using the backoff time of the distributed coordination function; therefore, a risk of collisions exists when overlapping point coordinators are present on the same PHY channel. This may be the case when multiple access points form an infrastructure network. To minimize these collisions, the point coordinator utilizes a random backoff time if the point coordinator experiences a busy medium when attempting to transmit the initial beacon.

NOTE

By default, all 802.11-compliant stations operate using the *distributed coordination function (DCF)*, which is a carrier sense access mechanism. As an option, you can initialize the stations to also implement the priority-based *point coordination function (PCF)*.

In most cases, the DCF will suffice; however, consider activation of the PCF if needing to support the transmission of time-bounded information, such as audio and video. The PCF, though, will impose greater overhead on the network because of the transmission of polling frames.

Joining a Network

Once a station is turned on, it needs to first determine whether another station or access point is present to join before authenticating and associating with an applicable station or access point. The station accomplishes this discovery phase by operating in a passive or active scanning mode. After joining with a BSS or an ESS, the station accepts the SSID (service set identifier), TSF (timing synchronization function) timer value, and PHY setup parameters from the access point.

With passive scanning, a station listens to each channel for a specific period of time, as defined by the ChannelTime parameter. The station just waits for the transmission of beacon frames having the SSID that the station wants to join. Once the station detects the beacon, the station can negotiate a connection by proceeding with authentication and association processes.

TIP

You can configure a station to scan passively for other stations for a particular amount of time before enabling the station to form its own network. The typical default time for this setting is 10 seconds.

Active scanning involves the transmission of a Probe frame indicating the SSID of the network that the station wants to join. The station that sent the probe will wait for a Probe Response frame that identifies the presence of the desired network.

Some vendors enable you to set up each radio card so that it associates with a preferred access point even if the signal from that particular access point is lower than the signals from other access points. This may be useful if there's a need to regulate the flow of traffic through particular access points. In most cases, the station will reassociate with another access point, though, if it doesn't receive beacons from the preferred access point.

A station can also send probes using a broadcast SSID that causes all networks within reach to respond. An access point will reply to all probe requests in the case of infrastructure-based networks. With independent BSS networks (that is, those with no access point), the station that generated the last beacon frame will respond to probe requests. The Probe Response frame indicates the presence of the desired networks, and the station can complete its connection by proceeding with the authentication and association processes.

Station Synchronization

Stations within the BSS must remain in synchronization with the access point to ensure that all stations are operating with the same parameters (such as using the correct hopping pattern) and enabling power-saving functions to work correctly. To accomplish this, the access point periodically transmits beacon frames.

The beacon contains information about the particular Physical layer being used. For example, the beacon identifies the frequency hopping sequence and dwell time so the station can implement the applicable demodulation. The beacon also contains the access point's clock value. Each station receiving the beacon will use this information to update its clock accordingly, so the station knows when to wake up (if in Sleep mode) to receive beacons.

Providing Authentication and Privacy

Because of the open broadcast nature of wireless LANs, designers need to implement appropriate levels of security. The 802.11 standard describes the two following types of authentication services that increase the security of 802.11 networks:

- **Open system authentication** The default authentication service that simply announces the desire to associate with another station or access point.

- **Shared key authentication** The optional authentication that involves a more rigorous exchange of frames, ensuring that the requesting station is authentic.

The following sections describe the operation of these authentication types, as well as the wired equivalent privacy (WEP) function.

> **NOTE**
>
> When setting up your wireless LAN, consider the type of authentication to use based on security requirements. Vendors enable you to configure a station or access point to operate using either open encryption, shared key, or no security. The default operation is generally open encryption. If you implement the shared key mode, you'll need to configure all stations with the same key.

Open System Authentication

An organization may want to use open system authentication if it is not necessary to validate positively the identity of a sending station. A station can authenticate with any other station or access point using open system authentication if the receiving station designates open system authentication via the MIB parameter aAuthenticationType.

Figure 4.4 illustrates the operation of open system authentication. The Status Code located in the body of the second authentication frame identifies success or failure of the authentication.

Shared Key Authentication

The optional shared key authentication approach provides a much higher degree of security than with the open system approach. For a station to use shared key authentication, it must implement WEP. Figure 4.5 illustrates the operation of shared key authentication. The secret shared key resides in each station's MIB in a write-only form to make it available to only the MAC coordination. The 802.11 standard, though, does not specify the process of installing the key in stations.

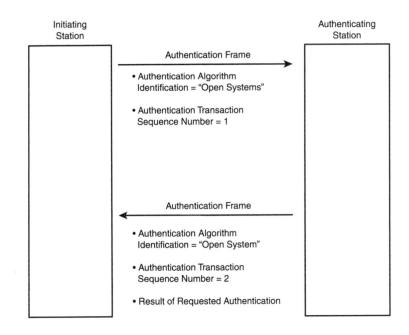

FIGURE 4.4

The first frame of the open system authentication service requests authentication, and the second frame transmission indicates acceptance or rejection.

The process is as follows:

1. A requesting station sends an authentication frame to another station.

2. When a station receives an initial authentication frame, the station will reply with an authentication frame containing of 128 octets of challenge text that the WEP services generate.

3. The requesting station will then copy the challenge text into an authentication frame, encrypt it with a shared key, then send the frame to the responding station.

4. The receiving station will decrypt the value of the challenge text using the same shared key and compare it to the challenge text sent earlier. If a match occurs, then the responding station will reply with an authentication indicating a successful authentication. If not, the responding station will send a negative authentication.

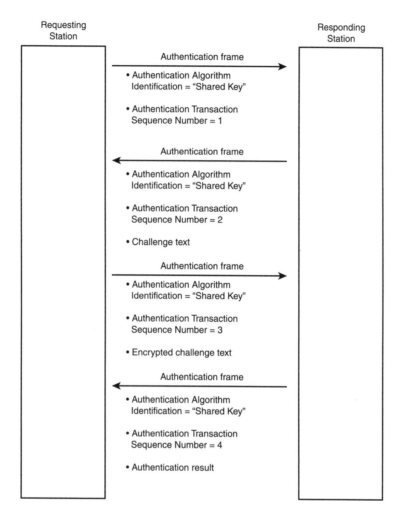

FIGURE 4.5

The shared key authentication service uses the transmission of frames that (1) request authentication, (2) deliver challenge text, (3) deliver an encrypted frame, including the challenge text, and (4) accept or reject the authentication.

Private Frame Transmissions

To offer frame transmission privacy similar to a wired network, the 802.11 specification defines optional WEP. WEP generates secret shared encryption keys that both source and destination stations can use to alter frame bits to avoid disclosure to eavesdroppers. This process is also known as *symmetric encryption*. Stations can use WEP alone without authentication services, but they should implement both WEP and authentication together to avoid making the LAN vulnerable to security threats.

Figure 4.6 shows the processing that occurs with the WEP algorithm.

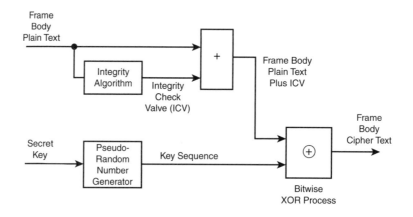

FIGURE 4.6

The wired equivalent privacy (WEP) safeguards data transmissions by performing a series of operations using a secret shared key.

The process is as follows:

1. At the sending station, the WEP encipherment first runs the unencrypted data located in the Frame Body of a MAC frame through an integrity algorithm. This algorithm generates a four-octet integrity check value that is sent with the data and checked at the receiving station to guard against unauthorized data modification.

2. The WEP process inputs the secret shared encryption key into a pseudo-random number generator to create a key sequence with length equal to the `plaintext` and integrity check value.

3. WEP encrypts the data by bitwise XORing the `plaintext` and integrity check value with the key sequence to create `ciphertext`. The pseudo-random number generator makes key distribution much easier because only the shared key must be made available to each station, not the variable length key sequence.

4. At the receiving station, the WEP process deciphers the `ciphertext` using the shared key that generates the same key sequence used initially to encrypt the frame.

5. The station calculates an integrity check value and ensures that it matches the one sent with the frame. If the integrity check fails, the station will not hand the MSDU off to the LLC, and a failure indication is sent to MAC management.

MAC Frame Structure

The following sections define each field and subfield of the MAC frame. For a formal description (using the ITU Specification and Description Language) of the MAC layer operation, refer to Appendix C of the 802.11 standard.

Overall MAC Frame Format

The IEEE 802.11 standard specifies an overall MAC frame format, as shown in Figure 4.7. This frame structure is found in all frames that stations transmit, regardless of frame type. After forming the applicable frame, the MAC coordination passes the frame's bits to the Physical Layer Convergence Protocol (PLCP), starting with the first bit of the Frame Control field and ending with the last bit of the frame check sequence (FCS).

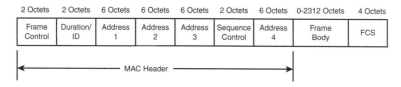

FIGURE 4.7

The MAC frame consists of a header, variable length Frame Body, and a 32-bit frame check sequence (FCS), all of which support MAC layer functionality.

The following defines each of the main MAC frame fields:

- **Frame Control**   This field carries control information being sent from station to station. Figure 4.8 illustrates specific subfields within the Frame Control field.

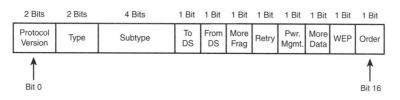

FIGURE 4.8

The Frame Control field defines the frame as a management, control, or data frame.

- **Duration/ID**   In most frames, this field contains a duration value, depending on the type of frame sent. (See the section "MAC Frame Types," later in this chapter, for possible values.) In general, each frame contains information that identifies the duration of the next frame transmission. As an example, the Duration/ID field in data and acknowledgment (ACK) frames specifies the total duration of the next fragment and acknowledgment. Stations on the network monitor this field and hold off transmissions based on the duration information.

In Power Save–Poll control frames only, the Duration/ID field carries the 14 least significant bits of the association identity of the sending station. The two remaining bits for this field are set to 1. Possible values for this identification are currently in the decimal range 1–2007.

- **Address 1, 2, 3, and 4**   The address fields contain different types of addresses, depending on the type of frame being sent. These address types may include the basic service set identification (BSSID), source address, destination address, transmitting station address, and receiving station address. IEEE standard 802-1990 defines the structure of the addresses, which are all 48 bits in length.

  The addresses can be either individual or group addresses. There are two types of group addresses: *multicast*, which associate with a group of logically related stations, and *broadcast* addresses, which refer to all stations on a given LAN. A broadcast address consists of all ones.

- **Sequence Control**   The leftmost four bits of this field consist of a Fragment Number subfield, indicating the fragment number of a particular MSDU. This number starts with 0 for the first fragment, then increments by 1 for each successive transmission. The next 12 bits of this frame are the Sequence Number subfield, starting at 0 and incrementing by 1 for each subsequent MSDU transmission. Each fragment of a specific MSDU will have the same sequence number.

  A station shall have one or more outstanding MDDUs concurrently. On reception of a frame, a station can filter duplicate frames by monitoring the sequence and fragment numbers. The station knows the frame is a duplicate if the sequence number and fragment number are equal to the frame immediately preceding, or the Retry bit is set to 1.

  Duplicate frames can occur when a station receives a frame without errors and sends an ACK frame back to the sending station, then transmission errors destroy the ACK frame en route. After not receiving the ACK over a specific time period, the sending station retransmits a duplicate frame. The destination station performs an acknowledgement of the retransmitted frame even if the frame is discarded due to duplicate filtering.

- **Frame Body**   This field has a variable length payload and carries information that pertains to the specific frame being sent. In the case of a data frame, this field may contain a LLC data unit (also called an MSDU). MAC management and control frames may include specific parameters in the Frame Body that pertain to the particular service the frame is implementing. If the frame has no need to carry information, then this field has length of zero. The receiving station will determine the frame length from a field within the applicable Physical layer headers (see Chapter 5, "IEEE 802.11 Physical (PHY) Layer").

- **Frame Check Sequence (FCS)**   The MAC layer at the sending station calculates a 32-bit frame check sequence (FCS) using a cyclic redundancy code (CRC) and places the result in this field. The MAC layer uses the following generator polynomial over all fields of the MAC header and Frame Body to calculate the FCS:

  $G(x)=X^{32}+X^{26}+X^{23}+X^{22}+X^{16}+X^{12}+X^{11}+X^{10}+X^{8}+X^{7}+X^{5}+X^{4}+X^{2}+X+1.$

  The result's highest-order coefficient is placed in the field at the leftmost bit. The receiver implements a CRC to check for transmission errors in the frame.

> **NOTE**
>
> The *basic service set identification (BSSID)*, also known as a network ID, is a six-byte address that distinguishes a particular access point from others. Most access points will ship with a default BSSID, and you can change the ID through configuration parameters if you're installing a network with multiple access points.
>
> Be sure to avoid conflicts by assigning a different BSSID for each access point. Typically, you can set up the access point via its management utility to automatically choose a BSSID that doesn't conflict with other BSSs operating in the same area.

Frame Control Field

The following defines each of the subfields with the Frame Control field:

- **Protocol Version field**   For the current standard, the protocol version is zero; therefore, the Protocol Version field always contains 0. IEEE will add version numbers in the future if a newer version of the standard is fundamentally incompatible with an earlier version.

- **Type field**   This field defines whether the frame is a management, control, or data frame as indicated by the bits in the following table:

bit3, bit2	Frame Type
0, 0	Management frame
0, 1	Control frame
1, 0	Data frame
1, 1	Reserved

> **NOTE**
>
> All reserved bits are transmitted as value 0 and are ignored by the receiving station.

- **Subtype field** This field defines the function of the frame, as shown in the following table:

Frame Type	Subfield (Bits 7,6,5,4)	Frame Function
Management Type (bit 3, bit 2)=00	0000	Association Request
	0001	Association Response
	0010	Reassociation Request
	0011	Reassociation Response
	0100	Probe Request
	0101	Probe Response
	0110–0111	Reserved
	1000	Beacon
	1001	Announcement Traffic Indication Map (ATIM)
	1010	Disassociation
	1011	Authentication
	1100	Deauthentication
	1101–1111	Reserved
Control Type (bit 3, bit 2)=01	0000–1001	Reserved
	1010	Power-Save (PS) Poll
	1011	Request to Send (RTS)
	1100	Clear to Send (CTS)
	1101	Acknowledgement (ACK)
	1110	Contention Free (CF) End
	1111	CF End + CF ACK
Data Type (bit 3, bit 2)=10	0000	Data
	0001	Data + CF ACK
	0010	Data + CF Poll

Frame Type	Subfield (Bits 7,6,5,4)	Frame Function
	0011	Data + CF ACK + CF Poll
	0100	Null (no data)
	0101	CF ACK
	0110	CF Poll
	0111	CF ACK + CF Poll
	1000–1111	Reserved
Reserved Type (bit 3, bit 2)=11	0000–111	

Limiting Multicast Traffic

A *delivery traffic indication message (DTIM)* determines how often the MAC layer forwards multicast traffic. This parameter is necessary to accommodate stations using Power Save mode. You can set the DTIM value via the access point. If you set the value to 2, the access point will save all multicast frames for the BSS and forward them after every second beacon.

Having smaller DTIM intervals delivers multicast frames in a more timely manner, causing stations in Power Save mode to wake up more often and drain power faster. Having higher DTIM values, though, delays the transmission of multicast frames.

- **To DS field** The MAC coordination sets this single-bit field to 1 in any frame destined for the distribution system. It is 0 for all other transmissions. An example of this bit being set would be when a frame's destination is in a radio cell (also called BSS) of a different access point.

- **From DS field** The MAC coordination sets this single-bit field to 1 in any frame leaving the distribution system. It is 0 for all other transmissions. Both the To DS and From DS fields are set to 1 if the frame is being sent from one access point through the distribution system to another access point.

- **More Frag field** This single-bit field is set to 1 if another fragment of the same MSDU follows in a subsequent frame.

Implementing Fragmentation

The MAC services provide fragmentation and defragmentation services to support the division of MSDUs into smaller elements for transmission. Fragmentation can increase the reliability of transmission because it increases the probability of a successful transmission due to smaller frame size. Each station can support the concurrent reception and defragmentation of fragments for up to three MSDUs. The MAC layer fragments only frames having a unicast receiver address. It never fragments broadcast and multicast frames because of significant resulting overhead on the network.

If the length of the MSDU needing transmission exceeds the aFragmentationThreshold parameter located in the MAC's management information base (MIB), then the MAC protocol will fragment the MSDU. Each fragmented frame consists of a MAC header, FCS, and a fragment number indicating its ordered position in the MSDU. Each of the fragments is sent independently and requires separate ACKs from the receiving station. The More Fragment field in the Frame Control field indicates whether or not a frame is the last of a series of fragments.

After decryption takes place (if the station is implementing WEP), the destination station will combine all fragments of the same sequence number in the correct order to reconstruct the corresponding MSDU. Based on the fragment numbers, the destination station will discard any duplicate fragments.

If there is significant interference present or collisions due to high network utilization, try setting the fragment size to send smaller fragments. This will enable the retransmission of smaller frames much faster. However, it is more efficient to set the fragment size larger if very little or no interference is present because it requires overhead to send multiple frames. The fragment size value can typically be set between 256 and 2,048 bytes.

- **Retry field**   If the frame is a retransmission of an earlier frame, this single-bit field is set to 1. It is 0 for all other transmissions. The reason for retransmission could be because the errors in the transmission of the first frame resulted in an unsuccessful FCS.

Setting the Transmission Retry Time

You can set the retry time on stations to govern the amount of time a station will wait before attempting to retransmit a frame if no acknowledgement appears from the receiving station. This time value is normally set between 1 and 30 seconds. You can also set the number of retries that will occur before the station gives up. This value can normally be set between 0 and 64.

- **Power Management field**   The bit in this field indicates the power management mode that the sending station will be in after the current frame exchange sequence. The MAC layer places 1 in this field if the station will be in a sleep mode (802.11 defines this as Power Save mode). A 0 indicates the station will be in full Active mode. A receiving station can use this information to adjust transmissions to avoid waking up sleeping stations. In most cases, battery-operated devices should be kept in Power Save mode to conserve battery power.

- **More Data field**   If a station has additional MSDUs to send to a station that is in Power Save mode, then the sending station will place 1 in this field. The More Data field is 0 for all other transmissions. The More Data feature alerts the receiving station to be ready for additional frames. An example of using this feature is when a station is sending a group of fragments belonging to a single MSDU.

- **WEP field**   A 1 in this field tells the receiving station that the Frame Body has been processed by the WEP algorithm—that is, the data bits have been encrypted using a secret key. The WEP field bit is 0 for all other types of transmissions. Refer to the section "Private Frame Transmissions," earlier in this chapter, to learn how the WEP algorithm works.

- **Order field**   This field is set to 1 in any data frame being sent using the StrictlyOrdered service class, which tells the receiving station that frames must be processed in order.

NOTE

The IEEE 802.11 standard makes use of the same 48-bit MAC address that is compatible with the entire 802 LAN family. The 802.11 architecture can handle multiple logical media and address spaces, which makes 802.11 independent of the distribution system implementation.

The vendor you purchase the radio card and access points from usually guarantees that the MAC address loaded in the radio is unique from all other radios, even those from other vendors. You normally have the option to change the MAC address of the card; however, you should use the factory-set address to avoid the potential of address conflicts.

IEEE 802.11 defines the following address types:

- **Destination Address (DA)**   The final destination of the MSDU that is in the Frame Body of the MAC frame.

- **Source Address (SA)**   The address of the MAC entity that initiated the MSDU transmission.

- **Receiver Address (RA)** The address of the access point that is to receive the frame next.
- **Transmitter Address (TA)** The address of the immediately preceding access point sending the frame.

MAC Frame Types

To carry out the delivery of MSDUs between peer LLCs, the MAC layer uses a variety of frame types, each having a particular purpose. The IEEE 802.11 specification divides MAC frames into three broad categories that provide management, control, and data exchange functions between stations and access points. The following sections describe the structure of each major frame type.

Management Frames

The purpose of management frames is to establish initial communications between stations and access points. Thus, management frames provide such services as association and authentication. Figure 4.9 depicts the common format of all management frames.

FIGURE 4.9

The management frame format includes destination address, source address, and BSSID in address fields 1, 2, and 3, respectively.

The Duration field within all management frames during the contention-free period (as defined by the point coordination function) is set to decimal 32,768 (hexadecimal value of 8000), giving management frames plenty of time to establish communications before other stations have the capability to access the medium.

During the contention period (as defined by the CSMA-based distributed coordination function), all management frames have the Duration field set as follows:

- If the destination address is a group address, the Duration field is set to 0.
- If the More Frag bit is set to 0 and the destination address is an individual address, then the Duration field contains the number of microseconds required to transmit one ACK frame plus one short interframe space. (The section "Access Spacing," earlier in this chapter, defines the interframe space.)

- If the More Frag bit is set to 1 and the destination address is an individual address, then the Duration field contains the number of microseconds required to transmit the next fragment, plus two ACK frames, plus three short interframe spaces.

A station receiving a management frame performs address matching for receive decisions based on the contents of the Address 1 field of the MAC frame, which is the destination address (DA). If the address matches the station, then that station completes the reception of the frame and hands it off to the LLC layer. If a match does not occur, the station ignores the rest of the frame.

The following defines each of the management frame subtypes:

- **Association request frame**   A station will send this frame to an access point if it wants to associate with that access point. A station becomes associated with an access point after the access point grants permission.

- **Association response frame**   After an access point receives an association request frame, the access point will send an association response frame to indicate whether or not it is accepting the association with the sending station.

- **Reassociation request frame**   A station will send this frame to an access point if it wants to reassociate with that access point. A reassociation may occur if a station moves out of range from one access point and within range of another access point. The station will need to reassociate (not merely *associate*) with the new access point so that the new access point knows that it will need to negotiate the forwarding of data frames from the old access point.

- **Reassociation response frame**   After an access point receives a reassociation request frame, the access point will send a reassociation response frame to indicate whether or not it is accepting the reassociation with the sending station.

- **Probe request frame**   A station sends a probe request frame to obtain information from another station or access point. For example, a station may send a probe request frame to determine whether a certain access point is available.

- **Probe response frame**   If a station or access point receives a probe request frame, the station will respond to the sending station with a probe response frame containing specific parameters about itself (such as parameter sets for the frequency hopping and direct sequence PHYs).

- **Beacon frame**   In an infrastructure network, an access point periodically sends a beacon (according to the aBeaconPeriod parameter in the MIB) that provides synchronization among stations utilizing the same PHY. The beacon includes a timestamp that all stations use to update what 802.11 defines as a timing synchronization function (TSF) timer.

If the access point supports the point coordination function, then it uses a beacon frame to announce the beginning of a contention-free period. If the network is an independent BSS (that is, it has no access points), all stations periodically send beacons for synchronization purposes.

- **ATIM frame**   A station with frames buffered for other stations sends an announcement traffic indication message (ATIM) frame to each of these stations during the ATIM window, which immediately follows a beacon transmission. The station then transmits these frames to the applicable recipients. The transmission of the ATIM frame alerts stations in sleep state to stay awake long enough to receive their respective frames.

- **Disassociation frame**   If a station or access point wants to terminate an association, it will send a disassociation frame to the opposite station. A single disassociation frame can terminate associations with more than one station through the broadcast address of all ones.

- **Authentication frame**   A station sends an authentication frame to a station or access point that it wants to authenticate with. The authentication sequence consists of the transmission of one or more authentication frames, depending on the type of authentication being implemented (open system or shared key). Refer to the section "Providing Authentication and Privacy," earlier in this chapter.

- **Deauthentication frame**   A station sends a deauthentication frame to a station or access point with which it wants to terminate secure communications.

The content of the Frame Body field of management frames depends on the type of management frame being sent. Figure 4.10 identifies the Frame Body contents of each management frame subtype.

Implementing Power Management

The power management function of an IEEE 802.11 network enables stations to go into sleep mode to conserve power for long periods of time without losing information. The 802.11 power management is supported with the use of access points; therefore, it's not available when implementing ad hoc networks. You should definitely consider implementing this feature if the conservation of batteries powering the radio card and appliance is a concern.

You implement power management on IEEE 802.11 LANs by first setting the access points and radio cards to power-save mode via the vendor's parameter initialization routines. The access points and radio cards will then carry out the power management functions automatically. As part of the power management routine, the access points will maintain a record of the stations currently working in power-save mode by monitoring the single-bit power management field in the Frame Control field of the MAC header for frames sent on the network. The access points will buffer packets addressed to the stations in power-save mode.

The access points will forward the buffered packets to the applicable stations when they return to active state (awake state) or when the stations request them. The access point knows when a station awakens because the station will indicate its active state by toggling the power management bit in the Frame Control field of the MAC frames.

A station can learn that it has frames buffered at the access point by listening to the beacons sent periodically by the access point. The beacons will have a list (called a *traffic indication map*) of stations having buffered frames at the access point. A station uses a power-save poll frame to notify the access point to send the buffered packets.

Frame Body Contents	Association Request	Association Response	Reassociation Request	Reassociation Response	Probe Response	Probe Request	Beacon	Disassociation	Authentication	Deauthentication
Authentication Algorithm Number									X	
Authentication Transaction Sequence Number									X	
Beacon Interval					X		X			
Current IP Address			X							
Listen Interval	X		X							
Reason Code								X		X
Association ID (AID)		X		X						
Status Code		X		X					X	
Timestamp					X		X			
Service Set Identity (SSID)	X		X		X	X	X			
Supported Rates	X	X	X	X	X	X	X			
FH Parameter Set					X		X			
DS Parameter Set					X		X			
CF Parameter Set					X		X			
Capability Information	X	X	X	X	X		X			
Traffic Indication Map (TIM)							X			
IBSS Parameter Set					X		X			
Challenge Text									X	

FIGURE 4.10

The Frame Body contents of a management frame depend on the frame subtype.

4

IEEE 802.11
MEDIUM ACCESS
CONTROL LAYER

The 802.11 standard describes the Frame Body elements of the management frame subtypes. Refer to the standard if you need detailed information, such as field formats. The following, however, summarizes each of the elements:

- **Authentication Algorithm Number**   This field specifies the authentication algorithm that the authenticated stations and access points are to use. The value is either 0 for open system authentication or 1 for shared key authentication.

- **Authentication Transaction Sequence Number**   This field indicates the state of progress of the authentication process.

- **Beacon Interval**   This value is the number of time units between beacon transmission times.

- **Capability Information**   This field announces capability information about a particular station. For example, a station can identify its desire to be polled in this element.

- **Current AP Address**   This field indicates the address of the access point that the station is currently associated with.

- **Listen Interval**   This value identifies, in units of Beacon Interval, how often a station will wake to listen to beacon management frames.

- **Reason Code**   This field indicates (via a numbered code) why a station is generating an unsolicited disassociation or deauthentication. Examples of the reasons are as follows:

  - Previous authentication no longer valid.

  - Disassociated due to inactivity.

  - Station requesting association is not authenticated with responding station.

- **Association ID (AID)**   This ID, which is assigned by an access point during association, is the 16-bit identification of a station corresponding to a particular association.

- **Status Code**   This code indicates the status of a particular operation. Examples of status are as follows:

  - Successful.

  - Unspecified failure.

  - Association denied because the access point is unable to handle additional associated stations.

  - Authentication rejected due to timeout waiting for next frame in sequence.

- **Timestamp**   This field contains the timer value at the sending station when it transmits the frame.

- **Service Set Identify (SSID)**   This field contains the identity of the extended service set (ESS).

- **Supported Rates**   This field identifies all data rates a particular station can accept. This value represents the data rate in 500Kbps increments. The MAC coordination has the capability to change data rates to optimize performance of frame transmissions.

- **FH Parameter Set**   This field indicates the dwell time and hopping pattern needed to synchronize two stations using the frequency-hopping PHY.

- **DS Parameter Set**   This field identifies the channel number that stations are using with the direct sequence PHY.

- **CF Parameter Set**   This field consists of a series of parameters that support the point coordination function (PCF).

- **TIM**   The traffic indication map (TIM) element specifies the stations having MSDUs buffered at the access point.

- **IBSS Parameter Set**   This field contains parameters that support the Independent Basic Service Set (IBSS) networks.

- **Challenge Text**   This field contains the challenge text of a shared key authentication sequence.

NOTE

Some vendors add optional extensions to 802.11 management frames that provide functionality beyond the standard. As an example, additional information of an association request could set priorities for which access point a station associates with.

If you're using access points from multiple vendors, you should disable the transmission of the extensions.

Control Frames

After establishing association and authentication between stations and access points, control frames provide functionality to assist in the deliver of data frames. A common flow of control frames is shown in Figure 4.11.

The following defines the structure of each control frame subtype:

- **Request to Send (RTS)**   A station sends an RTS frame to a particular receiving station to negotiate the sending of a data frame. Through the aRTSThreshold attribute stored in the MIB, you can configure a station to initiate an RTS frame sequence always, never, or only on frames longer than a specified length.

  Figure 4.12 illustrates the format of an RTS frame. The value of the Duration field, in microseconds, is the amount of time the sending station needs to transmit the frame, plus one CTS frame, plus one ACK frame, plus three short interframe space (SIFS) intervals.

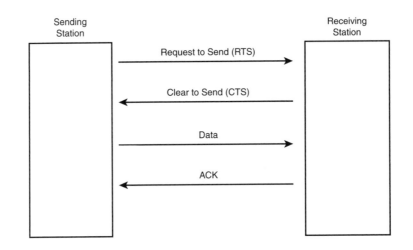

FIGURE 4.11

Control frames provide synchronization between sending and receiving stations.

2 Octets	2 Octets	6 Octets	6 Octets	4 Octets
Frame Control	Duration	RA	TA	FCS

FIGURE 4.12

The Request to Send frame format includes the receiver address (RA) and transmitter address (TA).

- **Clear to Send (CTS)**   After receiving an RTS, the station sends a CTS frame to acknowledge the right for the sending station to send data frames. Stations will always pay attention to the duration information and respond to an RTS frame, even if the station was not set up to initiate RTS frame sequences.

  Figure 4.13 illustrates the format of a CTS frame. The value of the Duration field, in microseconds, is the amount of time from the Duration field of the previous RTS frame, minus the time required to transmit the CTS frame and its SIFS interval.

2 Octets	2 Octets	6 Octets	4 Octets
Frame Control	Duration	RA	FCS

FIGURE 4.13

The Clear to Send and Acknowledgement frame formats include the receiver address (RA).

- **Acknowledgement (ACK)**   A station receiving an error-free frame must send an ACK frame to the sending station to acknowledge the successful reception of the frame. Figure 4.13 illustrates the format of an ACK frame.

  The value of the Duration field, in microseconds, is equal to 0 if the More Fragment bit in the Frame Control field of the previous data or management frame is set to 0. If the More Fragment bit of the previous data or management frame is set to 1, then the Duration field is the amount of time from the Duration field of the previous data or management frame minus the time required to transmit the ACK frame and its SIFS interval.

- **Power-Save Poll (PS Poll)**   If a station receives a PS Poll frame, the station updates its *network allocation vector (NAV)*, which is an indication of time periods during which a station will not initiate a transmission. The NAV contains a prediction of future traffic on the medium. Figure 4.14 illustrates the format of a PS Poll frame.

2 Octets	2 Octets	6 Octets	6 Octets	4 Octets
Frame Control	AID	BSSID	TA	FCS

FIGURE 4.14

The Power-Save Poll frame format includes the association identifier (AID), basic service set identification (BSSID), and the transmitter address (TA).

- **Contention–Free End (CF End)**   CF End designates the end of a contention period that is part of the point coordination function. Figure 4.15 illustrates the format of a CF End frame. In these frames, the Duration field is always set to 0, and the receiver address (RA) contains the broadcast group address.

2 Octets	2 Octets	6 Octets	6 Octets	4 Octets
Frame Control	Duration	RA	BSSID	FCS

FIGURE 4.15

The CF End and CF End + CF Ack frame formats include the receiver address (RA) and basic service set identification (BSSID).

- **CF End + CF Ack**   This frame acknowledges the contention-free end announcement of a CF End frame. Figure 4.15 illustrates the format of a CF End + CF Ack frame. In these frames, the Duration field is always set to 0, and the receiver address (RA) contains the broadcast group address.

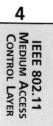

4

IEEE 802.11 MEDIUM ACCESS CONTROL LAYER

Using RTS/CTS

Because of the possibility of partial network connectivity, wireless LAN protocols must account for potential hidden stations. You can activate the RTS/CTS mode via the setup utility for the access point.

The RTS/CTS operation provides much better performance over basic access when there is a high probability of hidden stations. In addition, the performance of RTS/CTS degrades more slowly than basic access when network utilization increases. The use of RTS/CTS, though, will result in relatively low throughput in a situation where there is very little probability of hidden stations.

In the network depicted in Figure 4.16, station A and station B can both communicate directly with the access point; however, the barrier that represents lack of connectivity prevents stations A and B from communicating directly with each other. The problem is that a collision will occur when station A attempts to access the medium, because it will not be able to detect that station B is already transmitting.

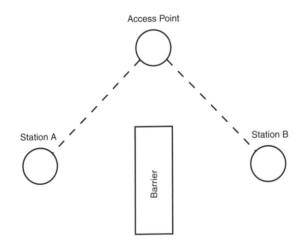

FIGURE 4.16

The barrier between stations A and B causes an access collision when station A attempts to access the medium while station B is transmitting a frame to the access point.

To guard against collisions based on hidden nodes and high utilization, the transmitting station B should send an RTS frame to the access point, requesting service for a certain amount of time. If the access point approves, it will broadcast a CTS frame announcing this time to all stations that hear the frame transmission. As a result, all stations, including station A, will not attempt to access the medium for the specified amount of time.

> **NOTE**
>
> You can set the minimum size packet that the station can use with the RTS/CTS function by accessing the configuration file of an access point or radio card. This value is normally within the range of 100 to 2048 bytes. Be aware that setting the minimum packet size too small may add excessive overhead to the network.

The RTS/CTS exchange also performs both a type of fast collision inference and a transmission path check. If the return CTS is not detected by the station originating the RTS, the originating station may repeat the process (after observing the other medium-use rules) more quickly than if the long data frame had been transmitted and a return ACK frame had not been detected. The RTS/CTS mechanism need not be used for every data frame transmission. Because the additional RTS and CTS frames add overhead inefficiency, the mechanism is not always justified, especially for short data frames.

Data Frames

The main purpose of data frames is to carry information, such as MSDUs, to the destination station for handoff to its applicable LLC layer (see Figure 4.17). These data frames may carry specific information, supervisory frames, or unnumbered frames from the LLC layer.

2 Octets	2 Octets	6 Octets	6 Octets	6 Octets	2 Octets	6 Octets	0-2312 Octets	4 Octets
Frame Control	Duration/ ID	Address 1	Address 2	Address 3	Sequence Control	Address 4	Frame Body	FCS

To DS	From DS	Address 1	Address 2	Address 3	Address 4
0	0	DA	SA	BSSID	N/A
0	1	DA	BSSID	SA	N/A
1	0	BSSID	SA	DA	N/A
1	1	RA	TA	DA	SA

FIGURE 4.17

The To DS and From DS subfields of the Frame Control field define the valid contents of the address fields.

The MAC layer is only part of the overall operations of the 802.11 protocol. A key to implementing a wireless network that fully satisfies requirements is to choose the appropriate PHY layer. Chapter 5 continues with the detailed coverage of the 802.11 standard by addressing each of the 802.11 PHYs.

IEEE 802.11 Physical (PHY) Layer

IN THIS CHAPTER

Physical Layer Architecture

The architecture of the Physical layer (see Figure 5.1) consists of the following three components for each station:

- **Physical layer management**   Physical layer management works in conjunction with MAC layer management and performs management functions for the Physical layer.

- **Physical Layer Convergence Procedure (PLCP) sublayer**   The MAC layer communicates with the PLCP via primitives through the Physical layer service access point (SAP). When the MAC layer instructs, the PLCP prepares MAC protocol data units (MPDUs) for transmission. The PLCP also delivers incoming frames from the wireless medium to the MAC layer.

  The PLCP appends fields to the MPDU that contain information needed by the Physical layer transmitters and receivers. The 802.11 standard refers to this composite frame as a *PLCP protocol data unit (PPDU)*. The frame structure of a PPDU provides for asynchronous transfer of MPDUs between stations. As a result, the receiving station's Physical layer must synchronize its circuitry to each individual incoming frame.

  Refer to the following sections later in this chapter for more detail on each specific PLCP: "FHSS Physical Layer Convergence Procedure," "DSSS Physical Layer Convergence Procedure (PLCP) Sublayer," and "IR Physical Layer Convergence Procedure (PLCP) Sublayer."

- **Physical Medium Dependent (PMD) sublayer**   Under the direction of the PLCP, the PMD provides actual transmission and reception of Physical layer entities between two stations via the wireless medium. To provide this service, the PMD interfaces directly with the wireless medium (that is, the air) and provides modulation and demodulation of the frame transmissions. The PLCP and PMD communicate via primitives to govern the transmission and reception functions.

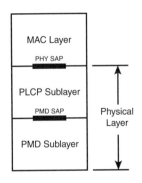

FIGURE 5.1

The Physical Layer Convergence Procedure (PLCP) sublayer minimizes the dependence of the MAC layer on the Physical Medium Dependent (PMD) sublayer by mapping MAC protocol data units into a frame format suitable for transmission by the PMD.

Physical Layer Operations

The general operation of the individual Physical layers is very similar. To perform PLCP functions, the 802.11 standard specifies the use of state machines. Each state machine performs one of the following functions:

- **Carrier sense**   To determine the state of the medium
- **Transmit**   To send individual octets of the data frame
- **Receive**   To receive individual octets of the data frame

The following sections describe each of the PLCP functions and the primitives used for transferring data between the MAC and Physical layers in more detail.

Physical Layer Service Primitives

The Physical layer provides its functionality to the MAC layer via the following service primitives:

- **PHY-DATA.request**   Transfers an octet of data from the MAC layer to the Physical layer. This primitive is possible only after the Physical layer issues a PHY-TXSTART.confirm.

- **PHY-DATA.indication**   Transfers an octet of received data from the Physical layer to the MAC layer.

- **PHY-DATA.confirm**   A primitive sent from the Physical layer to the MAC layer, confirming the transfer of data from the MAC layer to the Physical layer.

- **PHY-TXSTART.request**   A request from the MAC layer for the Physical layer to start transmission of a MPDU.

- **PHY-TXSTART.confirm**   A primitive sent from the Physical layer to the MAC layer, confirming the start of transmission of a MPDU.

- **PHY-TXEND.request**   A request from the MAC layer to the Physical layer to end the transmission of a MPDU. The MAC layer issues this primitive after it receives the last PHY-DATA.confirm primitive for a particular MPDU.

- **PHY-TXEND.confirm**   A primitive from the Physical layer to the MAC layer confirming the end of transmission of a particular MPDU.

- **PHY-CCARESET.request**   A request from the MAC layer to the Physical layer to reset the clear channel assessment state machine.

- **PHY-CCARESET.confirm**   A primitive sent from the Physical layer to the MAC layer confirming the resetting of the clear channel assessment state machine.

- **PHY-CCA.indication** A primitive sent from the Physical layer to the MAC layer to indicate the state of the medium. The status is either `busy` or `idle`. The Physical layer sends this primitive every time the channel changes state.
- **PHY-RXSTART.indication** A primitive sent from the Physical layer to the MAC layer to indicate that the PLCP has received a valid start frame delimiter and PLCP header (based on the CRC error checking within the header).
- **PHY-RXEND.indication** A primitive sent from the Physical layer to the MAC layer to indicate that the receive state machine has completed the reception of a MPDU.

Carrier Sense Function

The Physical layer implements the carrier sense operation by directing the PMD to check whether the medium is busy or idle. The PLCP performs the following sensing operations if the station is not transmitting or receiving a frame:

- **Detection of incoming signals** The PLCP within the station will sense the medium continually. When the medium becomes busy, the PLCP will read in the PLCP preamble and header of the frame to attempt synchronization of the receiver to the data rate of the signal.
- **Clear channel assessment** The clear channel assessment operation determines whether the wireless medium is busy or idle. If the medium is idle, the PLCP will send a PHY-CCA.indicate (with its status field indicating `idle`) to the MAC layer. If the medium is busy, the PLCP will send a PHY-CCA.indicate (with its status field indicating `busy`) to the MAC layer. The MAC layer can then make a decision whether to send a frame.

> **NOTE**
>
> With DSSS, the MAC layer performs the clear channel assessment via one of the following modes:
>
> - **Mode 1** The PMD measures the energy on the medium that exceeds a specific level, which is the energy detection (ED) threshold.
> - **Mode 2** The PMD detects a DSSS signal present on the medium. When this occurs, the PMD sends a PMD_CS (carrier sense) primitive to the PLCP layer.
> - **Mode 3** The PMD detects a DSSS signal present on the medium that exceeds a specific level (ED threshold). When this occurs, the PMD sends PMD_ED and PMD_CS primitives to the PLCP layer.
>
> After any of these modes occurs, the PMD sends a PMD_ED primitive to the PLCP layer, and the PLCP then indicates a clear channel assessment to the MAC layer.

IEEE 802.11–compliant stations and access points store the clear channel assessment operating mode in the Physical layer MIB attribute aCCAModeSuprt. A user can set this mode through station initialization procedures.

Transmit Function

The PLCP will switch the PMD to transmit mode after receiving the PHY-TXSTART.request service primitive from the MAC layer. The MAC layer sends the number of octets (0–4095) and the data rate instruction along with this request. The PMD responds by sending the preamble of the frame at the antenna within 20 microseconds.

The transmitter sends the preamble and header at 1Mbps to provide a specific common data rate at which the receiver listens. After sending the header, the transmitter changes the data rate of the transmission to what the header specifies. After the transmission takes place, the PLCP sends a PHY-TXSTEND.confirm to the MAC layer, shuts off the transmitter, and switches the PMD circuitry to receive mode.

Receive Function

If the clear channel assessment discovers a busy medium and valid preamble of an incoming frame, the PLCP will monitor the header of frame. The PMD will indicate a busy medium when it senses a signal having a power level of at least 85dBm. If the PLCP determines the header is error free, the PLCP will send a PHY-RXSTART.indicate primitive to the MAC layer to provide notification of an incoming frame. The PLCP sends the information it finds in the frame header (such as the number of octets and data rate) along with this primitive.

The PLCP sets an octet counter based on the value in the PSDU Length Word field in the header. This counter will keep track of the number of octets received, enabling the PLCP to know when the end of the frame occurs. As the PLCP receives data, it sends octets of the PSDU to the MAC layer via PHY-DATA.indicate messages. After receiving the final octet, the PLCP sends a PHY-RXEND.indicate primitive to the MAC layer to indicate the final octet of the frame.

The receive function will operate with single or multiple antenna diversities. You can select the level of *diversity* (that is, the number of antennas) via access point and radio card parameters. The strength of the transmitted signal decreases as it propagates to the destination. Many factors, such as the distance, heat, rain, and fog, cause this signal degradation. Multipath propagation can also lessen the signal strength at the receiver. Diversity is a method of improving reception by receiving the signal on multiple antennas and processing the superior signal.

IEEE 802.11 Frequency Hopping Spread Spectrum (FHSS) Physical Layer

The IEEE 802.11 Frequency Hopping Spread Spectrum (FHSS) Physical layer uses frequency hopping spread spectrum to deliver 1Mbps and 2Mbps data rates in the 2.4GHz band. FHSS and DSSS were the initial 802.11 Physical layers implemented in wireless LAN solutions in 1997, shortly after the finalization of the 802.11 standard. This section describes the architecture and operation of 802.11 FHSS.

FHSS Physical Layer Convergence Procedure

Figure 5.2 illustrates the format of a FHSS PPDU (also called a *PLCP frame*). In general, the preamble enables the receiver to prepare clocking functions and antenna diversity before the actual content of the frame arrives. The header field provides information about the frame, and the whitened PSDU (PLCP service data unit) is the MPDU the station is sending.

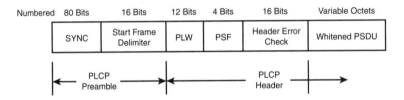

FIGURE 5.2

A FHSS Physical Layer Convergence Procedure (PLCP) frame consists of a PLCP preamble, PLCP header, and a PLCP service data unit.

The following describes each of the FHSS PLCP frame fields:

- **SYNC**   This field consists of alternating zeros and ones, alerting the receiver that a potentially receivable signal is present. A receiver will begin to synchronize with the incoming signal after detecting the SYNC.

- **Start Frame Delimiter**   The content of this field is always the 0000110010111101 bit pattern, defining the beginning of a frame.

- **PLW (PSDU Length Word)**   This field specifies the length of the PSDU in octets. The receiver will use this information to determine the end of the frame.

- **PSF (PLCP Signaling)**   This field identifies the data rate of the whitened PSDU portion of the frame. The preamble and header of the PPDU are always sent at 1Mbps, but the remaining portions of the frame can be sent at different data rates as indicated by this field. The PMD, though, must support the data rate.

The leftmost bit of the PLCP Signaling field, bit 0, is always 0. The following table identifies the data rate based on the value of bits 1, 2, and 3:

Bits 1–3	Data Rate
000	1.0Mbps
001	1.5Mbps
010	2.0Mbps
011	2.5Mbps
100	3.0Mbps
101	3.5Mbps
110	4.0Mbps
111	4.5Mbps

NOTE

The 1997 version of the IEEE 802.11 standard supports only 1Mbps and 2Mbps operation. The lower data rate will realize longer range transmission because the receiver has greater gain at lower data rates. The 802.11a and 802.11b supplements to the 802.11 standard provide higher data rates.

- **Header Error Check**   This field contains a 16-bit CRC result based on CCITT's CRC-16 error detection algorithm. The generator polynomial for CRC-16 is $G(x)=x^{16}+x^{12}+x^5+1$. The Physical layer does not determine whether errors are present within the PSDU. The MAC layer will check for errors based on the Frame Check Sequence (FCS).

  CRC-16 detects all single- and double-bit errors and ensures detection of 99.998% of all possible errors. Most experts feel CRC-16 is sufficient for data transmission blocks of 4 kilobytes or less.

- **Whitened PSDU**   The PSDU can range from 0–4095 octets in length. Before transmission, the Physical layer whitens the PSDU by stuffing special symbols every four octets to minimize DC bias of the data signal. The PSDU whitening process involves the use of a length-127 frame-synchronous scrambler and a 32/33 bias-suppression encoding algorithm to randomize the data. Figure 5.3 illustrates the process of whitening the PSDU.

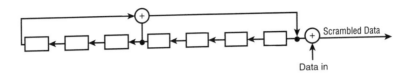

FIGURE 5.3

PSDU whitening at the transmitting station consists of inputting the PSDU into a scrambler, as shown here. All registers initialize with ones. This logic circuitry also performs the unscrambling necessary at the receiving station.

FHSS Physical Medium Dependent (PMD) Sublayer

The Physical Medium Dependent (PMD) sublayer performs the actual transmission and reception of PPDUs under the direction of the PLCP. To provide this service, the PMD interfaces directly with the wireless medium (that is, the air) and provides FHSS modulation and demodulation of the frame transmissions.

FHSS PMD Service Primitives

The PLCP and PMD communicate primitives, as shown in Figure 5.4, enabling the FHSS PLCP to direct the PMD when to transmit data, change channels, receive data from the PMD, and so on.

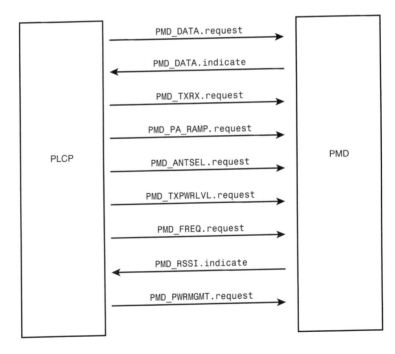

FIGURE 5.4

These primitives between the PLCP and PMD are commands that the FHSS Physical layer uses to operate the transmission and reception functions of the station.

The following defines each of the PLCP/PMD primitives:

- **PMD_DATA.request** This is a request from the PLCP to the PMD to transfer a 1 or 0 data bit. This action tells the PMD to modulate and send the data bit on the medium.

- **PMD_DATA.indicate** The PMD implements this primitive to transfer data bits to the PLCP. The value sent is either 1 or 0.

- **PMD_TXRX.request** The PLCP uses this request to place the PMD in transmit or receive mode. The value sent is either transmit or receive.

- **PMD_PA_RAMP.request** This request from the PLCP to the PMD initiates the ramp-up or ramp-down of the transmitter's power amplifier. The value sent is either on or off.

- **PMD_ANTSEL.request** The PLCP sends this primitive to select the antenna that the PMD will use. The value sent is a number from 1 to N, for which N is the total number of antennas the PMD supports. For transmit, this request selects one antenna. For receive, the PLCP can select multiple antennas for diversity.

- **PMD_TXPWRLVL.request** This request from the PLCP defines the transmit power level of the PMD. The value is Level1, Level2, and so on, up to Level8, and corresponds to power levels in the *management information base (MIB)*. Level1, for example, corresponds to the MIB value TxPowerLevel1.

- **PMD_FREQ.request** The PLCP sends this primitive to the PMD to define the transmit frequency. The value sent is the channel ID.

- **PMD_RSSI.indicate** The PMD uses this primitive to return a continual receiver signal strength indication of the medium to the PLCP. The PLCP uses this primitive for clear channel assessment functions. The value can range from 0 (weakest) to 15 (strongest) signal strength.

- **PMD_PWRMGMT.request** The PLCP sends this primitive to the PMD to place the radio in sleep or standby mode so it will drain less power. The value sent is either on for full operational mode, or off for standby or sleep mode.

Physical Sublayer Management Entity (PLME) Primitives

The Physical layer has access to the management information base (MIB) via the following Physical sublayer management entity (PLME) primitives:

- **PLME-GET.request** Requests the value of a specific MIB attribute.

- **PLME-GET.confirm** Returns the value of the applicable MIB attribute value that corresponds to a PLME-GET.request.

- **PLME-SET.request** Requests the MIB set a specific MIB attribute to a particular value.

- **PLME-SET.confirm** Returns the status of the PLME-SET.request.

FHSS PMD Operation

The operation of the PMD translates the binary representation of the PPDUs into a radio signal suitable for transmission. The FHSS PMD performs these operations via a frequency hopping function and frequency shift keying modulation technique. The following sections explain the FHSS PMD.

Frequency Hopping Function

The 802.11 standard defines a set of channels that are evenly spaced across the 2.4GHz ISM band. The number of channels depends on geography. For example, the number of channels for North America and most of Europe is 79, and the number of channels for Japan is 23.

The channels are spread across a band of frequencies, depending on geography. For example, 802.11-compliant stations in North America and most of Europe operate from 2.402 and 2.480GHz, and stations in Japan operate from 2.473 and 2.495GHz. Each channel is 1MHz wide; therefore, the center operating frequency for channel 2 (the first channel) in the U.S. is 2.402GHz, channel 3 is 2.403GHz, and so on.

The FHSS-based PMD transmits PPDUs by hopping from channel to channel according to a particular pseudo-random hopping sequence that uniformly distributes the signal across the operating frequency band. Once the hopping sequence is set in an access point, stations automatically synchronize to the correct hopping sequence. The 802.11 standard defines a particular set of hopping sequences. For example, it specifies 78 sequences for North America and most of Europe and 12 sequences for Japan. The sequences avoid prolonged interference with one another. This enables designers to collocate multiple PMDs to improve performance.

Setting the Hopping Sequence and Dwell Time

You can select the hopping sequence on the access point via a parameter accessible from its management utility. If the network has only one access point, then just use the default setting. If more than one access point is present, be sure to assign a different hopping sequence to each access point.

For each hop in the hopping sequence, the transmitter transmits at a specific center operating frequency for a particular amount of time, which is the *dwell time*. You can select the dwell time via configuration parameters on the access point that all stations will use:

- If there is not much chance of interference, select the longest dwell time possible.
- If significant interference is present, select a shorter dwell time to reduce the amount of time during which interference can occur.

The hop rate is adjustable, but the PMD must hop at a minimum rate that regulatory bodies within the country of operation specify. For the U.S., FHSS must operate at a minimum hop rate of 2.5 hops per second. In addition, the minimum hop distance in frequency is 6MHz in North America and most of Europe and 5MHz in Japan.

FHSS Frequency Modulation Function

The FHSS PMD transmits the binary data at either 1Mbps or 2Mbps using a specific modulation type for each, depending on which data rate is chosen. The PMD uses two-level Gaussian frequency shift key (GFSK) modulation, as shown in Figure 5.5, for transmitting data streams at 1Mbps. The concept of GFSK is to vary the carrier frequency to represent different binary symbols. Thus, changes in frequency maintain the information content of the signal. Noise usually affects the amplitude of the signal, not the frequency. As a result, the use of GFSK modulation reduces potential interference.

The input to the GFSK modulator is either a 0 or 1 coming from the PLCP. The modulator transmits the binary data by shifting the transmit frequency slightly above or below the center operating frequency (Fc) for each hop. To perform this operation, the modulator transmits on a frequency using the following rules:

> Transmit frequency = Fc+fd for sending a 1 bit
>
> Transmit frequency = Fc–fd for sending a 0 bit

In the equation, Fc is the operating center frequency for the current hop, and fd is the amount of frequency deviation. The value of fd will be greater than 110KHz. The 802.11 specification explains how to calculate exact values for fd, but the nominal value is 160KHz.

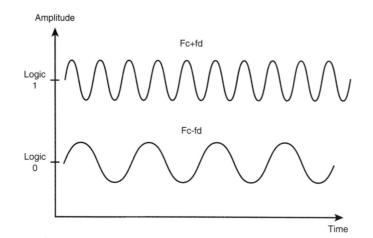

FIGURE 5.5

Two-level Gaussian frequency shift key (GFSK) modulation uses two possible frequencies at each hop to indicate whether a single data bit is a 1 or a 0.

The FHSS PMD uses four-level GFSK modulation, as shown in Figure 5.6, for transmitting data streams at 2Mbps. Stations implementing the 2Mbps version must also be able to operate at 1Mbps for the entire MSDU. For 2Mbps operation, the input to the modulator is combinations of two bits (00, 01, 10, or 11) coming from the PLCP. Each of these two-bit symbols is sent at 1Mbps, meaning each bit is sent at 2Mbps. Thus, the four-level modulation technique doubles the data rate while maintaining the same baud rate as a 1Mbps signal.

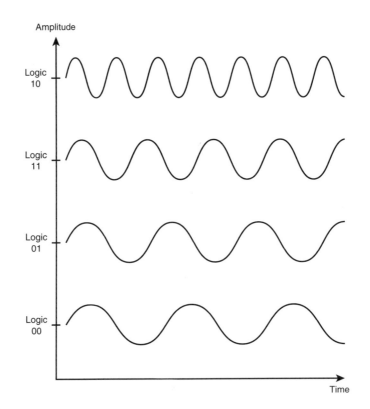

FIGURE 5.6

Four-level Gaussian frequency shift key (GFSK) modulation uses four possible frequencies at each hop to represent two data bits.

Similar to two-level GFSK, the modulator transmits the binary data bits by shifting the transmit frequency slightly above or below the center operating frequency for each hop. In this case, though, the transmitter can transmit at four possible frequencies, one for each two-bit combination. To perform this operation, the modulator will transmit on the operating center frequency with a frequency deviation equal to fd. There are two values of fd that move the transmit frequency above Fc and two values of fd that move the transmit frequency below Fc. The 802.11 standard describes how to calculate the exact value of fd.

Overall, the transmit power of the FHSS radio must comply with IEEE standard C95.1-1991. The 802.11 specification also limits the maximum amount of transmitter output power to 100 milliwatts of *isotropically radiated power* (meaning that the measurements are taken with an antenna having no gain). Apparently, this limit enables 802.11 radio products to comply with transmit power limits in Europe. The effective power will be higher, though, using antennas that offer higher directivity (gain).

The 802.11 specification also says that all PMDs must support at least 10 milliwatts of transmit power. Most access points and radio cards allow you to select multiple transmit power levels via initialization parameters.

NOTE

The 802.11 standard calls for wireless LAN hardware to be capable of operating in either office or industrial environments. The operating temperature range for office environments (referred to as Type 1) is 0–40 degrees C (32–104 degrees F). The operating temperature range for industrial environments (referred to as Type 2) is –30–+70 degrees C (–22–+158 degrees F).

IEEE 802.11 Direct Sequence Spread Spectrum (DSSS) Physical Layer

The IEEE 802.11 Direct Sequence Spread Spectrum (DSSS) Physical layer uses direct sequence spread spectrum to deliver 1Mbps and 2Mbps data rates in the 2.4GHz band. DSSS and FHSS were the initial 802.11 Physical layers implemented in wireless LAN solutions in 1997, shortly after the finalization of the 802.11 standard. This section describes the architecture and operation of 802.11 DSSS.

DSSS Physical Layer Convergence Procedure (PLCP) Sublayer

Figure 5.7 illustrates the DSSS PLCP frame format that the 802.11 specification refers to as a PLCP protocol data unit (PPDU). The preamble enables the receiver to synchronize to the incoming signal properly before the actual content of the frame arrives. The header field provides information about the frame, and the PSDU (PLCP service data unit) is the MPDU the station is sending.

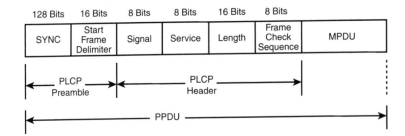

FIGURE 5.7

An IEEE 802.11 DSSS Physical Layer Convergence Procedure (PLCP) frame consists of a PLCP preamble, PLCP header, and a MPDU.

The following describes each of the DSSS PLCP frame fields:

- **Sync**   This field consists of alternating 0s and 1s, alerting the receiver that a potentially receivable signal is present. A receiver will begin to synchronize with the incoming signal after detecting the Sync.

- **Start Frame Delimiter**   This field defines the beginning of a frame. The bit pattern for this field is always 1111001110100000, which is unique for DSSS PLCPs.

- **Signal**   This field identifies the type of modulation that the receiver must use to demodulate the signal. The value of this field is equal to the data rate divided by 100Kbps. The only two possible values for the June 1997 version of 802.11 are 00001010 for 1Mbps DSSS and 00010100 for 2Mbps DSSS. The PLCP preamble and header are both always sent at 1Mbps.

- **Service**   The 802.11 specification reserves this field for future use; however, a value of 00000000 means 802.11 device compliance.

- **Length**   The value of this field is an unsigned 16-bit integer indicating the number of microseconds to transmit the MPDU. The receiver will use this information to determine the end of the frame.

- **Frame Check Sequence**   Similar to the FHSS Physical layer, this field contains a 16-bit CRC result based on CCITT's CRC-16 error detection algorithm. The generator polynomial for CRC-16 is $G(x)=x^{16}+x^{12}+x^{5}+1$. The CRC operation is done at the transmitting station before scrambling.

The Physical layer does not determine whether errors are present within the PSDU. The MAC layer will check for errors based on the FCS. CRC-16 detects all single and double-bit errors and ensures detection of 99.998% of all possible errors. Most experts feel CRC-16 is sufficient for data transmission blocks of 4 kilobytes or less.

- **PSDU** The PSDU, which is actually the MPDU being sent by the MAC layer, can range from zero bits to a maximum size that can be set by the aMPDUMaxLength parameter in the MIB.

DSSS Physical Medium Dependent (PMD) Sublayer

As with the FHSS and infrared Physical layers, the DSSS PMD performs the actual transmission and reception of PPDUs under the direction of the PLCP. To provide this service, the PMD interfaces directly with the wireless medium (that is, the air) and provides DSSS modulation and demodulation of the frame transmissions.

DSSS PMD Service Primitives

With direct sequence, the PLCP and PMD communicate via primitives, as shown in Figure 5.8, enabling the DSSS PLCP to direct the PMD when to transmit data, change channels, receive data from the PMD, and so on.

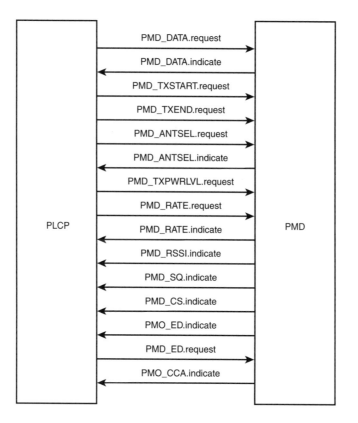

PLCP

PMD_DATA.request
PMD_DATA.indicate
PMD_TXSTART.request
PMD_TXEND.request
PMD_ANTSEL.request
PMD_ANTSEL.indicate
PMD_TXPWRLVL.request
PMD_RATE.request
PMD_RATE.indicate
PMD_RSSI.indicate
PMD_SQ.indicate
PMD_CS.indicate
PMO_ED.indicate
PMD_ED.request
PMO_CCA.indicate

PMD

FIGURE 5.8

These primitives between the PLCP and PMD are commands that the DSSS Physical layer uses to operate the transmission and reception functions of the station.

The following defines each of the PLCP/PMD primitives:

- **PMD_DATA.request**   This is a request from the PLCP to the PMD to transfer a data symbol. The value of the symbol sent with this request is 0 or 1 data bit if transmitting at 1Mbps or any combination of two data bits if transmitting at 2Mbps. The PMD_DATA.request primitive must be sent to the PMD before beginning the actual transmission of data with the PMD_TXSTART.request primitive.

- **PMD_DATA.indicate**   The PMD implements this primitive to transfer symbols to the PLCP. As with the PMD_DATA.request primitive, the value of the symbol sent with this request is 0 or 1 data bit if receiving at 1Mbps or any combination of two data bits if receiving at 2Mbps.

- **PMD_TXSTART.request**   The PLCP sends this primitive to the PMD to initiate the actual transmission of a PPDU.

- **PMD_TXEND.request**   The PLCP sends this primitive to the PMD to end the transmission of a PPDU.

- **PMD_ANTSEL.request**   The PLCP sends this primitive to select the antenna that the PMD will use. The value sent is a number from 1 to N, for which N is the total number of antennas the PMD supports. For transmit, this request selects one antenna. For receive, the PLCP can select multiple antennas for diversity.

- **PMD_ANTSEL.indicate**   This primitive indicates which antenna the Physical layer used to receive the latest PPDU.

- **PMD_TXPWRLVL.request**   This request from the PLCP defines the transmit power level of the PMD. The value is Level1, Level2, and so on, up to Level8, and corresponds to the power levels in the MIB. Level1, for example, corresponds to the MIB value TxPowerLevel1.

- **PMD_RATE.request**   The PLCP sends this primitive to the PMD to identify the data rate (either 1Mbps or 2Mbps) that the MPDU portion of the PPDU should be sent. This data rate applies only to the rate of transmission. The PMD must always be able to receive at all possible data rates.

- **PMD_RATE.indicate**   This primitive, sent from the PMD to the PLCP when the PMD detects the Signaling field within the PLCP preamble, identifies the data rate (either 1Mbps or 2Mbps) of a frame received.

- **PMD_RSSI.indicate**   The PMD uses this primitive during receive states to return a continual receiver signal strength indication (RSSI) of the medium to the PLCP. The PLCP uses this primitive for clear channel assessment functions. The value of the RSSI is one of 256 levels, represented by an eight-bit data word.

- **PMD_SQ.indicate**   This optional primitive provides a signal quality (SQ) measure of the DSSS PN code correlation. The value of the signal quality is one of 256 levels, represented by an eight-bit data word.

- **PMD_CS.indicate**   The PMD sends this primitive to the PLCP to indicate that demodulation of a data signal is occurring. This signals the reception of a valid 802.11 direct sequence PPDU.

- **PMD_ED.indicate**   This optional primitive indicates that the energy value indicated by a particular PMD_RSSI.indicate primitive is above a predefined threshold (stored in the aED_Threshold parameter in the MIB). The value of the PMD_ED.indicate primitive is either enabled, if the PMD_RSSI.indicate value is above the threshold, or disabled, if below the threshold. This primitive provides a means to detect the presence of non-802.11 direct sequence signals, at least those that exceed the threshold value.

- **PMD_ED.request**   The PLCP uses this primitive to set the value of the *energy detect threshold*—the minimum signal that the PMD can detect—in the PMD to the value of the aED_Threshold parameter in the MIB.

- **PMD_CCA.indicate**   The PMD sends this primitive to the PLCP to indicate the detection of RF energy adhering to the CCA algorithm.

DSSS PMD Operation

The operation of the DSSS PMD translates the binary representation of the PPDUs into a radio signal suitable for transmission. The DSSS Physical layer performs this process by multiplying a radio frequency carrier by a pseudo-noise (PN) digital signal. The resulting signal appears as noise if plotted in the frequency domain. The wider bandwidth of the direct sequence signal enables the signal power to drop below the noise threshold without loss of information.

As with FHSS, the DSSS Physical layer operates within the 2.4GHz to 2.4835GHz frequency range, depending on regulatory authorities in different parts of the world. The 802.11 standard specifies operation of DSSS on up to 14 channels of different frequencies (see Table 5.1). Channels are each 22MHz wide.

NOTE

Similar to FHSS, you can set the operating channel of a DSSS station or access point via a user-settable parameter. This enables designers to operate multiple direct sequence networks in the same area. Be sure, though, that you choose frequencies separated by at least 30MHz to avoid having the channels interfere with each other.

TABLE 5.1   The Specific DSSS Channels for Different Parts of the World

Channel No.	Frequency (GHz)	U.S. and Canada	Europe	Spain	France	Japan
1	2.412	✓	✓			
2	2.417	✓	✓			
3	2.422	✓	✓			
4	2.427	✓	✓			
5	2.432	✓	✓			
6	2.437	✓	✓			
7	2.442	✓	✓			
8	2.447	✓	✓			
9	2.452	✓	✓			
10	2.457	✓	✓	✓	✓	
11	2.462	✓	✓	✓	✓	
12	2.467		✓		✓	
13	2.472		✓		✓	
14	2.484					✓

The following sections explain the spreading sequence and modulation functions of the DSSS PMD.

DSSS Spreading Sequence

The general idea of direct sequence is to spread digitally the baseband data frame (PPDU) first, then modulate the spread data to a particular frequency. Figure 5.9 illustrates typical components of a DSSS transmitter.

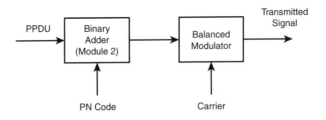

FIGURE 5.9

A direct sequence transmitter consists of a binary adder, PN code, and a modulator.

The transmitter spreads the PPDU by combining the PPDU with a pseudo-noise (PN) code (sometimes referred to as a *chip* or *spreading sequence*) via the binary adder. The PN sequence for direct sequence systems consists of a series of positive and negative 1s (ones). The specific PN code for 802.11 DSSS is the following 11-chip Barker sequence, with the leftmost bit applied first to the PPDU:

+1, -1, +1, +1, -1, +1, +1, +1, -1, -1, -1

The output of the binary adder is a DSSS signal having a higher rate signal than the original data signal. A 1Mbps PPDU at the input, for example, will result in an 11Mbps spread signal at the output of the adder. The modulator translates the baseband signal into an analog signal at the operating transmit frequency of the chosen channel.

DSSS is different than Code Division Multiple Access (CDMA). CDMA operates in a similar fashion; however, it uses multiple orthogonal spreading sequences to enable multiple users to operate at the same frequency. The difference is that 802.11 DSSS always uses the same spreading sequence, but it enables users to choose from multiple frequencies for concurrent operation.

A figure of merit for DSSS systems is known as *processing gain* (sometimes called *spreading ratio*), which is equal to the data rate of the spread DSSS signal divided by the data rate of the initial PPDU. The minimum allowable processing gain is 10 within the U.S. and Japan, according to applicable frequency regulatory agencies (FCC and MKK, respectively). To ensure compliance and minimize potential signal interference, the IEEE 802.11 standard minimum processing gain requirement is set at 11.

DSSS Frequency Modulation Function

A balanced modulator modulates the spread PPDU by combining it with a carrier set at the transmit frequency. The DSSS PMD transmits the initial PPDU at 1Mbps or 2Mbps using different modulation types, depending on which data rate is chosen. For 1Mbps (basic access rate), the PMD uses differential binary phase shift keying (DBPSK) modulation.

Phase shift keying varies the phase of the carrier frequency to represent different binary symbols. Thus, changes in phase maintain the information content of the signal. Noise usually affects the amplitude of the signal, not the phase. As a result, the use of phase shift key modulation reduces potential interference.

The input to the DBPSK modulator is either a 0 or 1 coming from the PLCP. The modulator transmits the binary data by shifting the carrier signal's phase, as shown conceptually in Figure 5.10.

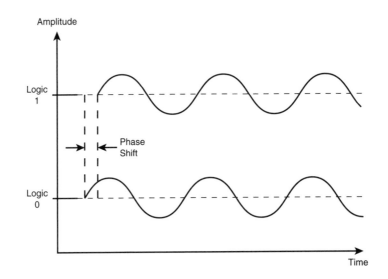

FIGURE 5.10

DBPSK (differential binary phase shift keying) modulation operates at a specific center frequency and varies the phase of the signal to represent single-bit symbols.

For 2Mbps transmission (enhanced access rate), the PMD uses *differential quadrature phase shift keying (DQPSK)* modulation to send data at 2Mbps. Figure 5.11 illustrates this concept. In this case, the input to the modulator is combinations of two bits (00, 01, 10, or 11) coming from the PLCP. Each of these two-bit symbols is sent at 1Mbps, resulting in a binary data rate of 2Mbps. Thus, the four-level modulation technique doubles the data rate while maintaining the same baud rate as a 1Mbps signal. This makes effective use of the wireless medium.

The transmit power levels for DSSS is

- 1,000 milliwatts for U.S. (according to FCC 15.247)
- 100 milliwatts for Europe (according to ETS 300-328)
- 10 milliwatts for Japan (according to MPT ordinance for Regulating Radio Equipment, Article 49-20)

The effective power will be higher, though, using antennas that offer higher directivity (that is, gain). Wireless LAN suppliers have optional antennas that provide a variety of radiation patterns. The 802.11 specification also says that all PMDs must support at least 1 milliwatt transmit power. Most access points and radio cards enable you to select multiple transmit power levels via initialization parameters. In fact, the standard calls for power level controls for radio that can transmit greater than 100 milliwatts. Higher-power radio must be able to switch back to 100 milliwatt operation.

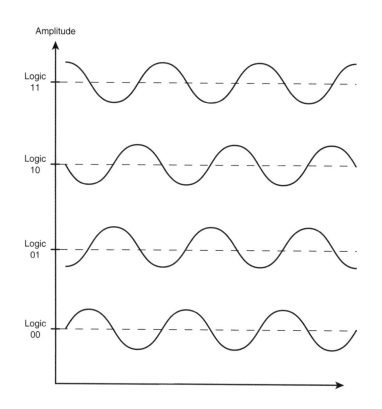

FIGURE 5.11

DQPSK modulation operates at a specific center frequency and varies the phase of the signal to represent double-bit symbols.

DSSS wireless LAN devices are capable of operating at relatively high data rates, supporting applications that require more range and bandwidth within a single cell. Be certain, however, to consider frequency hopping spread spectrum and infrared Physical layers before making a decision on which one to implement.

IEEE 802.11 High Rate Direct Sequence Spread Spectrum (HR-DSSS) Physical Layer

The IEEE 802.11 High Rate Direct Sequence Spread Spectrum (HR-DSSS) Physical layer is a rate extension to the 802.11 DSSS standard. HR-DSSS, commonly referred to as 802.11b, includes complementary code keying (CCK) and operates in the 2.4GHz band to achieve additional data rates of 5.5Mbps and 11Mbps. The HR-DSSS is the most common wireless LAN implementation today and is interoperable with 802.11 DSSS implementations. This section describes the architecture and operation of 802.11 HR-DSSS.

> **NOTE**
>
> The IEEE 802.11g working group is considering an extension of the 802.11b standard to double the data rate to 22Mbps. This version will implement all mandatory functions of the 802.11 MAC and Physical layers. As a result, it will be backward compatible with existing 11Mbps HR-DSS (802.11b) products.

The PLCP for the 802.11 HR-DSSS is the same as DSSS (refer to Figure 5.7) except for the following:

- **Alternate short SYNC field**   A shorter alternate SYNC field can be used in implementations in order to minimize overhead and maximize throughput. The short SYNC field consists of 56 scrambled bits.

- **Signal field contents**   The signal field value multiplied by 100Kbps indicates the data rate. The following are mandatory data rates specified by HR-DSSS:

Data Rate	Signal Field Value
1Mbps	00001010
2Mbps	00010100
5.5Mbps	00110111
11Mbps	01101110

- **Service field values**   Bit 2 of the Service field indicates whether the transmitter frequency and the symbol clocks are derived from the same oscillator. Bit 7 is used in conjunction with the Length field to eliminate ambiguity when converting the number of octets to corresponding transmit time for data rates greater than 8Mbps. For example, at 11Mbps, the Length field value equals the number of octets times 8, divided by 11, and rounded up to the next integer. Bit 7 of the Service field will be 0 if the rounding takes less than 8/11 and 1 if the rounding is equal to or greater than 8/11.

HR-DSSS Physical Medium Dependent Sublayer

The HR-DSSS PMD performs the actual transmission and reception of PPDUs under the direction of the PLCP. To provide this service, the PMD interfaces directly with the wireless medium and provides modulation and demodulation of the frame transmissions.

HR-DSSS PMD Service Primitives

The PLCP and PMD communicate primitives, as shown in Figure 5.12, enabling the PLCP to direct the PMD when to transmit data, change channels, receive data from the PMD, and so on.

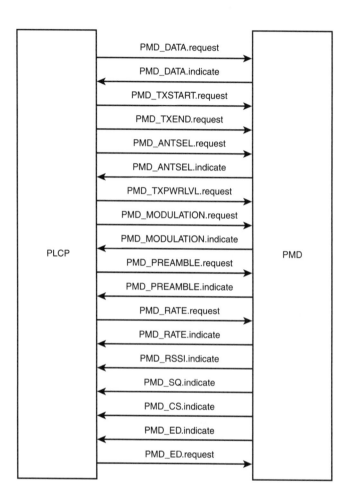

FIGURE 5.12

These primitives between the PLCP and PMD are commands that the HR-DSSS Physical layer uses to operate the transmission and reception functions of the station.

The following defines each of the PLCP/PMD primitives:

- **PMD_DATA.request**   This is a request from the PLCP to the PMD to transfer a data symbol. The value of the symbol sent with this request is 0 or 1 data bit if transmitting at 1Mbps, any combination of two data bits if transmitting at 2Mbps, any combination of four data bits if transmitting at 5.5Mbps, or any combination of eight data bits if transmitting at 11Mbps. The PMD_DATA.request primitive must be sent to the PMD before beginning the actual transmission of data with the PMD_TXSTART.request primitive.

- **PMD_DATA.indicate** The PMD implements this primitive to transfer symbols to the PLCP. As with the PMD_DATA.request primitive, the value of the symbol sent with this request is 0 or 1 data bit if receiving at 1Mbps, any combination of two data bits if receiving at 2Mbps, any combination of four data bits if receiving at 5.5Mbps, or any combination of eight data bits if receiving at 11Mbps.

- **PMD_TXSTART.request** The PLCP sends this primitive to the PMD to initiate the actual transmission of a PPDU.

- **PMD_TXEND.request** The PLCP sends this primitive to the PMD to end the transmission of a PPDU.

- **PMD_ANTSEL.request** The PLCP sends this primitive to select the antenna that the PMD shall use. The value sent is a number from 1 to N, for which N is the total number of antennas the PMD supports. For transmit, this request selects one antenna. For receive, the PLCP can select multiple antennas for diversity.

- **PMD_ANTSEL.indicate** This primitive indicates which antenna the Physical layer used to receive the latest PPDU.

- **PMD_TXPWRLVL.request** This request from the PLCP defines the transmit power level of the PMD. The value is Level1, Level2, and so on up to Level4 and corresponds to the corresponding power levels in the MIB. Level1, for example, corresponds to the MIB value TxPowerLevel1.

- **PMD_MODULATION.request** This request from the PLCP selects the modulation. The possible modulation types are Barker for 1Mbps or 2Mbps operation and CCK or PBCC for 5.5Mbps and 11Mbps operation. This primitive should be issued before the PMD_TXSTART.request.

- **PMD_MODULATION.indicate** This primitive indicates what modulation type was used to receive the PPDU.

- **PMD_PREAMBLE.request** The PLCP sends this primitive to identify whether to use the long or short preamble. The primitive value is either 0 for long preamble or 1 for short preamble.

- **PMD_PREAMBLE.indicate** This primitive indicates which preamble was used to send the PPDU.

- **PMD_RATE.request** The PLCP sends this primitive to the PMD to identify the data rate (either 1Mbps, 2Mbps, 5.5Mbps, or 11Mbps) at which the MPDU portion of the PPDU should be sent. This data rate applies only to the rate of transmission. The PMD must always be able to receive at all possible data rates.

- **PMD_RATE.indicate**   This primitive, sent from the PMD to the PLCP when the PMD detects the Signaling field within the PLCP preamble, identifies the data rate (either 1Mbps or 2Mbps) of a received frame.

- **PMD_RSSI.indicate**   The PMD uses this primitive during receive states to return a continual receiver signal strength indication (RSSI) of the medium to the PLCP. The PLCP uses this primitive for clear channel assessment functions. The value of the RSSI is one of 256 levels, represented by an eight-bit data word.

- **PMD_SQ.indicate**   This optional primitive provides a signal quality (SQ) measure of the DSSS PN code correlation. The value of the signal quality is one of 256 levels, represented by an eight-bit data word.

- **PMD_CS.indicate**   The PMD sends this carrier sense (CS) primitive to the PLCP to indicate that demodulation of a data signal is occurring. This signals the reception of a valid 802.11 direct sequence PPDU.

- **PMD_ED.indicate**   This optional primitive indicates that the energy value indicated by a particular PMD_RSSI.indicate primitive is above a predefined threshold (stored in the aED_Threshold parameter in the MIB). The value of the PMD_ED.indicate primitive is either enabled, if the PMD_RSSI.indicate value is above the threshold, or disabled, if below the threshold. This primitive provides a means to detect the presence of non-802.11 direct sequence signals, at least those that exceed the threshold value.

- **PMD_ED.request**   The PLCP uses this primitive to set the value of the *energy detect threshold*—which is the minimum signal that the PMD can detect—in the PMD to the value of the aED_Threshold parameter in the MIB.

HR-DSSS PMD Operation

The operation of the HR-DSSS PMD translates the binary representation of the PPDUs into a radio signal suitable for transmission. The HR-DSSS PMD is the same as DSSS PMD, except for a different modulation type necessary to deliver higher data rates. For 1Mbps and 2Mbps, the HR-DSSS PMD uses the Barker spreading sequence, which is the same for 802.11 DSSS implementations. HR-DSSS uses CCK to provide the spreading sequences for the 5.5Mbps and 11Mbps data rates. The HR-DSSS PMD uses the channel plan shown in Table 5.1.

CCK uses an I/Q modulation architecture with a spreading code 8 chips long at a chipping rate of 11 million chips per second. Each symbol (group of data bits) transmitted is represented by a particular CCK spreading code. Each chip of the spreading code is complex—that is, it has more than two possible phases. The spreading codes are known as complementary codes based on Walsh/Hadamard functions.

The formula that defines the code set for both the 5.5Mbps and 11Mbps data rates is shown in Figure 5.13.

$$C = \{e^{j(O_1 + O_2 + O_3 + O_4)}, e^{j(O_1 + O_3 + O_4)}, e^{j(O_1 + O_2 + O_4)},$$

$$- e^{j(O_1 + O_4)}, e^{j(O_1 + O_2 + O_3)}, e^{j(O_1 + O_3)},$$

$$- e^{j(O_1 + O_2)}, e^{j(O_1)}\}$$

FIGURE 5.13
Formula that defines the code set for both 5.5Mbps and 11Mbps data rates.

This formula represents the phase values for each of the spreading code chips represented as c0 to c7. The minus sign for chips 4 and 7 provides a 180-degree rotation to optimize the sequence correlation properties and minimize DC offsets.

For 5.5Mbps operation, CCK encodes four data bits (d0 to d3) per symbol onto the 8-chip spreading code. Data bits d2 and d3 encode the basic symbol as shown in Table 5.2. This encoding table satisfies the phase 2, 3, and 4 values show in the previous formula.

TABLE 5.2   CCK Encoding Table for 5.5Mbps Data Rates

d2,d3	c1	c2	c3	c4	c5	c6	c7	c8
00	1j	1	1j	-1	1j	1	-1J	1
01	-1j	-1	-1j	1	1j	1	-1J	1
10	-1j	1	-1j	-1	-1j	1	1J	1
11	1j	-1	1j	1	-1j	1	1J	1

CCK uses data bits d0 and d1 (as shown in Table 5.3) to encode the phase 1 term in the previous formula, using DQPSK to further encode the chips and obtain the actual spreading code. Thus, every other symbol is given an extra 180-degree rotation. This overall modulation provides nearly orthogonal spreading codes, which significantly improves the capability of the radio signal to survive multipath distortion and RF interference.

TABLE 5.3   DQPSK Encoding Table for Both 5.5Mbps and 11Mbps Data Rates

d0,d1	Even Symbols	Odd Symbols
00	0	PIE
01	PIE/2	3PIE/2

TABLE 5.3 Continued

d0,d1	Even Symbols	Odd Symbols
11	PIE	0
10	3PIE/2	PIE/2

For 11Mbps operation, Table 5.3 also provides the phase 1 value for the spreading code formula. Table 5.4 provides the phase values for the remaining data bits, based on QPSK, according to these dibit/phase value assignments:

d2, d3—phase 2 value

d4, d5—phase 3 value

d6, d7—phase 4 value

Thus, the overall process modulates eight data bits onto each 8-chip spreading code.

TABLE 5.4 QPSK Encoding Table for 11Mbps Data Rates

di, d(i+1)	Phase
00	0
01	$\pi/2$
10	π
11	$3\pi/2$

IEEE 802.11 Orthogonal Frequency Division Multiplexing (OFDM) Physical Layer

The IEEE 802.11 Orthogonal Frequency Division Multiplexing (OFDM) Physical layer delivers up to 54Mbps data rates in the 5GHz band. The OFDM Physical layer, commonly referred to as 802.11a, will likely become the basis for high-speed wireless LANs as 802.11a products are first available in late 2001 and early 2002. This section describes the architecture and operation of 802.11 OFDM.

> **NOTE**
>
> The benefits of OFDM are high spectral efficiency, resiliency to RF interference, and lower multipath distortion. The orthogonal nature of OFDM allows subchannels to overlap, having a positive effect on spectral efficiency. The subcarriers transporting information are just far enough apart to avoid interference with each other, theoretically.

OFDM Physical Layer Convergence Procedure

Figure 5.14 illustrates the format of an OFDM PPDU (also called a *PLCP frame*).

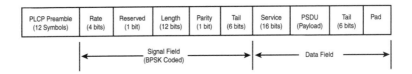

FIGURE 5.14

The OFDM Physical Layer Convergence Procedure (PLCP) frames consist of Preamble, Signal, and Data fields.

The following describes each of the OFDM PLCP frame fields:

- **PLCP Preamble**   This field enables the receiver to acquire an incoming OFDM signal and synchronize the demodulator. The preamble consists of 12 symbols. Ten of them are short for establishing AGC (automatic gain control) and the coarse frequency estimate of the carrier signal. The receiver uses the long symbols for fine-tuning. With this preamble, it takes 16 microseconds to train the receiver after first receiving the frame.

- **Rate**   The following identifies the data rate based on the value of bits 1, 2, 3, and 4:

Bits 1–4	Data Rate
1101	6Mbps
1111	9Mbps
0101	12Mbps
0111	18Mbps
1001	24Mbps
1011	36Mbps
0001	48Mbps
0011	54Mbps

- **Reserved**   This field is set to 0.

- **Length**   This field identifies the number of octets in the frame.

- **Parity**   This field is one bit based on positive (even) parity, based on the first 17 bits of the frame (Rate, Reserved, and Length fields).

- **Tail**   This field must be set to all zeros.

- **Service**   This field consists of 16 bits, with the first 7 bits as zeros to synchronize the descrambler in the receiver and the remaining 9 bits (all 0s) reserved for future use (and set to zeros).

- **PSDU**   The PSDU (PLCP service data unit) is the payload from the MAC layer being sent.

- **Tail**   This field consists of six bits (all zeros) appended to the symbol to bring the convolutional encoder to zero state.

- **Pad Bits**   This field contains at least six bits, but it is actually the number of bits that make the Data field a multiple of the number of coded bits in an OFDM symbol (48, 96, 192, or 288).

The PLCP Preamble and Signal fields are convolutional encoded and sent at 6Mbps using BPSK no matter what data rate the Signal field indicates. A data scrambler using a 127-bit sequence generator scrambles all bits in the data field to randomize the bit patterns in order to avoid long streams of ones and zeros.

> **NOTE**
>
> Some 802.11a chipset developers (for example, Atheros) are using proprietary techniques to combine OFDM channels for applications requiring data rates that exceed 54Mbps.

OFDM Physical Medium Dependent (PMD) Sublayer

The PMD performs the actual transmission and reception of PPDUs under the direction of the PLCP. To provide this service, the PMD interfaces directly with the wireless medium and provides OFDM modulation and demodulation of the frame transmissions.

OFDM PMD Service Primitives

The PLCP and PMD communicate primitives, as shown in Figure 5.15, enabling the PLCP to direct the PMD when to transmit data, change channels, receive data from the PMD, and so on.

The following defines each of the PLCP/PMD primitives:

- **PMD_DATA.request**   A request from the PLCP to the PMD to transfer a 1 or 0 data bit. This action tells the PMD to modulate and send the data bit on the medium.

- **PMD_DATA.indicate**   The PMD implements this primitive to transfer data bits to the PLCP. The value sent is either 1 or 0.

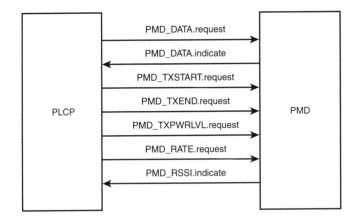

FIGURE 5.15

These primitives between the PLCP and PMD are commands that the 802.11 OFDM Physical layer uses to operate the transmission and reception functions of the station.

- **PMD_TXSTART.request**   A request from the PLCP layer to the PMD to start transmission of a PPDU.
- **PMD_TXEND.request**   A request from the PLCP layer to the PMD to end transmission of a PPDU.
- **PMD_TXPWRLVL.request**   A request from the PLCP that defines the transmit power level of the PMD.
- **PMD_RATE.request**   A request from the PLCP that selects the modulation rate the PMD should use for transmission.
- **PMD_RSSI.indicate**   The PMD uses this primitive to return a continual receiver signal strength indication of the medium to the PLCP. The PLCP uses this primitive for clear channel assessment functions. The value can range from 0 (weakest) to 255 (strongest) signal strength.

OFDM PMD Operation

The operation of the PMD translates the binary representation of the PPDUs into a radio signal suitable for transmission. The 802.11 OFDM PMD performs these operations by dividing a high-speed serial information signal into multiple lower-speed sub-signals that the system transmits simultaneously at different frequencies in parallel.

Operating frequencies for the 802.11s OFDM layer fall into the following three 100MHz unlicensed national information structure (U-NII) bands: 5.15–5.25GHz, 5.25–5.35GHz, and 5.725–5.825GHz. As shown in Table 5.5, there are 12 20MHz channels, and each band has different output power limits. In the U.S., the Code of Federal Regulations, Title 47, Section 15.407, regulates these frequencies.

TABLE 5.5   802.11 OFDM Defines Three Frequency Bands Having Different Power Limitations

Frequency Band	Channel Numbers	Center Frequency (MHz)	Maximum Output Power (with up to 6 dBi antenna gain)
U-NII lower band	36	5180	40mW (2.5mW/MHz)
	40	5200	
(5.15–5.25 MHz)	44	5220	
	48	5240	
U-NII middle band	52	5260	200mW (12.5mW/MHz)
	56	5280	
(5.25–5.35 MHz)	60	5300	
	64	5320	
U-NII upper band	149	5745	800mW (50mW/MHz)
	153	5765	
(5.725–5.825 MHz)	157	5785	
	161	5805	

The 802.11 OFDM Physical layer uses a combination of BPSK, QPSK, and QAM, depending on the chosen data rate (see Table 5.6). Data rates of 6Mbps, 12Mbps, and 24Mbps are mandatory for all 802.11-compliant products.

TABLE 5.6   802.11 OFDM Modulation Techniques

Data Rate (Mbps)	Modulation	Coding Rate	Coded Bits per Subcarrier	Code Bits per OFDM Symbol	Data Bits per OFDM Symbol
6	BPSK	1/2	1	48	24
9	BPSK	3/4	1	48	36
12	QPSK	1/2	2	96	48
18	QPSK	3/4	2	96	72
24	16-QAM	1/2	4	192	96
36	16-QAM	3/4	4	192	144
48	64-QAM	2/3	6	288	192
54	64-QAM	3/4	6	288	216

Figures 5.16, 5.17, 5.18, and 5.19 illustrate the 802.11 OFDM modulation types.

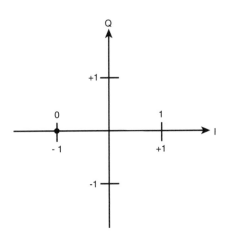

FIGURE 5.16

The 802.11 OFDM Physical layer uses BPSK for 6Mbps and 9Mbps data rate operation.

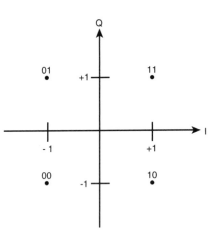

FIGURE 5.17

The 802.11 OFDM PMD uses QPSK for 12Mbps and 18Mbps data rate operation.

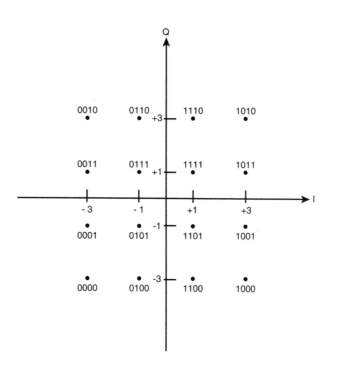

FIGURE 5.18

The 802.11 OFDM PMD uses 16-QAM for 24Mbps and 36Mbps data rate operation.

OFDM splits an information signal across 52 separate subcarriers. Four of them are pilot sub-carriers that the system uses as a reference to disregard frequency or phase shifts of the signal during transmission. A pseudo-binary sequence is sent through the pilot subchannels to prevent the generation of spectral lines. The remaining 48 subcarriers provide separate wireless path-ways for sending the information in a parallel fashion.

OFDM divides groups (symbols) of 1, 2, 4, or 6 bits, depending on data rate chosen, and con-verts them into complex numbers representing applicable constellation points, as shown in Figures 5.15, 5.16, 5.17, and 5.18. An inverse FFT (fast Fourier transform) combines the sub-carriers before transmission.

The 802.11 OFDM standard requires receivers to have a minimum sensitivity ranging from 82dBm to 65dBm, depending on the chosen data rate. Because of the relatively low power lim-its in the lower frequency bands, implementers should carefully consider range requirements of the application before choosing a particular band.

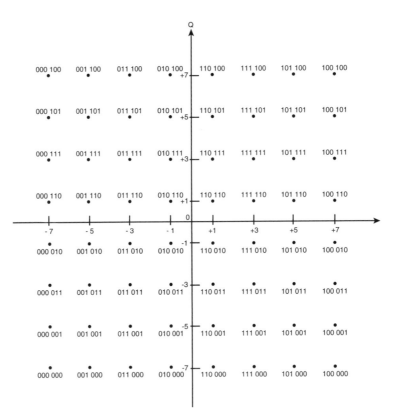

FIGURE 5.19

The 802.11 OFDM PMD uses 64-QAM for 48Mbps and 54Mbps data rate operation.

NOTE

The 802.11 OFDM Physical layer is very similar to the one used in HiperLAN/2.

IEEE 802.11 Infrared (IR) Physical Layer

The IEEE 802.11 Infrared (IR) Physical layer uses pulse position modulation to deliver 1Mbps and 2Mbps data rates via passive ceiling reflection using infrared light. Currently, no products have been released based on this standard; however, it is presented in this chapter as a matter of completeness. This section describes the architecture and operation of the 802.11 IR Physical layer.

IR Physical Layer Convergence Procedure (PLCP) Sublayer

Figure 5.20 illustrates the infrared PLCP frame format that the 802.11 specification refers to as a PLCP protocol data unit (PPDU). The preamble enables the receiver to synchronize properly to the incoming signal before the actual content of the frame arrives. The header field provides information about the frame, and the PSDU (PLCP service data unit) is the MPDU the station is sending.

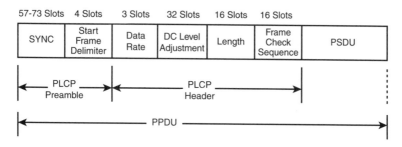

FIGURE 5.20

Infrared Physical Layer Convergence Procedure (PLCP) frames consist of a PLCP preamble, a PLCP header, and a PLCP service data unit (PSDU).

The following describes each of the PLCP frame fields:

- **Sync**   This field consists of alternating presence of a pulse in consecutive time slots. The 802.11 standard specifies that the Sync field must have a minimum length of 57 time slots and a maximum length of 73 time slots. A receiver will begin to synchronize with the incoming signal after first detecting the Sync.

- **Start Frame Delimiter**   The content of this field defines the beginning of a frame. The bit pattern for this field is always the 1001bit pattern, which is unique for infrared PLCPs. One (1) represents the presence of a pulse, whereas zero (0) represents no pulse for information conveyed in infrared PPDUs.

- **Data Rate**   This field identifies the data rate at which the PMD will transmit the frame. The only two possible values, based on the June 1997 version of 802.11, are 000 for 1Mbps and 001 for 2Mbps. The PLCP preamble and header are both always sent at 1Mbps.

- **DC Level Adjustment**   This field consists of a bit pattern that enables the receiving station to stabilize the DC level of the signal. The bit patterns for the two supported rates are as follows:

  1Mbps   00000000100000000000000010000000

  2Mbps   00100010001000100010001000100010

- **Length**   The value of this field is an unsigned 16-bit integer indicating the number of microseconds to transmit the MPDU. The receiver will use this information to determine the end of the frame.

- **Frame Check Sequence**   Similar to the FHSS Physical layer, this field contains a 16-bit CRC result based on CCITT's CRC-16 error detection algorithm. The generator polynomial for CRC-16 is $G(x)=x^{16}+x^{12}+x^{5}+1$. The CRC performs the operation on the Length field before transmitting the frame.

  The Physical layer does not determine whether errors are present within the PSDU. The MAC layer will check for errors based on the FCS. CRC-16 detects all single- and double-bit errors and ensures detection of 99.998% of all possible errors. Most experts feel CRC-16 is sufficient for data transmission blocks of 4 kilobytes or less.

- **PSDU**   This is actually the MPDU being sent by the MAC layer, which can range from zero to a maximum size of 2500 octets.

IR Physical Medium Dependent (PMD) Sublayer

The operation of the PMD translates the binary representation of the PPDUs into an infrared light signal suitable for transmission. The 802.11 infrared Physical layer operates using non-directed transmission, as shown in Figure 5.21, eliminating the need for line-of-sight operation. Most radio LAN suppliers refer to this type of transmission as *diffused infrared*.

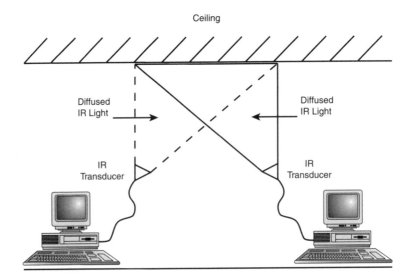

FIGURE 5.21

An 802.11-based infrared LAN system uses the ceiling as a reflection point for supporting carrier sense access protocols.

Because of this form of transmission, the infrared Physical layer is intended only for indoor operation where a ceiling is present to reflect the signals. Windows can significantly attenuate the infrared signals, so be sure to test the operation of infrared devices in the facility before installing the entire system. Because of the use of a ceiling as a reflection point, 802.11 infrared devices are limited in transmission range. A typical range is 30 to 60 feet (10 to 20 meters), depending on ceiling height.

The infrared Physical layer transmits its signals in the nearly visible 850–950 nanometers range at a maximum transmit power level of 2 watts peak optical power. Because of the relatively high transmission frequency, there are no frequency regulatory restrictions for infrared-based systems. In fact, the only regulatory standards that apply to the 802.11 infrared-based system are safety regulations, namely IEC 60825-1 and ANSI Z136.1.

> **NOTE**
>
> The 802.11 specifications make it possible for inexpensive development of 802.11-compliant infrared products using LED emitters and PIN diode detectors.

The infrared PMD transmits the binary data at either 1Mbps (basic access rate) or 2Mbps (enhanced access rate) using a specific modulation type for each, depending on which data rate is chosen. For 1Mbps operation, the infrared PMD uses 16-pulse position modulation (PPM). The concept of *pulse position modulation* is to vary the position of a pulse to represent different binary symbols. Thus, changes in pulse positions maintain the information content of the signal.

Noise usually affects the amplitude of the signal, not the phase. As a result, the use of pulse position modulation reduces potential interference. As shown in Table 5.7, 16-PPM maps each possible group of four bits in the PPDU to one of 16 symbols. The 1 bit in the 16-PPM symbol illustrates the position of a pulse representing a particular group of four PPDU data bits. The transmission order is from left to right. A 0 (zero) represents no pulse.

TABLE 5.7   16-Pulse Position Modulation

Data Bits	16 PPM Symbol
0000	0000000000000001
0001	0000000000000010
0011	0000000000000100
0010	0000000000001000
0110	0000000000010000

TABLE 5.7 Continued

Data Bits	16 PPM Symbol
0111	0000000000100000
0101	0000000001000000
0100	0000000010000000
1100	0000000100000000
1101	0000001000000000
1111	0000010000000000
1110	0000100000000000
1010	0001000000000000
1011	0010000000000000
1001	0100000000000000
1000	1000000000000000

For 2Mbps operation, the infrared PMD uses 4-PPM, as shown in Table 5.8. The order of the data fields in both Table 5.7 and Table 5.8 is based on the gray code, which ensures that there is only a single bit error in the data if a pulse of the transmitted signal gets out of position by one time slot. This is why the bits forming the data bit words look out of order. The 1 bit in the 4-PPM symbol illustrates the position of a pulse representing a particular group of two PPDU data bits. The transmission order is from left to right.

TABLE 5.8 4-Pulse Position Modulation

Data Bits	4 PPM Symbol
00	0001
01	0010
11	0100
10	1000

An infrared wireless LAN offers excellent noise immunity and more security than spread spectrum radio implementations; however, the lack of products forces you to use proprietary devices. Thus, be sure to consider 802.11 spread spectrum radio Physical layers before deciding which one to implement.

As discussed in this chapter, there are several Physical layers to consider when implementing a wireless LAN. Chapter 8, "Implementing a Wireless LAN," will explain how to choose the most appropriate standard based on wireless LAN requirements.

Deploying Wireless LANs

PART
III

IN THIS PART

Wireless System Integration

IN THIS CHAPTER

Wireless System Architecture

A complete wireless system consists of more than what IEEE 802.11 specifies. Other components are necessary to fully depict an architecture that satisfies application requirements. Figure 6.1 illustrates additional components that might be necessary to complete a wireless system. You need to specify these components when designing the system. Some of these components, such as the distribution system, might already be present. Companies generally have existing distribution systems, such as ethernet LANs and WAN connectivity.

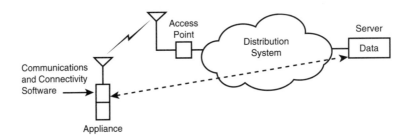

FIGURE 6.1

In addition to IEEE 802.11 components, a wireless system includes a distribution system, communications protocols (such as TCP/IP), connectivity software, and network-management protocols.

The remaining sections in this chapter explain the wireless system components that are beyond the scope of 802.11.

Network Distribution Systems

Designers of the 802.11 standard purposely avoided the definition of a particular distribution system for connecting access points, leaving system architects the freedom to implement 802.11-compliant networks the most effective way. As a result, you'll need to decide what technologies and products will constitute the distribution system if multiple access points are necessary to extend the range of the complete wireless system. A network distribution system is also necessary if databases and applications reside on systems accessible only from a wired network (refer to Figure 6.2).

In most cases, you can specify a wired LAN backbone to act as the distribution system. Typically, vendors sell access points capable of connecting to either IEEE-compliant ethernet or token ring LANs. In addition, wide area network (WAN) components might be necessary to connect LANs separated by longer distances. The following sections explain alternatives you have for LAN and WAN distribution systems.

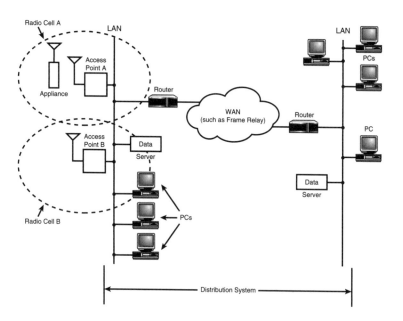

Figure 6.2

The network distribution system might include common LAN and WAN systems to connect access points and access to resources located on other networks.

IEEE 802.3 Carrier Sense Multiple Access (CSMA)

IEEE 802.3 is based on the Ethernet product developed by Xerox Corporation's Palo Alto Research Center (PARC) in the 1970s. In 1980, the IEEE released the IEEE 802.3 Carrier Sense Multiple Access (CSMA) LAN standard, often called ethernet, which has now become by far the most preferred wired LAN. Ethernet operates at 10, 100, and 1,000Mbps, depending on the type of physical layer chosen. The use of ethernet satisfies most performance requirements, and, because of its high degree of proliferation, applicable products are low cost compared to other networks, such as Token Ring. Figure 6.3 illustrates the frame header fields of the IEEE 802.3 protocol.

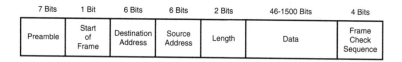

7 Bits	1 Bit	6 Bits	6 Bits	2 Bits	46-1500 Bits	4 Bits
Preamble	Start of Frame	Destination Address	Source Address	Length	Data	Frame Check Sequence

Figure 6.3

IEEE 802.3 specifications describe a MAC frame header that is common to all 802.3 PHYs.

The following list describes each of the IEEE 802.3 MAC frame header fields:

- **Preamble**—Both Ethernet and IEEE 802.3 frames begin with an alternating pattern of 1s and 0s called the preamble, which tells receiving stations that a frame is arriving. This provides time for the receiving station to synchronize to the incoming data stream.

- **Start-of-Frame**—The start-of-frame delimiter ends with two consecutive 1 bits, which serve to synchronize the frame reception functions of all stations on the LAN.

- **Destination and Source Address**—The Destination and Source Address fields are 6 bytes long and refer to the addresses contained in the Ethernet and IEEE 802.3 network interface cards. The first 3 bytes of the addresses are specified by the IEEE on a vendor-dependent basis, and the last 3 bytes are specified by the Ethernet or IEEE 802.3 vendor. The source address is always a unicast (single-node) address. The destination address can be unicast, multicast, or broadcast.

- **Data**—The Data field contains the actual data carried by the frame that will eventually be given to an upper-layer protocol at the destination station. With IEEE 802.3, the upper-layer protocol must be defined within the data portion of the frame, if necessary. The Data field can be up to 1,500 bytes long. At a minimum, the field will be at least 46 bytes long because it will contain at least the header of the higher-layer protocol data unit.

- **Frame Check Sequence**—The 4-byte Frame Check Sequence field contains a cyclic redundancy check (CRC) value so that the receiving device can check for transmission errors.

The operation of 802.3 ethernet is very similar to what IEEE 802.11 defines. Ethernet stations share a common physical wire medium instead of air. If an ethernet station wants to transmit a data frame, it must first sense the medium to determine whether another station is already transmitting. If the medium is idle, the station may transmit. The station must wait a random amount of time, however, if the medium is busy.

Traditional ethernet operates at a wire speed of 10Mbps. Fast ethernet, which is part of the 802.3 standard and operates at 100Mbps, is cost-effective in situations that require higher data rates. The strengths of fast ethernet include multiple-vendor product support, high data rates with small price premium over 10Mbps versions, compatibility with existing 10Mbps networks, and the capability to utilize existing UTP cable (category 3 or higher). Gigabit ethernet, with a PHY based on ANSI X3T11 Fibre Channel technology, is a recent addition to the 802.3 family. Gigabit ethernet is a strong alternative to Asynchronous Transfer Mode (ATM) and shares similar advantages as fast ethernet.

Some suppliers offer full-duplex versions of their ethernet products at a higher price than standard half-duplex products. Full duplex can double the data rate between two ethernet network devices by enabling simultaneous transmission in both directions. In most cases, though, applications and servers do not take advantage of the full bandwidth in both directions when communicating with each other. Thus, be sure that you are able to gain the advantages of full-duplex operation before spending the additional money.

Of course, ethernet is not subjected to the perils of wireless communications, such as hidden stations and radio interference, but other factors common to both 802.11 and 802.3 still apply. Ethernet operates at relatively high data rates; however, specified data rates deal with wire speed, not throughput. For example, a 10Mbps ethernet link enables an ethernet station to transmit a data packet to another ethernet station at 10Mbps only when the station is actually transmitting the data. The aggregate data rate (that is, throughput) for a shared ethernet link will, at best, be 1–2 Mbps. This is because stations must take turns transmitting and collisions might occur, causing gaps in the delivery of information.

Ethernet products are available that support a variety of physical mediums and data rates. Options for ethernet wiring include the following:

- Unshielded twisted-pair (UTP) wire
- Optical fiber cable
- Coaxial cable

These options are described in the succeeding sections.

Unshielded Twisted-Pair (UTP) Wire

UTP wire uses metallic conductors, providing a path for current flow that represents information. As the name implies, UTP wiring doesn't include shielding found in other forms of twisted-pair wires. The wire is twisted in pairs to minimize the electromagnetic interference resulting from adjacent wire pairs and external noise sources. A greater number of twists-per-foot increases noise immunity.

UTP is inexpensive to purchase and easy to install, and it is currently the industry standard for wiring LANs. Consider the use of twisted-pair wiring for all wired connections inside buildings. Figure 6.4 illustrates the topology of a typical UTP-based ethernet LAN.

- **Category 1**—Old-style phone wire, which is not suitable for data transmission. This includes most telephone wire installed in the United States before 1983.
- **Category 2**—Certified for use with the 4Mbps version of IEEE 802.5 Token Ring networks.
- **Category 3**—Certified for 10Mbps (10Base-T) and some 100Mbps (100Base-T) versions of IEEE 802.3 ethernet networks. Many facilities that have an initial installation of a 10Mbps ethernet network have an installed base of category 3 cabling.

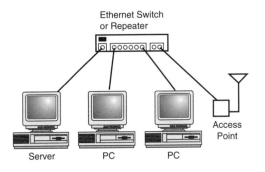

FIGURE 6.4

IEEE 802.3 ethernet stations that utilize UTP connect to an ethernet switch or repeater (hub), forming a star topology.

- **Category 4**—Certified for use with the 16Mbps version of IEEE 802.5 Token Ring networks.

- **Category 5**—Certified for use with ANSI FDDI Token Ring, as well as 100 and 1,000Mbps versions of IEEE 802.3 ethernet networks. Category 5 UTP is the most popular form of wiring for wired LANs.

TIP

There's very little difference in price between category 5 wiring and the other lower-category wiring, and labor costs to install them are the same. Therefore, you should install category 5 cable for all UTP-based network installations, regardless of whether you need the extra bandwidth. This will avoid the expensive rewiring if you require higher performance in the future.

Understanding Ethernet Repeaters and Switches

An ethernet repeater (commonly called a *shared ethernet hub*) refers to a component that provides ethernet connections among multiple stations sharing a common collision domain (see Figure 6.5). Consider utilizing a hub when connecting local user stations (that is, a workgroup) to a single server that has only one connection to the LAN.

A switch is more intelligent than a hub because it has the capability to connect the sending station directly to the receiving station (see Figure 6.6). This results in multiple collision domains and significantly increases throughput. A switch is generally more expensive than a hub; however, consider utilizing a switch if you need to connect user stations if multiple server connections exist or high utilization is impacting the performance of a repeater-based LAN.

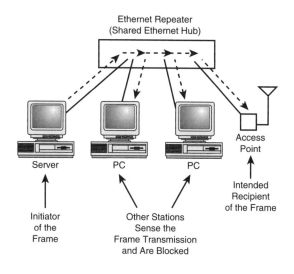

FIGURE 6.5

When stations connect to a shared ethernet hub, the transmission of a frame from one station blocks all other stations from transmitting.

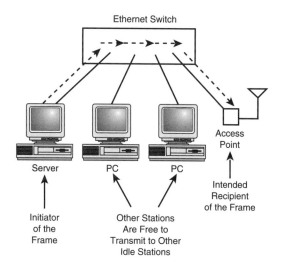

FIGURE 6.6

When stations connect to a switch, the transmission of a frame from one station doesn't block the other stations from transmitting.

Optical-Fiber Cable

If you need a very high degree of noise immunity or information security, consider the use of optical fiber instead of UTP. Optical fiber is a medium that uses changes in light intensity to carry information from one point to another. An optical-fiber system consists of a light source, optical fiber, and a light detector. A light source changes digital electrical signals into light (that is, on for a logic 1 and off for a logic 0), the optical fiber transports the light to the destination, and a light detector transforms the light into an electrical signal.

The main advantages of optical fiber are very high bandwidth (megabits per second and gigabits per second), information security, immunity to electromagnetic interference, lightweight construction, and long-distance operation without signal regeneration. As a result, optical fiber is superior for bandwidth-demanding applications and protocols, operation in classified areas and between buildings, and installation in airplanes and ships. IEEE 802.3's 10Base-F and 100Base-F specifications identify the use of optical fiber as the physical medium. Of course, FDDI identifies the use of optical fiber as well.

> **TIP**
>
> Utilize optical fiber to connect hubs and switches and provide connections between buildings. This will be more expensive than using UTP, but benefits such as higher data rates and less possibility of interference on interbuilding links generally outweigh the higher cost.

Coaxial Cable

The construction of coaxial cable includes a solid metallic core with a shielding as a return path, offering a path for electrical current representing information to flow. The shielding does a good job of reducing electrical noise interference within the core wire. As a result, coaxial cable can extend to much greater lengths than UTP. The disadvantage of coaxial cable, though, is its bulky shape, making it difficult to install. Also, coaxial cable doesn't lend itself very well to centralized wiring topologies, making it difficult to maintain.

During the 1980s, coaxial cable was very popular for wiring LANs; therefore, you might find some still existing in older implementations. Very few, if any, new implementations will require the use of coaxial cable; however, you should be aware of these types of networks in case you have to interface the wireless users to it.

IEEE 802.3 defines two physical-layer specifications, 10Base-2 and 10Base-5, based on the use of coaxial cable. 10Base-2 uses RG-58 cable, the same used to connect your television to a cable outlet, and it will operate over a distance of up to 200 meters (600 feet). 10Base-5 uses a much larger cable than RG-58, but it is capable of operating up to 500 meters (1500 feet) without the use of repeaters. Both 10Base-2 and 10Base-5 utilize a bus topology, as shown in Figure 6.7.

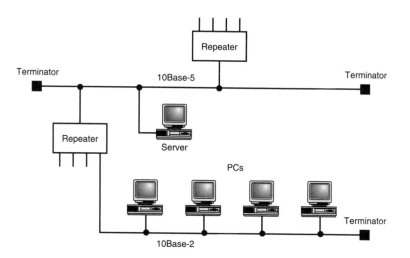

FIGURE 6.7

10Base-2 and 10Base-5 ethernet network configurations are less reliable than 10Base-T networks because a break at one point in the cable can bring down the network.

NOTE

Access points typically have the capability to connect to ethernet networks via 10Base-T, 10Base-2, and 10Base-5 connectors, as shown in Figure 6.8.

IEEE 802.5 Token Ring

The IEEE 802.5 standard specifies a 4 and 16Mbps token ring LAN. The first token ring network was developed by IBM in the 1970s, and then IEEE released the 802.5 specification based on IBM's work. Because of the IBM orientation of Token Ring, you'll find that most Token Ring networks in facilities deploy IBM mainframes and servers.

Today, IBM Token Ring and IEEE 802.5 networks are compatible, although there are minor differences. For instance, IBM's Token Ring network specifies a star configuration, with all end stations attached to a device called a *multistation access unit* (MSAU). IEEE 802.5 does not specify a topology, but most 802.5 implementations are based on a star configuration similar to the UTP version of ethernet. Also, IEEE 802.5 does not specify a media type, but IBM Token Ring identifies the use of UTP wire (see the section "Unshielded Twisted-Pair (UTP) Wire," earlier in this chapter).

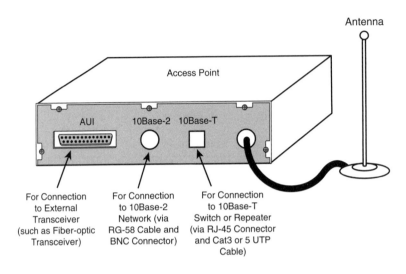

FIGURE 6.8
Access points generally provide the capability of connecting to multiple ethernet network types.

Token Ring protocols ensure that only one station transmits at a time through the use of a token. The token, which is a distinctive group of bits, circulates the ring. If a station wants to transmit data, it must first wait its turn to receive the token, and then it can transmit its data. The capturing of the token ensures that no other station will transmit. The data circulates the ring, and the appropriate destination senses its address and processes the data. When finished, the sending station forwards the token to the next station downline.

Because of the token-passing mechanism, 802.5 operates with more stability under heavier traffic than 802.3 ethernet. The predictable access method of 802.5 enables it to handle synchronous-type information transfers. IEEE 802.5 is the second most popular LAN medium access technique and is slightly more expensive to implement than ethernet.

Figure 6.9 illustrates the token ring frame formats, and the following lists explains the purpose of each field.

The following list describes the fields of an 802.5 token:

- **Start Delimiter**—The start delimiter alerts each station that a token (or data frame) is arriving. This field includes signals that distinguish the byte from the rest of the frame by violating the encoding scheme used elsewhere in the frame.
- **Access Control**—The access control byte contains the priority and reservation fields, as well as a token bit that is used to differentiate a token from a data or command frame. The monitor bit is used by the active monitor to determine whether a frame is endlessly circling the ring.

- **End Delimiter**—The end delimiter identifies the end of the token or data/command frame. It also contains bits to indicate a damaged frame, as well as the last frame in a logical sequence.

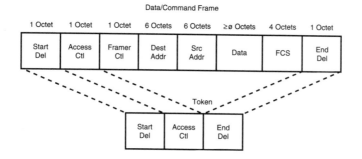

FIGURE 6.9
Token ring protocols utilize a token and standard MAC frame structure to implement token-passing protocols.

The following list describes the field of an 802.5 MAC frame:

- **Frame Control**—The frame control byte indicates whether the frame contains data or control information. In control frames, the frame control byte specifies the type of control information.

- **Destination and Source Address**—As with IEEE 802.3, the destination and source address are 6 bytes long and designate the source and destination stations.

- **Data**—The Data field contains the data being sent from source to destination. The length of this field is limited by the ring token holding time, which defines the maximum time that a station may hold the token.

- **Frame Check Sequence (FCS)**—The 4-byte FCS field contains a cyclic redundancy check (CRC) value so that the receiving device can check for errors.

- **End Delimiter**—The end delimiter identifies the end of the data/command frame. It also contains bits to indicate a damaged frame, as well as the last frame in a logical sequence.

ANSI Fiber Distributed Data Interface (FDDI)

The Fiber Distributed Data Interface (FDDI) standard was produced by the ANSI X3T9.5 standards committee in the mid-1980s, and it specifies a 100Mbps dual token ring campus network. FDDI specifies the use of optical-fiber medium and will support simultaneous transmission of both synchronous and prioritized asynchronous traffic. The Copper Data Distributed Interface (CDDI) version of FDDI operates over category 5 twisted-pair wiring. FDDI is an effective solution as a reliable high-speed interface within a LAN or corporate network.

FDDI is an expensive solution, but it is effective for supporting high-speed deterministic access to network resources. Some organizations find it necessary to use FDDI for connecting servers in a server pool. It's also beneficial to use FDDI as the backbone for a campus or enterprise network. The synchronous mode of FDDI is used for applications whose bandwidth and response time limits are predictable in advance, permitting them to be preallocated by the FDDI Station Management Protocol. The asynchronous mode is used for applications whose bandwidth requirements are less predictable or whose response time requirements are less critical. Asynchronous bandwidth is instantaneously allocated from a pool of remaining ring bandwidth that is unallocated, unused, or both.

ANSI is currently developing FDDI II, which is an extension of FDDI. It is unclear when ANSI will release this standard. FDDI II has two modes: Basic mode, which is the existing FDDI, and hybrid mode, which will incorporate the functionality of basic mode plus circuit switching. The addition of circuit switching enables the support of isochronous traffic. Isochronous transmission is similar to synchronous transmission, but, with isochronous, a node is capable of sending data at specific times. This simplifies the transmission of real-time information because of decreased source buffering and signal processing.

Wide Area Networking Concepts

A wide area network might be necessary when deploying a wireless system to provide wired connections between facilities (refer to Figure 6.10). For example, a department store chain in Texas maintains its pricing information in a centralized database in Dallas. Each of the 100 individual retail stores retrieves pricing information from the central database each night over a Frame Relay WAN, making the pricing information available to wireless handheld data collectors that clerks use to price items.

The components of a WAN consist of routers and links. Routers receive routable data packets, such as Internet Protocol (IP) or Internetwork Packet Exchange (IPX) packets, review the destination address located in the packet header, and decide which direction to send the packet next to forward the packet closer to the final destination. Routers maintain routing tables that adapt, via a routing protocol, to changes in the network.

Routing Information Protocol (RIP)

The Routing Information Protocol (RIP) is currently the most common type of routing protocol. RIP bases its routing path on the distance (number of hops) to the destination. In 1982, RIP appeared in the Berkeley Software Distribution (BSD) version of UNIX as part of TCP/IP protocol suite. Today, many other routing protocols, such as AppleTalk's routing protocol, use RIP as a foundation. Other companies, such as Novell and Banyan, have RIP-like routing protocols as well. Also, Microsoft expanded NT's WAN capabilities by adding support for routing packets based on RIP.

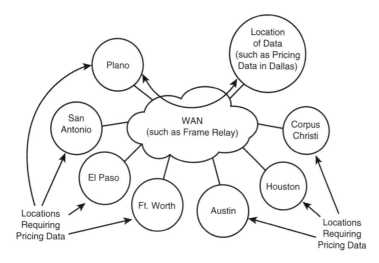

FIGURE 6.10

The WAN-based distribution system is necessary to connect facilities separated by large distances.

A router implements RIP by storing information in its routing table. A destination column indicates all possible destination networks, a next-hop field identifies the router port to send the packet next, and the distance field refers to the number of hops it will take to reach the destination network. A RIP routing table contains only the best route to a particular destination. If the router receives new routing information from another node, it will overwrite the entry.

RIP maintains optimum routing paths by sending out routing update messages if the network topology changes. For example, if a router finds that a particular link is faulty, it updates its routing table and then send a copy of the modified table to each of its neighbors. The neighbors update their tables with the new information and send updates to their neighbors, and so on. Within a short period, all routers have the new information.

Open Shortest Path First (OSPF) Protocol

The problem with RIP is that it's not very robust, meaning that it lacks the capability to handle larger networks and the capability to effectively determine alternate paths. As a result, the Internet Engineering Task Force developed Open Shortest Path First (OSPF) to replace the RIP protocol. The basis of OSPF is the Shortest Path First algorithm developed by Bolt, Beranek, and Newman (BBN) in 1978 for the Advanced Research Project Agency Network (ARPANET).

OSPF is quickly becoming the industry-standard protocol because of its robustness; it supports the requirements of larger networks, such as special service requests, support for multiple network-layer protocols, and authentication. OSPF is an efficient protocol, supporting speedy recovery from topology changes because OSPF routers can reroute data traffic as necessary. OSPF also minimizes overhead packet traffic when announcing changes by sending only information regarding the change instead of the entire routing table.

OSPF maintains a topological database that stores information related to the state of links within an autonomous network, and it uses this information to calculate the shortest path. Many companies incorporate OSPF into their routers. For example, Novell's Multiprotocol Router (MPR) Version 3 for NetWare is a NetWare Loadable Module (NLM) software-based router for NetWare 3.x and 4.1 that implements OSPF. In addition, Cisco's routers, including its 7000 family of routers, support OSPF.

With OSPF, a router announces its presence by sending a Hello message to each of its possible neighbors. Periodically, each neighbor sends a Hello message to show that it's still operational. Therefore, the new router will soon learn of its neighbors as well.

OSPF responds to upper-layer type of service (TOS) requests found in the header of an IP packet. Based on the TOS, OSPF calculates the best route. For example, OSPF can respond to all eight combinations of IP's TOS bits, which can represent all combinations of delay, throughput, and reliability. If the TOS bits specify low delay, high throughput, and low reliability, OSPF will calculate a route that best satisfies these requirements.

Private Versus Public WANs

When implementing wide area networking, you need to decide whether to utilize a private or a public WAN. A private WAN consists of routers and links that the company (containing the system end users) owns and operates. This is the traditional approach to wide area networking. Private WANs often consist of leased T1 and 56Kbps digital circuits that provide connections between user-owned and user-maintained routers.

With public WANs, the company leases connections to a WAN architecture that supports multiple unrelated companies. Generally, these public networks utilize Frame Relay, SMDS, or ATM protocols. Figure 6.11 illustrates conceptual differences between private and public WANs.

In general, there are tradeoffs between the private and public approaches. The benefits and drawbacks of the *private WAN* are as follows:

- More suitable for WANs requiring a low degree of meshing (very few links, as in the case of a centralized topology)
- Service fees that are economically feasible for metropolitan areas
- Higher initial cost because of a greater number of hardware interfaces and circuit installations

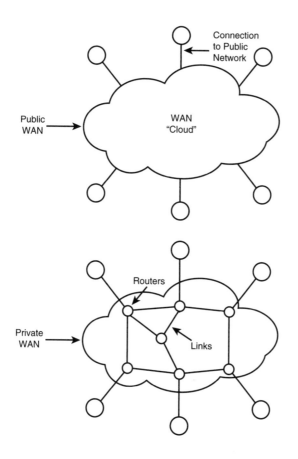

FIGURE 6.11

An MIS group of a company views a public WAN as a connection to a network "cloud," whereas it views a private WAN as a collection of routers and links (communications lines).

- Lease fees sensitive to the distance between sites
- In-house management required; therefore, potentially higher operating costs
- Fixed bandwidth

The benefits of the *public WAN* are as follows:

- More suitable for a WAN requiring a high degree of meshing (a large number of links, as in a distributed topology)
- Lower initial cost because of a fewer number of hardware interfaces and circuit installations
- Potentially lower operating cost because of less staffing requirements

- Lease fees not sensitive to the distance between sites
- Variable bandwidth offered (bandwidth on demand)
- Management provided by the carrier; therefore, potentially lower operating costs
- Service fees that are most economical for long-haul (outside the metropolitan area) distances
- Very little control, if any, over network restoration in the event of network failure

Traditionally, organizations have implemented private point-to-point WANs to support communications between remote terminals to centralized mainframe-based applications. T1 is a common communications circuit that companies lease to provide links between routers in a private network. Bell Labs originally developed the T1 standard to mulitplex multiple phone calls into a composite signal, suitable for transmission through a digital communications circuit. A T1 signal consists of a serial transmission of T1 frames, with each frame carrying 8-bit samples of 24 separate channels. You can lease an entire T1 circuit (1.544Mbps) or only single fractional T1 channels (64Mbps each) from a telephone service carrier.

With the development of distributed client/server applications, most organizations now require technologies suitable for highly meshed topologies. There's a greater need to support communications among the remote sites, not just to a centralized data center. Thus, you should seriously consider leasing the use of a public packet-switching WAN to support today's demand for distributed computing.

There are many technologies to choose from when implementing a WAN. The following sections define the most common technologies for public WANs.

X.25

X.25 was the first public packet-switching technology, developed by the CCITT and offered as a service during the 1970s; it is still available today. X.25 offers connection-oriented (virtual circuit) service and operates at 64Kbps, which is too slow for some high-speed applications. Designers of this protocol made it very robust to accommodate the potential for transmission errors resulting from the transport over metallic cabling and analog systems used predominately in the 1970s. Thus, X.25 implements very good error control, which takes considerable overhead.

Some companies have a significant investment in X.25 equipment and are still supporting the technology. However, you should consider other packet-switching technologies, such as Frame Relay, SMDS, or ATM for new implementations.

Frame Relay

Frame Relay is today's most popular and widely available public WAN technology, providing a packet-switching interface operating at data rates of 56Kbps to 2Mbps. Actually, Frame Relay is similar to X.25, minus the transmission error control overhead. Thus, Frame Relay assumes that a higher-layer, end-to-end protocol will check for transmission errors. Carriers offer Frame Relay as permanent connection-oriented (virtual circuit) service. In the future, Frame Relay will be available as a switched virtual circuit service as well.

To interface with Frame Relay service, you need to purchase or lease a *Frame Relay Attachment Device (FRAD) or* router with a Frame Relay interface. The FRAD or router interfaces a LAN (typically ethernet) to the local Frame Relay service provider via a T1 circuit. Frame Relay is currently overall the most feasible technology you can use for connecting geographically disparate sites, especially if these sites span several metropolitan areas and have distributed applications.

Switched Multimegabit Data Service (SMDS)

SMDS is a packet-switching interface that operates at data rates ranging from 1.5Mbps to 45Mbps. SMDS is similar to Frame Relay, except that SMDS provides connectionless (datagram) service. Some companies utilize SMDS to support highly spontaneous multimedia applications. You can access a local SMDS service provider via T1 or T3 (45Mbps) circuits. SMDS is not available in all areas.

Asynchronous Transfer Mode (ATM)

Some companies construct private networks using ATM technology and products; however, ATM is now available from most carriers as a public network offering. ATM is a circuit-switching protocol that transmits small data packets called cells passing through devices known as *ATM switches.* An ATM switch analyzes information in the header of the cell to switch the cell to the output interface that connects to the next switch as the cell works its way to its destination. ATM operates at relatively high data rates (up into the range of gigabits per second).

Choosing a Distribution System

The ultimate selection of the distribution system depends on requirements for connecting wireless users to applications and data storage located on wired networks. Be sure to carefully analyze user requirements and existing system designs before making a decision on which wired LAN and WAN technology to implement. In most cases, ethernet will satisfy LAN needs, and Frame Relay will work best for WAN connections.

Roaming Protocols

A critical function in a multiple-cell wireless LAN (that is, ESS) is *roaming*, which enables wireless users to move from cell to cell seamlessly. Because the 802.11 standard does not provide specifications for roaming, it is up to the radio LAN vendors to define roaming protocols.

Companies that manufacture radio LAN access points have their own flavor of roaming. This often forces 802.11 users to standardize on one particular vendor for access points to ensure seamless roaming. In some cases, wireless LAN companies have established partnerships to standardize on a common roaming protocol to enable interoperabilty between multivendor access points.

> **NOTE**
>
> Many wireless LAN product vendors enable you to indicate the degree of mobility of each station so that the access point can optimize roaming algorithms. If you set up the station as being mobile, the roaming protocols will enable the station to reassociate as it moves from cell to cell. Stationary devices might experience a short episode of radio interference and falsely reassociate with a different access point. As a result, the roaming protocols take this into consideration when dealing with stations that you indicate as stationary.

Through the collaboration of companies led by Lucent, the Inter-Access Point Protocol (IAPP) specification provides a common roaming protocol enabling wireless users to move throughout a facility while maintaining a connection to the network via multivendor access points. Today, interoperability tests and demonstrations show that IAPP works with a variety of access points. As a result, IAPP could become the industry standard if other vendors and users embrace the protocol. The Wireless Ethernet Compatibility Alliance (WECA) includes interoperable roaming as a requirement to receiving Wi-Fi certification.

The IAPP specification builds upon the capabilities of the IEEE 802.11 standard, using the distribution system interfaces of the access point that 802.11 provides. IAPP operates between access points, using the User Datagram Protocol (UDP) and the Internet Protocol (IP) as a basis for communications. UDP is a transport-layer protocol that provides connectionless and unacknowledged end-to-end data transfers. See the section "Internet Protocol (IP)," later in this chapter, for an explanation of IP.

IAPP defines two basic protocols: the Announce Protocol and the Handover Protocol. The Announce Protocol provides coordination between access points by performing the following functions:

- Inform other access points about a new active access point
- Inform the access points of network-wide configuration information

The Handover Protocol informs an access point that one of its stations has reassociated with a different access point. The old access point forwards buffered frames for the station to the new access point. The new access point then updates filter tables to ensure that MAC-level filtering (bridging) will forward frames appropriately.

Implementing Roaming

Normally, you won't have the luxury to choose a type of roaming protocol for the wireless system you're implementing. Vendors generally implement a proprietary roaming protocol that works only with their products. When deciding which access points to use, be sure to include the presence of a multiple-vendor roaming protocols (IAPP) as a factor when comparing access points.

As with other product procurements, though, it is most effective to plan on purchasing components, such as access points and radio cards, from a common vendor. As with implementing an ethernet network with common hubs and switches, this will make the resulting wireless system easier to manage.

Communications Protocols

The wireless and wired networking technologies provide lower-level connections among the network interface cards located in end-user appliances, access points, servers, and printers. A communications protocol operates at a higher level (typically the transport and network layers) and establishes end-to-end connections between the application software within devices on the network. This is necessary to provide a common path for entities to communicate.

The most common protocols for providing communication among network devices and applications are the Transmission Control Protocol (TCP) and the Internet Protocol (IP). These protocols are the basis of standards for connecting to the Internet and providing open-systems connectivity in other systems. The IETF has many request for comments (RFCs) that explain the operation of TCP/IP protocols. You can purchase TCP/IP software from a variety of vendors for different platforms. In fact, UNIX includes TCP/IP as part of the operating system.

Transmission Control Protocol (TCP)

The Transmission Control Protocol (TCP) operates at the OSI transport layer and is commonly used for establishing and maintaining communication between applications on different computers. TCP provides highly reliable, full-duplex, connection-oriented, acknowledged, and flow-control services to upper-layer protocols and applications. For example, a mainframe computer employing TCP software enables a user with TCP software as well to log in to the mainframe and run the application using Telnet. Connection-oriented services, such as Telnet, FTP, rlogin, X Window, and SMTP, require a high degree of reliability and therefore use TCP. Figure 6.12 illustrates the header of the TCP protocol.

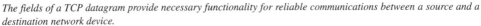

Figure 6.12

The fields of a TCP datagram provide necessary functionality for reliable communications between a source and a destination network device.

The following list describes the fields of TCP datagram:

- **Source Port and Destination Port**—Identifies the service access points at which upper-layer source and destination processes and applications receive TCP services. Most server processes associate with a fixed-port number (23 for Telnet and 161 for SNMP) to provide application developers a standard port to point to when communicating with a server. Most client processes, though, request a port number from its operating system at the beginning of execution. This enables the server processes to differentiate which client process it is communicating with.

- **Sequence Number**—Specifies the sequence number of the datagram being sent.

- **Acknowledgement Number**—Contains the sequence number of the next datagram that the sender of the immediate packet expects to receive.

- **Header Information**—Carries information about the TCP header, such as TCP header length and control flags.

- **Window**—Specifies the size of the sender's receive window (that is, buffer space available for incoming data).

- **Checksum**—Used to determine whether there are any errors in the header.

- **Urgent Pointer**—Points to the first data in the packet byte that the sender wanted to mark as urgent.

- **Options**—Specifies various TCP options.

- **Data**—Contains upper-layer information and control data.

Tip

Firewalls can filter incoming datagrams based on the port addresses found in the TCP header. This enables system designers to restrict access to specific applications on a network residing behind the firewall. Be sure to incorporate a firewall with appropriate TCP filters to block access to specific applications.

The operation of the TCP protocol is fairly straightforward:

1. Entity A wanting to establish a connection with Entity B initiates a three-way handshake protocol starting with a connection request datagram sent to Entity B.

2. Entity B responds to Entity A with an acknowledgement containing control information (such as window size).

3. Entity A finishes the TCP connection by sending an acknowledgement containing control information back to Entity B.

4. The two entities send TCP datagrams back and forth to each other associated to a particular port address.

Internet Protocol (IP)

The Internet Protocol (IP) operates at the OSI network layer. Routers commonly use IP to route TCP datagrams from source to destination. Figure 6.13 illustrates the fields of an IP packet, which are explained as follows:

- **Version**—The version number of the IP protocol. For example, a value of 4 represents IPv4, and a value of 6 represents IPv6.

- **Internet Header Length**—The length of the IP header in 32-bit words.

- **Type of Service**—the level of service (such as precedence, delay, throughput, and reliability) that the IP datagram should be given as it traverses the network.

- **Total Length**—The length of the datagram in bytes.

- **Identification**—The identification number of the datagram for purposes of combining datagram fragments.

- **Flags**—Data bits for controlling whether fragmentation should take place.

- **Fragment Offset**—The location of a datagram (if it's a fragment) within the complete datagram. The receiving entity uses this to combine fragments.

- **Time-to-Live**—The maximum amount of time the datagram can exist as the datagram traverses the network.

- **Protocol**—The protocol that associates with the data in the Data field of the datagram. For example, a value of 6 indicates that the Data field contains a TCP datagram, and a value of 17 indicates that the Data field contains a UDP datagram.

- **Header Checksum**—16-bit checksum of the datagram header (up to and including the Protocol field).

- **Source IP Address**—The IP address of the sender of the datagram.

- **Destination IP Address**—The IP address of the destination of the datagram.

- **Options**—A set of fields that describe specific processing that must take place on the packet. The use of options are generally used for debugging and testing.

- **Padding**—Additional data bits to ensure that the packet is a complete set of 32-bit words.

FIGURE 6.13
The fields of an IPv4 packet provide necessary functionality for routing across dissimilar networks.

If you plan to utilize applications requiring TCP/IP interfaces, or if users will need access to the Internet, you'll have to assign a unique IP address to each device connected to the network (handheld appliance, access point, workstation, printer, server, and so on). Actually, the IP address corresponds to a network connection; therefore, a server that has two network interface cards would require two IP addresses, one for each card.

The IP packet header contains the source and destination IP address that routers will use, along with a routing table, to determine where to send the packet next. The IP address is 32 bits longs; therefore, there are 4,294,967,296 unique IP addresses.

IP Address Classes

The developers of the Internet decided to base IP addressing on the hierarchical format shown in Figure 6.14, distinguishing the address into three classes: Class A, Class B, and Class C. If users never plan to interface with the Internet, you're free to utilize the IP address space in any way. Otherwise, you must obtain official IP addresses (ones that are unique from others assigned) to operate over the Internet. You can obtain an official IP address through an Internet service provider (ISP) in your nearest metropolitan area. For an official IP address, you'll be given a unique network number, and you're free to assign addresses within the domain. For example, if you're assigned a Class C address, you'll be free to assign up to 255 addresses.

When planning the allocation of address, make sure that you obtain enough official unique IP addresses for each network connection. For example, an organization with 350 users, 10 access points, and 4 servers requires at least 364 addresses. You could satisfy this requirement by obtaining one Class B address or two Class C addresses.

Because of the vast number of organizations deploying Web servers and gaining access to the Internet, unique IP addresses are quickly running out. In fact, it's impossible to obtain a Class A address and very difficult, if not impossible, to obtain a Class B address. Therefore, you'll probably need to be issued multiple Class C addresses. The problem, though, is that it's difficult to manage multiple Class C addresses if they are not contiguous. Therefore, you'll need to predict the number of addresses that you'll need for the future to obtain a contiguous series of addresses.

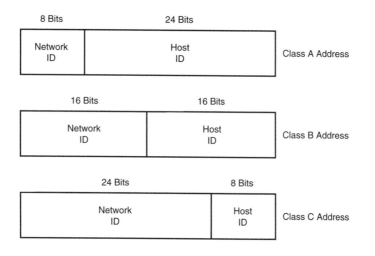

FIGURE 6.14

A router forwards packets on to a particular network segment based on the network ID portion of the IP address. When the packet arrives at the correct network, the network delivers the packet to the final destination based on the host ID.

NOTE

Most systems currently use IPv4, which has been in use since the early 1980s. Some companies, though, are beginning to migrate their systems to a newer version, IPv6. The main differences are that IPv6 offers much larger IP addresses—128 bits each— providing a solution to the small number of IPv4 IP addresses. IPv6 includes extensions to support authentication, data integrity, and data confidentiality.

Implementing IP Address Assignment with a Limited Number of Official IP Addresses

If your network implementation requires a large number of IP addresses, or if it's difficult to predict the number of addresses needed in the future, consider private addressing techniques. The Network Information Center has set aside a single Class A address (10.X.X.X) that you can utilize within your network, giving you a large number of addresses to assign to network devices. You have to agree, however, to not use these addresses on the Internet.

> If you need Internet access, you can deploy a proxy server that translates your private addresses into legal Internet addresses. This means that you need to obtain at least one Class C address to support the connections to the Internet. As a result, the outside world sees only a few IP addresses and not the many used within the company.

Static Versus Dynamic IP Addresses

For smaller wireless LANs (with less than 50 users), it might be feasible to install static IP addresses within the configuration files for each appliance. The problem with installing static IP addresses in larger LANs, though, is that you'll more than likely make a mistake and accidentally use a duplicate address or an IP address that doesn't correspond to the immediate network. The wrong IP address will cause problems that are difficult to troubleshoot. In addition, it is tedious and time-consuming to change the IP address on all network devices if you must alter the address plan in the future.

For larger LANs, consider the use of a dynamic address assignment protocol, such as the Dynamic Host Configuration Protocol (DHCP). DHCP issues IP addresses automatically within a specified range to devices such as PCs when they are first powered on. The device retains the use of the IP address for a specific license period that the system administrator can define. DHCP is available as part of the Microsoft Windows NT Server NOS and UNIX operating systems, and it offers the following advantages over manual installation:

- **Efficient implementation of address assignments**—With DHCP, there is no need to manually install or change IP addresses at every client workstation during initial installation or when a workstation is moved from one location to another. This saves time during installation and avoids mistakes in allocating addresses (such as duplicate addresses or addresses with the wrong subnet number). It is very difficult to track down address-related problems that might occur when using permanently assigned addresses.

- **Central point of address management**—With DHCP, there is no need to update the IP address at each client workstation if making a change to the network's configuration or address plan. With DHCP, you can make these changes from a single point in the network. For example, if you move the Domain Name Service software to a different platform (such as from a Sun to an NT platform), you would need to incorporate that change for each client workstation if using permanently assigned addresses. With DHCP, you just update the configuration screen from a single point at the NT server or remote location. Again, this advantage is strongest for larger networks.

Issues with TCP/IP over Wireless LANs

TCP/IP-based protocols provide an excellent platform for high-speed wired LANs with constant connections; however, the use of TCP/IP protocols over wireless LANs poses significant problems. The following list explains issues that could affect the performance of the wireless LAN when using standard TCP/IP protocols:

- **High overhead**—Because of TCP's connection-oriented protocol, it often sends packets that only perform negotiations or acknowledgements and that do not contain real data. This additional overhead consumes a relatively large amount of the limited wireless bandwidth, deteriorating the performance over the wireless LAN.

- **Incapability to adjust under marginal conditions**—TCP is fairly rigid when posed with changes in wireless coverage. With TCP, a marginal connection between the wireless appliance and an access point can cause the TCP/IP protocol to terminate the connection, requiring the application or user to re-establish a connection.

- **Difficulty in dealing with mobile node addresses**—Traditional IP addressing assumes that the network device will always permanently connect to the network from within the same network domain (that is, the same router port). Problems arise when an appliance associated with an IP address roams to an access point located within a different network domain, separated from the original network domain by a router.

  In most cases, this will confuse the router and possibly other devices located within the new network domain. The result is a network that cannot route the packets to the destination of the mobile station, unless you physically change the IP address in the appliance when it's being operated within a different domain. However, this is not feasible in most cases.

If the wireless system will consist of a larger number of appliances (usually greater than 10) per access point, contemplate the use of wireless *middleware* to deal with the limited bandwidth and need to operate in marginal conditions. Middleware products provide communication over the wireless network using a lightweight non-TCP/IP protocol between the appliances and middleware software residing on a server or separate PC. The gateway then communicates to the devices on the higher-speed wired network using standard TCP/IP-based protocols. For more information on the advantages of middleware, see the "Middleware" section later in this chapter.

Mobile IP

Consider the use of Mobile IP if users need to roam to parts of the network associated with a different IP address than what's loaded in the appliance. IETF's RFC 2002 defines Mobile IP, an enhancement to the standard IP protocol. The main goal of Mobile IP is to enable mobile stations to roam transparently throughout networks, automatically maintaining proper IP-based connections to their home networks. This avoids the impracticality of changing the IP address in the appliance when operating in a different area of the network.

The need for Mobile IP arises most often in wireless WAN systems. For example, a user might need to roam temporarily with a wireless appliance in a foreign network that has a completely different IP network address than the home network. This situation can also occur in a LAN when users roam from an access point located on one subnet (that is, router port) of a network to an access point on another subnet. In these cases, be sure to consider the use of Mobile IP.

Mobile IP uses an address-forwarding mechanism to continue the delivery of packets to a mobile station as it moves from network to network. This operation is similar to the postal mail delivery service. Imagine that you're moving temporarily from Dayton, Ohio, to Washington, D.C., for a six-month consulting assignment. After you arrive in D.C. and obtain a new mailing address, you drop off a change of address card at your new D.C. post office, which notifies the Dayton post office of your new address. Now when the Dayton post office receives mail for you, it knows to forward the mail to you at your new address in D.C.

The operation of Mobile IP is very similar to this analogy. For example, imagine that you're a doctor working in a hospital and you need to wander from your office to the emergency room to assist a new patient:

1. You carry your mobile station (a wireless pen-based computer), which has an IP address associated with the part of the network where your office is located, toward the emergency room. (The wireless access points in the emergency room reside on a different subnet of the hospital's network.)

2. As you walk closer to your destination, your pen-based computer associates with the emergency room's network.

3. The Mobile IP protocol notifies your home network of a care-of address (IP address located within the emergency room subnet) that your home network should send packets relevant to your mobile station.

4. Your home network forwards all packets destined to you to the emergency room's network (via the care-of address), which will deliver them to your mobile station.

A positive attribute of Mobile IP is that its implementation does not require changes to routers or the Domain Name Service (DNS). To implement Mobile IP, you have to include only a few software elements as the following describes (refer to Figure 6.15):

- **Mobile node**—The mobile node is an entity contained within a particular wireless mobile station (such as a handheld PC or data collector) that communicates with other Mobile IP components. A mobile node is built into a TCP/IP protocol stack or can exist as a "shim" under a TCP/IP stack.

- **Home agent**—The home agent resides within the mobile station's home subnet, intercepts packets addressed to the mobile station, and forwards applicable packets to the applicable foreign agent.
- **Foreign agent**—The foreign agent receives packets from home agents and delivers the packets to the mobile node. The foreign agent resides somewhere within the foreign network. In some modes, the foreign agent is not necessary.

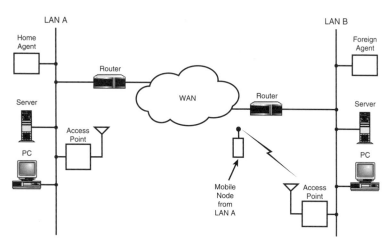

FIGURE 6.15

Mobile IP enables mobile stations to roam from network to network without your needing to manually reassign an IP address to the mobile station.

The Mobile IP protocol performs several functions, as detailed in the following sections.

Agent Discovery

The agent discovery process is necessary to bind the mobile node to a foreign agent or, in some cases, directly to the home agent. Foreign and home agents periodically advertise their availability to mobile nodes via broadcast messages. A mobile node can also broadcast a message indicating its presence and discover whether a foreign agent is available.

After receiving communication from a foreign or home agent, the mobile node determines whether it's located on the home network or a foreign network. If the mobile node is within the home network, the mobile station will not utilize the mobility functions. A mobile node returning to its home network, though, will deregister with the applicable foreign agent. If the mobile node finds that it's on a foreign network, it will obtain a care-of address from the foreign network.

Assignment of Care-of Address

Before the home network can forward packets to the remote network, it must know the appropriate care-of address. With Mobile IP, there are two methods to assign a care-of address:

- With the first method, a foreign agent maintains a single care-of address for all mobile nodes that fall within its domain. This makes best use of the limited number of addresses available with IPv4 because all mobile nodes share the same care-of address. When the foreign agent advertises its presence, the broadcast message contains the care-of address of the foreign agent.

- With the second method, the mobile node acquires the care-of address through some external means. For example, the mobile node might obtain the address dynamically through a protocol such as the Dynamic Host Configuration Protocol (DHCP). The advantage of this method of address assignment is that it enables a mobile node to function without a foreign agent; however, you need to specify a pool of addresses that can be available to the visiting nodes.

Registration

After receiving its new care-of address, the mobile node (or foreign agent) registers it with the home agent. This establishes a link (also referred to as a tunnel) between the foreign and home networks.

For security purposes, the mobile node and the home agent encrypt messages sent back and forth to each other. In addition, the home and foreign agents may reject the registration requests to guard against attacks such as packet forgery and modification.

Tunneling and Encapsulation

Mobile IP transports packets back and forth between the home and foreign networks via a tunnel. The tunnel has two endpoints: one at the home agent IP address and the other at the care-of address (either of the foreign agent or of the mobile node). The home agent intercepts datagrams sent to the mobile node's home address and then encapsulates and transmits the datagrams (generally as the payload of an IP packet) to the care-of address entity.

After reception at the foreign network, the foreign agent de-encapsulates the datagram and sends it to the mobile node. Datagrams sent by the mobile node are generally handled using standard IP routing without passing through the home agent.

Implementing Mobile IP

Don't expect Mobile IP to work everywhere. You must carefully plan the use of Mobile IP to ensure that the external networks will support wireless mobile stations, at a minimum, with the correct type of access point (that is, direct sequence or frequency hopping) and will implement TCP/IP protocols.

If the external network doesn't support a foreign agent, the network will need to have a dynamic address-assignment mechanism, such as DHCP, to issue a temporary IP address to the visiting mobile appliance. Also, you'll need to ensure that the TCP/IP software product you're using supports Mobile IP. If not, most wireless product vendors can supply you with the appropriate shim for your existing TCP/IP protocol stack.

IPv6 incorporates the Mobile IP protocols, making it much easier to implement support for mobile nodes. So, as you migrate to IPv6-based TCP/IP software and routers, Mobile IP services will already be available.

With Mobile IP, you must also properly configure firewalls protecting both the home and the foreign networks to enable Mobile IP traffic to flow. Some firewalls are set up to prevent internal users from sending packets destined to external networks that have source addresses that do not correspond with the internal network (such as when a user is trying to spoof another external network). These firewalls block the transmission of packets from the mobile node because its source address does not correspond to the internal (that is, foreign) network. For this case, you'll need to set up the firewall to allow the Mobile IP traffic to pass.

In addition, mobile nodes and foreign agents utilize the Internet Control Message Protocol (ICMP) to register care-of addresses with the home agent. Therefore, you might need to configure the firewall protecting the home network to enable ICMP datagrams to pass through to the home agent.

Connectivity Software

The radio card, access point, and communications software provide lower midlevel connections, but another higher level of functionality is necessary to map the application software, keyboard, display, and peripherals of the appliance to the application software or database residing on the network. This other system component is often referred to as *connectivity software*, which mostly deals with presentation-layer functions.

Connectivity software comes in many forms, such as terminal emulation, direct database connectivity, Web browsers, and middleware. These are very different approaches to interfacing with applications and databases, and their implementation depends on many factors (see the sidebar "Implementing Connectivity Software," at the end of this chapter).

Terminal Emulation

The idea behind terminal emulation is to make the appliance appear as a terminal to application software running on a host-based operating system, such as UNIX and AS/400. For example, you need virtual terminal (VT) emulation running on the appliance to interface with an application running on a UNIX host. Likewise, 5250 emulation software will interface with an application running on an IBM AS/400. This form of connectivity is common in the traditional terminal/host system. Figure 6.16 illustrates the concept of terminal emulation.

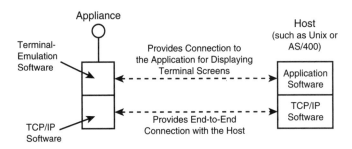

FIGURE 6.16

Terminal-emulation software on the appliance interfaces the keyboard and display of the appliance to the application software on the host via a terminal session.

Terminal-emulation software on wireless appliances generally communicates with the host using Telnet over TCP/IP protocols. The appliance appears to the host as a terminal session. After a connection is made with the host, the application software residing on the host can send display information (such as logon prompts, menus, and data) to the appliance, and keyboard strokes will be sent to the application. Thus, the software on the host provides all application functionality.

TIP

If a wireless appliance running terminal-emulation software does not connect to the host, be sure that the host is running TCP/IP protocols. It's common to not implement TCP/IP software for host computers (especially mainframes) if the original implementation did not interface with a network. In these cases, you'll have to install the TCP/IP software to establish communications between the appliance and the host.

The following are attributes of terminal emulation:

- **Very little, if any, programming needed to interface with existing host-based applications**—The implementation of appliances that utilize terminal emulation to interface with the host does not require any software programming on the appliance. You can often purchase appliances with terminal emulation factory-loaded, and the only setup needed on the appliance is to load the IP address and some configuration parameters.

  In most cases, you can establish a terminal session with existing host-based application without even making any changes to the application software. Many smaller appliances, though, have small displays, requiring users to scroll around the larger displays that programmers might have developed for desktop-based computer monitors. In this case, many companies rewrite their applications to fit the smaller displays of portable appliances.

  If printing is necessary from the appliance, you will probably need to embed the print streams of the particular appliance in the application on the host. If programming is needed on the host, you can leverage existing knowledge in the host application-development environment.

- **Central application software control**—With terminal emulation, all application software is updated only at the host, not at the individual appliances. All users automatically can take advantage of changes to the application without needing updates to the software on the appliance. This makes configuration management much easier, especially when there are hundreds of appliances.

- **Low cost**—Terminal emulation is generally less expensive than implementing a middleware approach. Most companies charge a couple hundred dollars per appliance for terminal emulation.

- **Limited availability of terminal-emulation software for DOS-based appliances**—Terminal-emulation software is widely available for Microsoft Windows operating systems; however, it is very difficult to find DOS-based appliance operating systems. This is because the DOS-based versions of TCP/IP software do not have a standard interface to appliance software. Many companies have ported their specific appliances to DOS-based terminal-emulation software, though.

- **Inflexible programming environment**—When developing or modifying the application on the host, the terminal-emulation specification limits the control of the appliance from the host-based application.

- **Limited support for migration to client/server systems**—Terminal-emulation software does not interface directly to databases, which makes it unsuitable for client/server implementations. Thus, terminal emulation enables users to access only the screens that the application provides.

- **Difficulty in supporting the appliances**—With standard terminal emulation, there is no effective way to monitor the performance of the wireless appliances. This makes it difficult to troubleshoot network problems.

- **Significant effect on wireless networks**—With terminal emulation, all screens and print streams must traverse the wireless network, affecting the performance of the overall system. In addition, terminal emulation utilizes TCP to maintain a connection with the host. TCP does not operate efficiently over wireless networks (see the section "Issues with TCP/IP over Wireless LANs," earlier in this chapter).

A police station in Florida was losing track of evidence that it acquired through the investigation of crimes. This had become a big problem because when the court needed the evidence, police officials couldn't find the evidence in a timely manner. This often delayed trial proceedings. As a result, the police chief decided to implement an asset-tracking system to manage the items and their specific locations. This system, based on the use of bar codes and handheld scanning equipment, needed a wireless network to support mobility when performing asset-management functions (such as picking and inventory) in the relatively large room that contained the evidence.

Because no IS staff members were available to do the project, the police chief outsourced the complete system implementation to a reliable system integrator. After careful analysis of functionality requirements and the existing system, the integrator developed a design that specified the use of off-the-shelf asset-management software, two 802.11-compliant handheld scanners, an 802.11 access point, and connectivity software. The asset-management software was hosted on the existing UNIX server that supported the police station's jail management software. The access point interfaced the wireless handheld scanners to an existing ethernet network, providing a network connection to the UNIX server.

When dealing with the connectivity software, the integrator narrowed the choices to either terminal emulation or middleware. Direct database connectivity was not an option because there was no way to interface directly with the database. All interaction with the database was done through the application software only.

The integrator decided to utilize terminal emulation (VT220) for several reasons. First, there would have been no significant gain in performance by using middleware with only two wireless appliances sending data over the wireless network. The relatively small amount of data sent between appliances and the UNIX application offered very little impact to the 2Mbps wireless network. In addition, the price for two terminal-emulation licenses for the appliances was much less expensive than the cost of purchasing middleware software. Also, the police station had no plans to move to a client/server system. Overall, terminal emulation was the least-cost form of connectivity software based on the police station's requirements.

Direct Database Connectivity

Direct database connectivity encompasses application software on the appliance (the client) that interfaces directly with a database located on a server. With this configuration, the software on the appliance provides all application functionality. Figure 6.17 illustrates the concept of direct database connectivity.

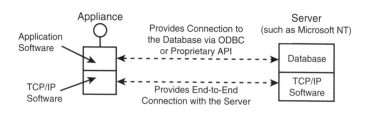

FIGURE 6.17

Direct database connectivity fits the very popular client/server system model.

The appliance generally uses TCP/IP software as a basis for communicating with the server for direct database connectivity. After a connection is made with the server, the application software residing on the appliance communicates with the database using vendor-specific database protocols (that is, the application program interface) or a common protocol such as Open Database Connectivity (ODBC).

The following are attributes of direct database connectivity:

- **Flexible programming environment**—Direct database connectivity enables the programmer to interact directly with database records rather than be limited to what the application software on the host provides (as is the case with terminal emulation). Direct database connectivity provides the most flexible programming environment as compared to other connectivity approaches.

- **A moderate amount of programming needed to interface new appliances with existing applications**—With direct database connectivity, you must often develop a program that runs on the appliance to interface with the existing database, especially if you're incorporating new appliances into an existing database. This requires the developer to understand how to write software that interfaces with the appliance's specific display, keyboard, scanner, and peripherals.

- **Distributed application software control**—New releases of application software must be installed on each of the appliances when using the direct database connectivity approach. This offers challenges with distributing new application software releases. One method that helps overcome this problem is to store the current version of the appliance application software on a server and have the application software running on the appliance compare its current version with the one located on the server. If the one on the server is a newer release, the application software on the appliance can automatically download and install the newer version of software.

In addition, modifications to the central database structure might require changes to the application software on the appliance. Care must be taken to ensure that these application changes are made so that the application works properly.

- **Low cost**—Direct database connectivity is generally less expensive than implementing a middleware approach.

- **Good support for client/server systems**—Direct database connectivity fits well into the client/server system model, enabling programmers to develop front-end applications that run on the appliance.

- **Application size limited to the amount of appliance memory**—With direct database connectivity, the appliance must have sufficient storage for the application software.

- **Wireless network impacts**—With direct database connectivity, only the database inquiries and data records must traverse the wireless network, making efficient use of the wireless network performance in terms of data transfers. All print streams and screen interfaces are handled within the appliance. However, most direct database implementations utilize TCP to maintain a connection with the host. As mentioned before, TCP does not operate efficiently over wireless networks (see the section "Issues with TCP/IP over Wireless LANs," earlier in this chapter).

Implementing Client/Server Systems with ODBC

The advantage of writing the appliance software to interface with ODBC is that it provides an open interface to the many databases that are ODBC-compliant. This enables you to write one application that can interface with databases from different vendors. With direct database connectivity, a programmer can interface directly with the database using the database's proprietary language or can utilize the common industry standard Open Database Connectivity (ODBC) interface. If you plan to interface with multiple database types, certainly consider using an ODBC interface.

ODBC Microsoft's implementation of the X/Open and SQL Access Group (SAG) Call Level Interface (CLI) specification provides interactive database functions such as adding, modifying, and deleting data. ODBC provides a generic, vendor-neutral interface to relational and nonrelational databases, alleviating the need for developers to learn multiple application programming interfaces (APIs).

The architecture of ODBC encompasses the following components:

- **Host application**—Is the application software located on the appliance that is responsible for calling ODBC functions to execute statements, retrieve results, and gather statistics

- **Driver manager**—Loads the specific database drivers, depending on the data source in use
- **DBMS-specific drivers**—Translates the database function call, submits a request to a data source, and produces results
- **Data sources**—Is the specific database that stores data relevant to the application

Intranet-Based Connectivity Software

If your wireless system needs to interface with an application on a Web server, the connectivity software can simply consist of a Web browser that runs on the appliance (refer to Figure 6.18) and communicates with the Web server using the Hypertext Transfer Protocol (HTTP). This is very similar to the concept of using terminal emulation. This works fine for appliances that run Microsoft Windows appliances that have larger screens: A variety of browsers are available that run on Windows and most existing intranet applications are written to fill a full-size monitor.

It's more difficult to integrate a DOS-based appliance (such as a data collector) with a smaller display with an existing intranet application. Browsers are difficult to find for specific DOS-based appliances. In addition, the intranet application must be written to fill a much smaller area of the screen to work effectively with the smaller screens of some appliances.

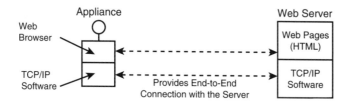

FIGURE 6.18

With intranet-based connectivity, a Web browser runs on the appliance and interfaces with an application on the Web server, fitting in well with existing Web applications.

The following are attributes of intranet-based connectivity. (Many of these are similar to the use of terminal emulation.)

- **Very little, if any, programming needed to interface with existing host-based applications**—A wireless system implementation using intranet-based connectivity with a Web server does not require any software programming on the appliance. This enables companies to leverage their knowledge of Web-based programming for the development of the application.

- **Central application software control**—With intranet-based connectivity, all application software is updated only on the Web server, not on the individual appliances. All users automatically can take advantage of changes to the application without needing updates to the software on the appliance. This makes configuration management much easier, especially when there are hundreds of appliances.

- **Low cost**—Intranet-based connectivity is generally less expensive than implementing a middleware approach. You can purchase Web browsers for the appliances for a relatively small fee.

- **Strong support for client/server systems**—Intranet-based connectivity software (that is, a Web browser) offers a thin-client front end to an application residing on the server.

- **Potential effect on wireless network performance**—Intranet-based connectivity can consume large amounts of the limited wireless bandwidth, depending on the type of application. For example, the browser on the appliance might point to a Web page containing large graphic files that must be sent from the server to the appliance. Most intranet-based implementations may also utilize TCP to maintain a connection with the host. As mentioned before, TCP does not operate efficiently over wireless networks (see the section "Issues with TCP/IP over Wireless LANs," earlier in this chapter).

Middleware

Wireless network middleware is an intermediate software component generally located on the wired network between the wireless appliance and the application or data residing on the wired network (refer to Figure 6.19). The overall goal of middleware is to increase performance of applications running across a wireless network. To accomplish this, middleware attempts to counter wireless network impairments, such as limited bandwidth and disruptions in network connections.

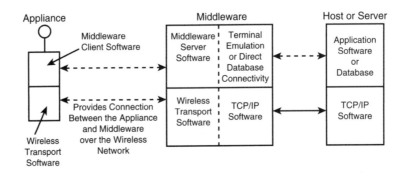

FIGURE 6.19

With middleware, the appliance communicates with middleware software using a protocol optimized for wireless networks. The middleware then communicates with the actual application or database using applicable connectivity software.

The following are common features found in middleware products that go beyond the basic functionality of connecting appliances to applications and databases located on the wired network:

- **Optimization techniques**—Many middleware products include data compression at the transport layer to help minimize the number of bits sent over the wireless link. Vendors use a variety of compression algorithms to perform the compression, including V.42bis, Hoffman encoding, run-length encoding, and proprietary compression techniques. Some implementations of middleware use header compression, in which mechanisms replace traditional packet headers with a much shorter bit sequence before transmission.

- **Intelligent restarts**—With wireless networks, a transmission may be cut at midstream due to interference or operation in fringe areas. An intelligent restart is a recovery mechanism that detects when a transmission has been cut. When the connection is re-established, the middleware resumes transmission from the break point instead of at the beginning of the transmission.

- **Data bundling**—Some middleware is capable of combining (bundling) smaller data packets into a single large packet for transmission over the wireless network. This is especially beneficial in helping lower transmission service costs of wireless WANs. Because most wireless data services charge users by the packet, data bundling results in a lower aggregate cost.

- **Embedded acknowledgements**—Rather than send acknowledgements as separate small packets, middleware products tend to embed acknowledgements in the header of larger information-carrying packets, to reduce the number of packets traversing wireless network. Many network protocols (including Novell's IPX) require stations to send acknowledgements to each other to continue data flows.

- **Store-and-forward messaging**—Middleware performs message queuing to ensure message delivery to users who might become disconnected from the network for a period of time. When the station comes back online, the middleware sends the stored messages to the station.

- **Screen scraping and reshaping**—The development environment of some middleware products enables the developer to use visual tools to "scrape" and "reshape" portions of existing application screens to more effectively fit within the smaller display of data collectors.

- **Support for Mobile IP**—Some middleware products offer home-agent and foreign-agent functions to support the use of Mobile IP protocols.

- **Operational support mechanisms**—Some middleware products offer utilities and tools to monitor the performance of wireless appliances, enabling MIS personnel to better troubleshoot problems.

> **NOTE**
>
> A wireless *gateway* consists of the wireless middleware, operating system, and hardware platform.

The following are attributes of middleware connectivity:

- **Highly efficient operation over wireless networks**—Middleware reduces the load on the wireless network through the use of optimization techniques such as data compression and screen scraping.

- **No programming required on the appliance or host/server**—Most middleware products offer a development environment that shields the developer from understanding appliance and host-based development environments.

- **Support for migration from terminal/host to client/server systems**—Many companies are migrating from terminal/host (that is, mainframes) to client/server systems. Middleware is a cost-effective solution for supporting these migrations, enabling connections to both terminal-based systems and client/server databases simultaneously.

- **Support of multiple-vendor appliances**—Middleware products interface with a wide variety of appliances.

- **Long-term cost savings**—Because of easier support of operational wireless applications, middleware provides considerable long-term cost savings.

- **Higher initial costs for implementations with smaller numbers of appliances**—The cost for middleware is $5,000 to $10,000 per site, making it relatively expensive for implementing wireless systems that have fewer than 10 appliances. Be sure, though, to consider all the advantages of middleware before finalizing a business case.

A boat-building company in Maine decided to implement a quality-assurance system to improve the efficiency of performing periodic inspections. Several times throughout the manufacturing process of each boat, inspectors need to walk throughout the plant and record flaws as the boats are being assembled. The new system includes a handheld PC with an 802.11-compliant radio card that communicates back to the corporate information system. For each boat, the inspector enters the boat's serial number, and then the system prompts the inspector through a series of questions that pertain to the quality of specific items of that particular boat. As the inspector answers the questions, the wireless network transports the data back to the corporate information system for viewing by construction managers.

The company's corporate information system consists of an IBM mainframe that supports most of the company's application software, servers that host databases, 3270 terminals that interface with the mainframe applications, PCs that run client application software that interface with the databases, and an ethernet network that ties everything together. The information that the new quality-assurance system uses is located on both the mainframe and the database servers. As a result, the corporate IS group had to pay close attention to the type of connectivity software to use to satisfy the requirements of both operating environments.

As alternatives for connectivity software, the IS group evaluated the use of terminal emulation, direct database connectivity, and middleware. 3270 terminal emulation for the handheld PCs would interface easily with the mainframe system, but it would not provide an interface to the database servers. Likewise, direct database connectivity would interface with the database servers but not the mainframes. For this project, middleware was clearly the best alternative. The need to seamlessly interface with both the mainframe and the database server systems was imperative.

Implementing Connectivity Software

Choosing a form of connectivity software depends on several factors, including the following:

- The existing system (application software, database, and operating system)
- Future system migration plans
- The number of appliances
- The presence of multiple-vendor appliances

If there are very few appliances (fewer than five) associated with a particular terminal/host system, terminal emulation is the most economical solution for connectivity software. For client/server systems that have very few appliances, a direct database solution is probably most effective. If larger numbers of appliances are present, especially if there's a mix of vendor types, investigate the use of middleware.

TIP

Maximize caching of data on the appliance to minimize transmissions across the wireless network.

Planning a Wireless LAN

IN THIS CHAPTER

Managing a Wireless LAN Implementation

In most cases, organizations accomplish work in functional groups, which perform parts of an operation that are continuous and repetitive. As the system administrator for a client/server system, for example, you might perform daily backups of databases. This task, as well as others, is part of the operation of a system-management function. Projects are similar to functional operations: They are performed by people, are constrained by limited resources, and should be planned, executed and controlled. Projects, however, are temporary endeavors that people undertake to develop a new service or product. Thus, you should classify network implementations as projects because they have a definite beginning and end.

> **NOTE**
>
> A common case study surfaces periodically throughout this chapter to provide real examples of key planning steps of wireless LAN projects. This case study continues in Chapter 8, "Implementing a Wireless LAN."

> **NOTE**
>
> Because of the complexities of wireless networks, most end-user companies outsource the implementation of the wireless LAN to a system integrator.

Establishing Project-Management Principles

The Project Management Institute (PMI) defines project management as "the art of directing and coordinating human and material resources throughout the life of a project." Project management primarily consists of planning, monitoring, and controlling the execution of the project. Planning involves identifying project goals and objectives, developing work plans, budgeting, and allocating resources. Project monitoring and control ensure that the execution of the project conforms to the plan by periodically measuring progress and making corrections to the project plan, if necessary.

> **NOTE**
>
> PMI offers a certification titled Project Management Professional (PMP) that you can earn through work experience, education, and successful completion of the PMP examination. The PMP certification ensures that you've mastered the skills necessary to manage a project of any type. Many corporations are beginning to recognize the

importance of PMP-certified professionals. You should consider completing the PMP certification process as part of your continuing professional education. Learn more about PMI from its Web site, www.pmi.org.

The use of sound project-management principles results in many benefits, such as the following:

- Clarification of project goals and activities
- Better communication among project team members, executives, and the customer
- Accurate projections of resource requirements
- Identification and reduction of risks
- More effective resolution of contingencies

Such benefits help an organization complete a quality wireless system implementation on time and within budget.

Planning a System Project

Planning is an important part of any activity. It provides a time at the beginning of a project to think about what could go wrong and to visualize solutions that will keep the project on the right track. Specifically, project planning is a process consisting of analysis and decisions for the following purposes:

- Directing the intent of the project
- Identifying actions, risks, and responsibilities within the project
- Guiding the ongoing activities of the project
- Preparing for potential changes

In the planning stage of a wireless system project, visualize the goals you have for implementing the network and the actions necessary to maximize a successful outcome. In some cases, you will need to determine the requirements and any necessary products before you can complete the project plan.

You should produce a project plan by performing the following steps:

1. Define the project scope.
2. Develop a work plan.
3. Create a schedule.
4. Identify resources.

7

**PLANNING A
WIRELESS LAN**

5. Develop a budget.

6. Define project operations.

7. Evaluate risks.

After evaluating risks, you might need to refine some of the other elements of the plan. For example, the project might require the team to interface a handheld wireless data terminal to an existing IBM mainframe computer containing a centralized application or database. If the team's design engineer has no experience working with mainframe databases, you should consider the project at risk and should attempt to mitigate the problem. Most likely, you would modify the resource plan by either assigning another employee to the project or utilizing a consultant to assist when necessary.

In fact, you should treat the project plan as a *living document*—one that you should update as more information, such as detailed requirements and design, becomes available.

Identifying Project Scope

Before determining project tasks, staffing, and creating the schedule and budget, you must first define the project's scope, which provides a basis for future project decisions. The project scope gives a project team high-level direction, allowing an accurate development of remaining planning elements and execution of the project. For each project, you should prepare a project scope that has at least the following items:

- **Project charter**—The project charter formally recognizes the existence of the project, identifies the business need that the project is addressing, and gives a general description of the resulting solution. This description should show the relationship between the solution and the business needs of the organization.

    The requirements phase of the project will define more details of the solution. A manager external to the project should issue the charter and name the person who will be the project manager. The project charter should provide the project manager with the authority to apply people and material resources to project activities.

- **Assumptions**—The project team should state assumptions for unknown or questionable key factors that could affect the project. For example, a product vendor might tell you that a new wireless device will be available on a specific date. If the success of the project depends on this product, then you should identify its availability as an assumption. This will assist you when evaluating project risks (see the section "Dealing with Project Risks," later in this chapter).

- **Constraints**—Constraints limit the project team's options in completing the project. Common constraints are funding limits, technical requirements, availability of resources, type and location of project staff, and schedules. Be sure to fully define constraints to keep the visualized outcome of the project within an acceptable scope.

Case Study 7.1:

Developing a Project Scope for an Enterprise-wide Wireless LAN

An auto parts manufacturing company based in Atlanta, Georgia, has nine distribution centers located throughout the United States. As the manufacturing company produces the parts, it ships them to the distribution centers for temporary storage. When resellers and retail stores order more parts, the company can react quickly by shipping them to the requester from the nearest distribution center. Profits for this $800-million-per-year company had been high the previous year; therefore, the company was looking seriously at investing some of the profits to improve its stance with customers and take on more market share.

The president of the company, Bob, had met with one of his friends who operates a manufacturing company that makes and distributes hydraulic pumps. While fishing, Bob's friend mentioned that had he just finished the implementation of a wireless system that supports automation with his distribution centers and wireless mobility in the executive office areas. His friend had found that the automated system, which included receiving and inventory functions, was saving him more than a $1 million per year in labor. The wireless system in the executive offices cost approximately the same as installing wired Ethernet, but he was seeing definite benefits for his staff to have wireless mobility with their laptops throughout the offices. After returning from the visit with his friend, Bob immediately notified his warehouse operations manager, Denise, and the head of information systems, Chris, to consider a similar system for their parts distribution centers and professional office areas.

Because they had never implemented wireless systems and had limited resources within their information systems group, Chris and Denise decided to contract a system integration company to manage the entire project—from project planning through implementation. After a couple meetings with the system integrator, Chris decided to contract Debra, an employee of the system integrator and a certified project manager, to develop a project plan and feasibility study so that Bob could decide on funding. The project plan, which consists of a work plan, resource identification, a preliminary budget, and risk identification, will provide a basis for the costs shown within the feasibility study. A business process analysis will provide information regarding the benefits of implementing the system.

As the first step for planning the project, Debra developed a project scope to ensure that everyone would be focusing on the same basic requirements throughout the project and to provide a basis for determining the following:

- Project tasks
- Staffing
- Scheduling
- Budgeting

Debra met with Bob to clearly understand his perspective of the project. She asked questions that probed the business problem and addressed the constraints that will limit the project. Debra also met with both Denise and Chris to gain a basic understanding of the issues and needs of the warehouse staff, office workers, and information systems group concerning the proposed project.

After gathering this information, Debra prepared a project scope. The following are the main points of the document:

- **Project charter**—The purpose of this project is to develop a wireless bar code system to automate functions that result in a significant return on investment within the distribution-center warehouses. In addition, the project will implement a wireless LAN in the office areas to support mobility with end users who have laptops. The warehouse staff currently utilizes paper-based methods to manage all aspects of the warehouse, resulting in inefficient use of labor and higher delays than competitors when processing orders for customers. A wireless automatic identification and data capture (AIDC) system is a solution that will decrease delays in getting parts to customers by enabling the warehouses to keep more accurate records of parts in stock, shorten order-picking time, and speed up the shipping-preparation process. The AIDC system will consist of a wireless LAN, applicable application software, and database. The AIDC will need to interface with the company's existing corporate information system to feed management and reporting systems already in place. The office system will consist of a wireless LAN and existing laptops and applications.

  This project will consist of a requirements analysis and feasibility study phase that the president (Bob) and his financial officers will use to decide whether the expense for the system is in the best interest of the company. If the feasibility of implementing the system is positive, the project will also include steps for designing, installing, and supporting the system.

- **Constraints**—The manufacturing company will fund the analysis and feasibility study and will spend up to $500,000 during the next year to implement the system. There are no restrictions on the selection of hardware and software for this project.

Developing a Work Breakdown Structure

To reach the goals of the project, plan a series of activities that produce the end product with a minimum amount of time and money. The development of a *work-breakdown structure (WBS)* is a good way of planning the tasks, as well as tracking the progress of the project. A WBS has a tree-like structure and identifies the tasks that the team members will need to perform and the products they must deliver. The first level of the WBS should indicate major phases, followed by lower layers that identify tasks and subtasks. The WBS also provides a basis for other planning elements, such as resource allocations and schedules.

A common question is, what level of detail should the WBS include? At a minimum, you should specify enough detail so that it is possible to determine the length of time to complete and estimate the cost of each phase and task. This will make it possible to more accurately plan the project.

Case Study 7.2:

Developing a Work-Breakdown Structure (WBS) for an Enterprise-wide Wireless LAN

Debra, the project manager developing the project plan and feasibility study for the wireless LAN, received acceptance of the project scope from upper management of the manufacturing company. She is now ready to develop a WBS identifying the necessary actions the project needs to accomplish.

The following list gives an overview of each phase of WarehouseTrack:

- **Requirements phase**—Defines the needs of the eventual users of the wireless LAN and existing systems (if any). This phase provides the basis for the solution.

- **Design phase**—Consists of selecting a set of technologies, standards, and products that satisfy the requirements.

- **Development phase**—Consists of developing application and connectivity software that resides on the appliances and server.

- **Operational support preparation phase**—Consists of the planning necessary to effectively support the system after it is installed. Preparations include training development and delivery, and plans for support elements, such as maintenance, system administration, and security.

- **Installation and testing phase**—Consists of physically installing the system components and running tests to verify proper operation.

The following represents a WBS for the implementation of the wireless LAN:

1. Requirements phase
    1.1 Elicit end user information
    1.2 Elicit system information
    1.3 Define the requirements
    1.4 Update the project plan
2. Design phase
    2.1 Perform a site survey
    2.2 Define system elements
    2.3 Select products

2.4 Identify the location of access points

2.5 Verify the design

2.6 Document the design

2.7 Update the project plan

2.8 Obtain approvals for the design

2.9 Procure components

3. Development phase

3.1 Develop appliance software

3.2 Develop database

3.3 Develop PC application software

3.4 Develop connectivity software

3.5 Perform system testing

3.6 Perform pilot testing

4. Operational support preparation phase

4.1 Prepare training courses

4.2 Define system administration staffing and procedures

4.3 Establish help desk support

4.4 Define network-management methods and procedures

4.5 Establish a maintenance process

4.6 Define configuration control procedures

5. Installation and testing phase

5.1 Plan the installation

5.2 Stage system components

5.3 Install the components

5.4 Test the installation

5.5 Perform acceptance testing

5.6 Transfer the network to operational support

Creating a Schedule

The schedule indicates the element of timing in a project, making it possible for the project manager to coordinate work activities. The schedule and WBS are the basis for selecting and coordinating resources, as well as the primary tools for tracking project performance. A schedule should contain the following information:

- Names of the phases and tasks listed on the WBS
- Starting date, duration, and due date of each task
- Relationships between phases and tasks

The project manager should create the schedule by first recording the phase names listed in the WBS and assigning someone to be responsible for each. The next step, working with the responsible team members, is to determine the starting date, duration, and due date for each task. If you cannot determine these characteristics for each task, consider further division of the task into subtasks to accommodate a more accurate assessment. You should also indicate the relationships between tasks using precedence relationships. In other words, show conditions that must be met (such as the completion of a particular task) before starting each task.

A project team must often deal with unrealistic schedules; therefore, there might not be enough time to complete a quality implementation. In this case, you might want to consider decreasing the scope of the project.

7

Case Study 7.3:

Developing a Schedule for an Enterprise-wide Wireless LAN

The next step for Debra, the project manager developing the project plan and feasibility study for the wireless LAN, is to create a schedule. After reviewing the project scope and WBS, Debra created the schedule in Figure 7.1.

Identifying Resources

Resources are the people and materials you need to perform the activities identified in the work plan. The goal of resource allocation, like most other planning activities, is to assign people and materials that maximize the success of the project, while minimizing the cost and time to complete the project. As you identify the resources, confirm their availability and schedule them to ensure that they are ready when needed.

To properly plan resources, you need to do two things:

1. Establish a project team
2. Identify necessary materials

Figure 7.2 illustrates recommended members of a wireless system-implementation project team.

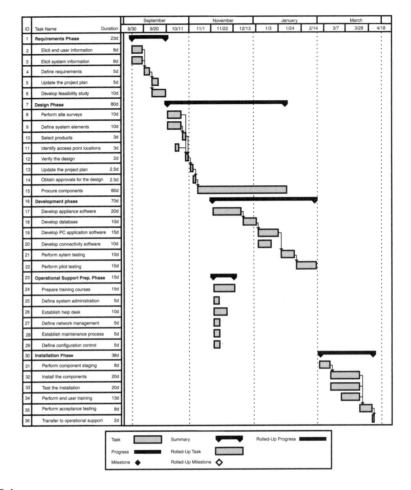

FIGURE 7.1

A schedule in the form of a Gantt chart is an invaluable tool for managing the project.

The following list describes the team members of a wireless system-implementation project:

- **Project manager**—The team should have one project manager who manages, directs, and is ultimately responsible for the entire project. This person coordinates the people and resources, ensuring that all objectives of the project are met on time and within budget. The project manager should have experience and education in managing projects, have excellent communication skills, be familiar with wireless networking concepts, and be familiar with the customer's environment.

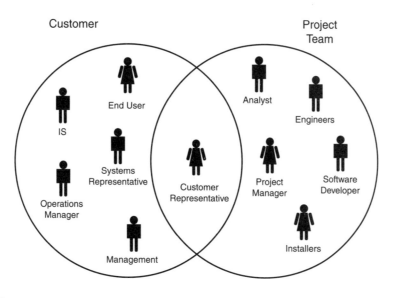

FIGURE 7.2

A project team should include members capable of completing the project tasks.

- **Customer representative**—The team should have a customer representative who portrays the interests of the users of the network and aims the project team in the right direction when determining requirements. The customer focal point should be very familiar with the user population and be able to honestly speak for the users.

- **Analysts**—Analysts gather information and define the needs of the users and the organization. The analyst should have good interviewing skills and be able to translate user and organizational needs into system requirements. It is also beneficial to have at least one analyst on the team fully understand the customer's business area.

- **Engineers**—Engineers provide the technical expertise necessary to fulfill the objectives of the project. Engineers should be part of analyzing needs, but primarily they should work on designing solutions that satisfy requirements. Thus, engineers should be very familiar with wireless technologies and should understand how to interface wireless products to existing networks and systems. In addition, engineers can assist with installing the network components.

- **Implementors**—The implementors are the software engineers and technicians who develop application software and install and test the network. Installers set up and interface network hardware, software, and wiring; therefore, they should be familiar with reliable installation practices. Testers should be independent from the design and development of the system, and they ensure that the installation meets user expectations, system requirements, and quality standards.

- **Operations representative**—The project team should have one operations representative to coordinate the project with existing network support organizations, ensuring that the implementation integrates well into the existing network infrastructure and support mechanisms. Thus, the operations representative should have a good knowledge of the existing network and should understand current network support mechanisms.

How many analysts, engineers, and implementors should you have on the team? There are no accurate rules because the level of staffing depends on the complexity of the customer organization, the scope of the project, schedule constraints, and the experience of the people you have available to perform the work. For smaller projects, very few people might fill the role of all project team members. In other cases, several team members might be needed to complete the project activities. For example, if you are planning to deploy a wireless data entry system for a business with 50 employees, you can probably get by with one or two team members. A deployment of this system to a company with 5,000 users, however, will require several analysts and engineers to define requirements and design the system, as well as a cadre of installers. The most important thing, though, is to make certain that the team is composed of people who can complete the project on time.

Case Study 7.4:

Developing a Resource Plan for an Enterprise-wide Wireless LAN

The next step for Debra, the project manager developing the project plan and feasibility study for the wireless LAN, is to assign resources for the project. To accomplish this, she had to look over the project scope, WBS, and schedule to determine the type of resources necessary and when they would be needed. Chris, the head of information systems at the manufacturing company, had decided to outsource the entire project; therefore, the system integration company will plan to provide all the resources except the customer and operations representatives. Debra proceeded by coordinating the availability of resources with the manufacturing company and her functional manager. The following is a list of resources that Debra assigned to the project and their primary responsibility:

- **Project manager**—Debra, to manage the entire project
- **Customer representative**—Denise, to be the primary focal point for the manufacturing company
- **Business analyst**—Brian, to define the needs of the end users and the organization to support the development of functional requirements and benefits for the feasibility study

- **System analyst**—Evan, to define the existing system as part of the requirements analysis
- **Engineer**—Jared, to provide the technical expertise necessary to design the system
- **Software developer**—Eric, to develop the software for the system
- **Software developer**—Pete, to perform independent system testing.
- **Operations representative**—Sophie, the system operations manager at the manufacturing company, to assist with preparing for operational support of the wireless LAN.

In addition to human resources, Debra identified other resources, such as PCs and application development tools, necessary for completing the project.

Developing a Budget

As part of the decision to begin a project, managers might have performed an economic analysis and allocated a specific amount of funding for the project. Thus, the project team might need only to validate and refine the budget, given the knowledge of the work plan and staff availability. If no previous budgeting has been done, the team will need to start from scratch. For this case, estimate hardware and software costs by performing some requirement assessment and preliminary design. Most system integrator and value-added reseller (VAR) companies refer to these as *presale activities*, providing a basis for a preliminary budget.

The WBS, schedule, and resource plan provide the basis for determining the cost of a wireless project. Before estimating the cost, you will need to assign resources to each WBS task. The next step is to calculate labor, material, travel, and shipping costs for each task and phase of the entire project. Again, you might need to perform at least a preliminary requirements assessment and design before being able to determine costs associated with the hardware and software of the system being implemented. Be sure to include sufficient travel costs for site surveys, onsite installations, and periodic onsite post-installation support.

During the execution of the project, you will need to track whether the project is being completed within budget. To facilitate budget control, assign unique account codes to project phases and subcodes to each WBS task. During the planning stages of the project, the initial budget is likely to be merely an estimate. After completing the requirements and design stages, the team might need to adjust the budget to reflect more precise information. The following are the major items of a project budget:

- Labor costs
- Hardware and software costs

- Travel costs
- Meeting costs

TIP

To minimize budget overruns, ensure that the contract with the customer states a process for handling changes and enhancements that the customer voices after the project is underway. As a minimum, the process should include provisions for assessing the impacts on the project resources, schedule, and cost.

Defining Project Operations

The scope, work plan, schedule, resources, and budget of the project are its physical makeup. To ensure that a project runs smoothly, however, you should also define project operations by developing an operations plan. This plan covers the rules and practices that people should follow during the project.

What aspects of the project should the operations plan cover? Generally, you should specify procedures for project actions that need to be followed each time the action is required. For instance, you should include these items in the operations plan:

- Roles and responsibilities of team members
- Methods for coordinating with other organizations
- Staffing procedures
- Travel policies
- Engineering drawing standards
- Document sign-off procedures

To develop a project operations plan, review existing corporate and local policies and regulations, and then define procedures for items that team members must accomplish in a unique manner. Also be sure to identify any restrictions that corporate policies and other regulations place on the project.

Dealing with Project Risks

The success of a project is often jeopardized by unforeseen elements that crop up at inopportune times. The nasty truth is that many projects are not completed on time, within schedule, or as expected. As an example, a project team might successfully complete the design stage of the project and be ready to purchase the components when it discovers that the customer's upper management has lost interest in the project and has withheld further funding. Or, you might do a thorough job of defining user needs, and then the team is not successful at determining a set of technologies and products that will fulfill the requirements.

To maximize the success of a project, the project team must not only develop a WBS, project schedule, and resource plan, but also continually identify and manage risks. Risk management should begin early in the project, even during the planning stage, and then continue throughout the project. A risk factor usually has more impact if you don't attempt countermeasures until later in the project. To avoid negative consequences, the team can manage risks by identifying risk factors and determining methods to reduce them. A risk factor is anything that might have adverse effects on the outcome of the project.

You can control risks by following these steps:

1. Review the project's WBS, schedule, resource plan, and budget, and assess the status of the preceding potential risk factors.

2. Define the potential impact that each risk has on the successful completion of the project.

3. Pinpoint the causes of the risks.

4. Refine the work plans to reflect the risk-reduction strategy.

   Periodically re-evaluate the potential risk factors, especially those found earlier in the project, and take necessary counteractive measures.

Case Study 7.5:

Identifying Risks for an Enterprise-wide Wireless LAN

Before finalizing a project plan, Debra, the project manager for the wireless LAN, felt that she needed to identify and resolve any risks that could impact the project before finalizing a project plan. She decided to hold a meeting with the entire team and go through a list of potential risks.

The following is a list of risks that she the team discussed:

- Project factors
  - **Clarity of project objectives**—The objectives of the project seem clear enough, as stated in the project scope. The requirements analysis would provide much greater detail.
  - **Project team size**—The project team size, as indicated in the resource plan, seems adequate based on the size of the project.
  - **Team geographical disbursement**—The project team is located within the same city, making the project easy to manage.
  - **Project duration**—The duration of the project seems adequate to meet all requirements.

- **Project manager's previous experience**—Debra, the project manager for the wireless LAN, has experience managing similar projects of this scope. She also has a project management certification from the Project Management Institute.

- Resource factors

  - **Experience of project team members**—All project team members have adequate experience to fulfill their roles, except possibly the operations representative, Sophie. She was new to the manufacturing company and didn't have a complete understanding of the existing systems; therefore, she might not be able to fully determine the impact of the new wireless system on the existing corporate information system. As a result, Debra will need to ensure that Sophie utilizes others' knowledgeable about the systems within the manufacturing company to consider all operational elements of the new wireless LAN.

  - **Working relationships among project team members**—All the team members from the system-integration company had worked on projects together before. In fact, they've been through a series of team-building exercises in the past. The system-integration company, however, had not implemented a system for this manufacturing company. Thus, Debra decided to set up a few team-building exercises with the entire team as it began the project.

  - **Use of contractors**—This could be an issue with this project. It will take the system integration company some time to become familiar with this manufacturing company. The team-building and analysis phase of the project will provide time for ramping up the project.

  - **Potential loss of team members due to other projects**—This could be a problem with this project, especially with the resources supplied by the system-integration company. The availability of the software developer, Eric, and the system tester, Pete, is at risk because their active part of the project doesn't occur until later in the schedule, providing time for them to become unavailable due to other projects that last longer than expected. Debra will have to remind Eric's and Pete's functional manager about their future work on the wireless LAN project from time to time.

- Organizational risk factors

  - **Level of management and customer commitment**—The company president, Bob, is fully backing this project.

  - **Funding constraints**—The funding of $1.2 million will limit the amount of the system that can be deployed during the first year.

  - **Level of user involvement and support during the project**—The operations manager, Denise, will be available throughout the project, but she has stated that only one warehouse clerk per distribution center will be available to answer questions concerning the project to ensure that productivity levels remain high enough to reach operational goals. This will be acceptable, assuming that Denise chooses clerks that have a good understanding of the operations of their individual warehouses.

- **Firmness of benefits**—The benefits of implementing this wireless LAN are unclear, making this a high-risk item. The team will need to carefully consider the cost benefits of this project before requesting capital.

- **Length of time necessary to receive a return on investment for implementing the project**—The return on investment for implementing this wireless LAN is unclear, making this a high-risk item.

- Technical factors

  - **Range of technologies available to satisfy requirements**—The technologies that provide the basis for implementing a wireless LAN within a warehouse and office area are mature; however, they are rapidly changing. The project team will need to carefully consider the competition among wireless LAN standards (such as 802.11a vs. 802.11b vs. HiperLAN/2). The decision of which specific wireless LAN technology to use is risky; therefore, Debra, the project manager, will have an independent consultant assist with the technology selection and design stage of this project.

  - **Availability of crucial hardware and software**—Hardware and software are readily available.

  - **Complexity of the interfaces to existing systems**—This is unknown at this point in the project; therefore, it is a high-risk item.

Case Study 7.6:

Developing a Project Plan for an Enterprise-wide Wireless LAN

At this point in the wireless LAN project, Debra, the project manager, assembled a project plan consisting of the following elements:

- Project scope (refer to Case Study 7.1, "Developing a Project Scope for an Enterprise-wide Wireless LAN")

- Work-breakdown structure (refer to Case Study 7.2, "Developing a Work-Breakdown Structure [WBS] for an Enterprise-wide Wireless LAN")

- Schedule (refer to Case Study 7.3, "Developing a Schedule for an Enterprise-wide Wireless LAN")

- Resource plan (refer to Case Study 7.4, "Developing a Resource Plan for an Enterprise-wide Wireless LAN")

- Preliminary budget. Provides costs of all elements of the project. At this point, the budget is accurate for the requirements analysis and design phases, but not the development and installation phases. Debra feels comfortable in showing precise labor costs for Brian, the business analyst; Evan, the systems analysis; and Jared, the design engineer, because the amount of time they need to perform the analysis and design is well known based on other projects of similar size.

  The exact amount of time and associated labor costs for Eric, the software developer, will not be known until after the design phase of the project. In addition, the cost of hardware and software will be unclear. A rough order of magnitude was given for the development and installation phases so that the decision makers would have some idea of the cost for the entire system.

  The cost of the requirements analysis phase is $30,000, and the cost of the design phase is $20,000. A rough order of magnitude for the development and installation, including hardware and software, for all nine distribution centers and the main office area is $2.5 million. This amount was based on a preliminary design defining the use of handheld scanner/printers, radio cards, radio LAN access points, database, and application software. The system would also cost approximately $400,000 per year to maintain.

- Risk assessment (refer to Case Study 7.5, "Identifying Risks for an Enterprise-wide Wireless LAN")

Debra presented the project plan to Denise, the warehouse manager, and Chris, the information systems manager, to obtain their feedback before presenting the plan to Bob, the company president. Bob approved the project plan and provided enough funding to complete the analysis phase of the project. After all requirements and exact costs were known, Bob and the rest of the executive staff would consider allocating the capital to complete the project.

Executing the Project

After completing the planning stage of the project, the project manager can begin work activities with a kick-off meeting and can guide the project through the activities identified in the WBS. The project team should periodically hold status meetings to assess the progress to date and to make changes to the plan, if necessary, to keep the project on course. These project-management actions include the following:

- Kick-off meeting
- Status checks
- Technical interchange meetings
- Progress reporting

The Kick-Off Meeting

The entire project team should have a kick-off meeting to review the project plan and officially start the project. This starts the team off together and avoids having people stray away from the primary objectives. At the kick-off meeting, discuss and agree on the following items:

- Project scope
- Task descriptions
- Schedule
- Staffing
- Budget
- Policies and procedures
- Risks

The key to an effective kick-off meeting (or any meeting, for that matter) is to stay focused by keeping discussions within scope of the specific agenda items. Spend a few minutes at the beginning of the meeting to review the agenda and ensure that everyone agrees that the topics are applicable and to see if anything is missing. It's not too late at this time to make alterations to the agenda, if necessary.

Periodic Activities

Periodically, the team should check the status of the project, perform technical interchange meetings, and report progress to upper management. The following list explains each of these activities:

- **Status checks**—For most projects, a weekly or biweekly status check is often enough to review project progress. You can normally accomplish this at a project staff meeting. The project manager should at least review completed tasks and check whether the project is on time and within budget. It's also a good idea to review risk factors and take action to minimize their impact.

- **Technical interchange meetings (TIMs)**—TIMs address technical issues that need attention by project team members and customer representatives. A TIM is effective if the solution to a technical requirement or problem cannot be adequately solved by a single team member. In this case, schedule a TIM and invite the people needed to solve the problem.

- **Progress reports**—Progress reports summarize the technical, schedule, and cost status of the project. The main idea is to show a comparison between planned and actual elements. Project managers should periodically send progress reports to upper management to keep them abreast of the status of the network development.

It is normally best to alert management of conditions that might affect the project as early as possible. This allows enough time for upper management to assist in countering the problems. Also be sure to include tasks that the project team still needs to complete, especially the ones that are planned to take place up until the next progress report.

Management reports should focus on current accumulative costs and the schedule status, past and present resource utilization, negative impacts on the project schedule, and identification of successful and unsuccessful tasks, as well as major changes made to the project plan. Any major changes should also be thoroughly explained. The progress report should explain how the project team will counter all deficiencies.

Enhancing Communication

During the execution of the project, take steps to maximize the flow of information among team members when determining requirements, designing the system, and performing installations. The problem with many project organizations is that they operate in a serial communication form, as shown in Figure 7.3. As a result, they depend heavily on documentation to convey requirements, solutions, and ideas. In this case, the customer represents the needs of potential end users of the system or product under development.

In companies that develop software products, sales and marketing staff typically express customer needs in terms of requests and requirements. Otherwise, requirements generally flow directly from the customer. Project managers are often responsible for managing the overall development, installation, and support of the product or system. Typically they produce the first specification that the development group uses to design, code, and install the system.

Several problems exist with this process, which lead to systems and products that don't adequately meet the users' needs. The series of hand-offs between the different players in the process, for example, can take a long time, delaying the creation of a prototype for validation purposes. In addition, the process doesn't engage the customer continually throughout the process, forcing developers to guess at missing or incomplete requirements. The process also dilutes the clarity of requirements as they flow via documentation and the spoken word from one element to the next.

The solution to this serial communication problem is to utilize team meetings that incorporate representatives from all organizational groups, especially when defining requirements. Sometimes this is referred to as *joint application design (JAD)*. See the section "Conducting a Joint Application Design Meeting," later in this chapter, for a detailed description of this process.

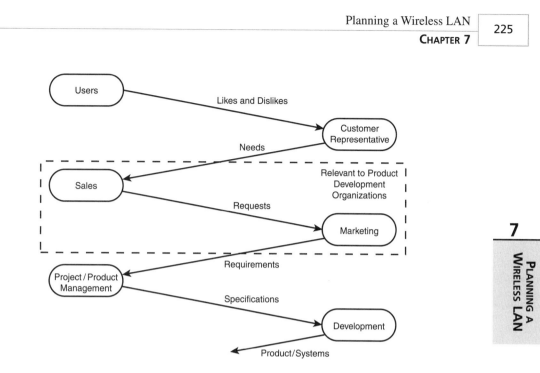

FIGURE 7.3
Serial communication significantly limits the effective flow of information.

Requirements Analysis Steps

Incomplete or missing requirements are the major reasons for unsuccessful projects, resulting in 60–80% of system defects that eventually surface late in the development phase or after delivery to the users. These system defects are very time-consuming and expensive to correct. Shabby upfront requirements also lead to the continual stream of new requirements that fill in for inadequacies throughout the project. New requirements cause a great deal of rework, extending development time and costs.

Requirements that are ambiguous, untestable, and, most of all, not capable of fully satisfying needs of potential users contribute to high development costs, lagging time to market, and unhappy users and customers. Thus, organizations must emphasize the definition of requirements to keep their heads above water. Figure 7.4 illustrates the concept of requirements for wireless system projects.

A project team should follow these steps when analyzing requirements for a wireless LAN product or integration of a wireless LAN into a corporate information system:

1. Elicit information
2. Define the requirements
3. Update the project plan

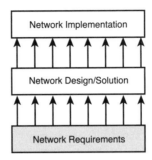

FIGURE 7.4
Requirements are the foundation of design, implementation, and support of a wireless system project.

Eliciting Information

The objective of eliciting information is to gather as many facts as you can relating to each of the requirement types. This information will enable you to define each of the requirements during a later step. The following is a checklist of items that you should consider performing when eliciting requirements:

- Review user needs
- Review existing systems
- Review the environment

The following sections explain each of these steps.

Reviewing User Needs

It's imperative that you determine the needs of potential end users before designing or deploying a wireless LAN system. The most effective method of reviewing the needs of potential users is to interview them. It's generally not practical to interview every user—just a cross-section will do. Talk with managers to obtain a high-level overview of what the people do and how they interact with other organizations. During the interview, ask questions that enable you to define specific requirements. The following sections give samples of good questions and describe the requirements that you need to define.

> **NOTE**
>
> In some cases, reviewing needs of users will identify weaknesses in the current business processes, motivating business process re-engineering, which is a realignment of the way a company operates. In fact, the introduction of wireless networking makes it possible to redesign the current paper-intensive methods to a more mobile and electronic form.

Reviewing Existing Systems

User needs are only part of the requirements; existing systems also portray important requirements. Reviewing existing systems helps you to define the system interface and operational support. If you're implementing a wireless LAN for a specific company, the project team should review current documentation that provides an accurate description of existing systems. For instance, review the concept of operations to examine system-level functionality, operational environment, and implementation priorities for an organization's information system.

Also review the strategic information system plan, which provides a long-term vision and the general procedures necessary to manage the efficient evolution of the corporate information system. This provides policies and standards that the design team might need to follow. In addition, the organization might have other plans, such as business and employee projections, that the team can consider. Business plans describe the future markets and strategies that the company wants to pursue, which is useful in determining the types of applications and services the users might require.

Reviewing the Environment

To determine environmental requirements, look at the conditions in which the network will operate. Gather information by interviewing company facility managers, and visually inspect areas where the wireless network will operate. For example, the obvious unseen hindrance to a radio-based wireless network is radio interference and multipath distortion.

Thus, in addition to talking with the facility manager or frequency manager about potential interference, consider using a radio-based site-survey tool to evaluate the radio wave activity in the part of the radio spectrum in which your components will operate. Most wireless LAN vendors include these site-survey tools with their products. You can use a spectrum analyzer to measure the amplitude of signals at various frequencies. A site survey of several different types of facilities will lend valuable information as the basis for designing a robust wireless product. If you are installing a wireless LAN, the site survey will detect potential RF interference and multipath propagation, enabling the system integrator to implement countermeasures to avoid significant operational problems.

7

PLANNING A
WIRELESS LAN

> **NOTE**
>
> Refer to the section "Questions for Defining Wireless LAN Requirements," later in this chapter, for questions you should answer before developing wireless LAN products or integrating wireless LANs into corporate information systems.

Defining Requirements

After gathering information, you're ready to define the requirements that will provide the basis for the design. To define the requirements, perform these steps:

1. Determine potential requirements
2. Validate and verify the requirements
3. Baseline the requirements

Determining Potential Requirements

The first step in defining requirements is to identify potential requirements by specifying each requirement using the information gathered during interviews, review of documents, and inspections. You can accomplish this by doing the following:

- Conducting a joint application design meeting
- Assessing constraints
- Documenting requirements

Conducting a Joint Application Design Meeting

An effective method for drafting requirements is to conduct a series of team meetings using joint application design (JAD) techniques. With JAD, all the active participants work together in the creation of requirements. Figure 7.5 illustrates the concept of JAD that uses a team approach for defining requirements.

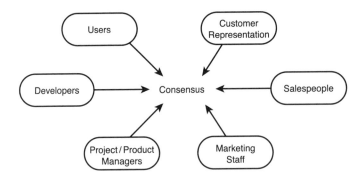

FIGURE 7.5

JAD is a parallel process, simultaneously defining requirements in the eyes of the customer, users, sales, marketing, project managers, analysts, and engineers.

The goal of JAD is to reach consensus on requirements among all team members, especially the customer and developers. JAD ensures the early definition of accurate requirements, minimizing later rework.

JAD is extremely effective for defining requirements because the customers and users become partners in the development project, producing an effective customer-developer team. This breaks down communication barriers and increases levels of trust and confidence. Because JAD helps you to determine requirements quickly, developers can start prototyping earlier. This is important because it provides a vision of the system for the users, fueling the refinement of requirements. JAD also keeps the customer accurately informed on what can and can't be done because engineers can validate the requirements as the customer states them.

In addition to the active participants, JAD consists of a facilitator, a scribe, and optional observers, as follows:

- **Facilitator**—The facilitator manages the overall meeting, acting as a mediator and guide to guarantee that the group stays focused on objectives and follows all JAD meeting rules. The facilitator should have good communication skills, be impartial to the project, have team-building experience and leadership skills, be flexible, and be an active listener.

- **Scribe**—The scribe records the proceedings of the JAD and should have good recording skills and some knowledge of the subject matter.

- **Observers**—It might be beneficial to have impartial observers monitor the JAD sessions and provide feedback to the facilitator and project manager. In addition, managers as observers can spot and take action on problems that go beyond the scope of the facilitator's and project manager's domains. However, to ensure appropriate interaction among the customer and developers, observers must not actively participate during the JAD meeting.

The following are some tips in preparing for a JAD:

- **Obtain the appropriate level of coordination and commitment to using JAD**—In many cases, participation in a JAD will stretch across organizational boundaries. Engineers are often from the information systems (IS) group, and the customer might represent users spanning several functional groups. Without concurrence of all group managers, the JAD meetings will appear to be biased to those who don't buying into the idea, causing some people to not participate or not accept the outcome. Therefore, to receive commitment to the method, the initiators of the JAD should discuss the benefits and purpose of the JAD with applicable managers of each group.

- **Ensure that there are clear objectives for the JAD meeting**—If there are not, the JAD proceedings will flounder and lead to unnecessary results.

- **Consider using an independent consultant as a facilitator**—This ensures neutrality and avoids siding with one particular group. Be certain, though, to avoid the selection of a consultant closely allied with the department responsible for development. A close alliance here could tempt the facilitator to favor the engineers, letting them dominate the meeting and inhibit ideas from the customer. It doesn't hurt to have internal people in mind to groom as facilitators; however, be sure that they have proper training and are not connected to the project they're facilitating.

- **Talk to all participants before the JAD**—Discuss the issues, such as potential conflicts, involved with the particular project. Give all new participants an orientation to JAD, if it's their first time attending one. In some cases, it might be the first time businesspeople and engineers work together. Therefore, minimize communication problems by preparing participants to speak the same language. Avoid using computer jargon. Otherwise, communication could be difficult and customer participation will decline.

- **Establish rules**—This is absolutely necessary because the different agendas of the customer, users, and developers can often derail the JAD and raise conflicts. Rules should state that all members will conform to an agenda, all participants are equal, observers will remain silent, and the bottom line is to reach consensus on requirements. Be sure to have the participants contribute to the formation of rules.

- **Don't let developers dominate the meeting**—Many JADs tend to have too many developers and not enough representation of the potential end users. This usually blocks users from expressing their ideas. In addition, there's a tendency of IS departments using JAD to "rubber-stamp" the requirements—that is, to have the customer merely review and approve them. You should limit the developers to architects and engineers because programmers might push the team toward a design too soon. The facilitator must ensure that everyone has fair time to voice their ideas.

Assessing Constraints

As part of the requirements definition, you should identify which of the requirements are constraints. Figure 7.6 illustrates the effects of constraints on solution alternatives. *Constraints* are usually requirements dealing with money, regulations, environment, existing systems, and culture. However, any requirement could be a constraint if that requirement is absolutely necessary and not subject to change.

Regulations are constraints because they often carry a mandate directing a particular form of conformance. The environment, such as building size and construction, establishes constraints because the facility might be too expensive to change to accommodate certain solutions. Existing systems are not always easy to change; therefore, solutions will have to conform to particular platform constraints, memory, and so on.

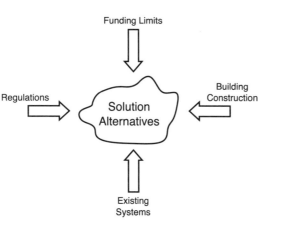

FIGURE 7.6
Constraints are firm requirements that limit the choice of solution alternatives.

Documenting Requirements

To support the remaining phases of the project adequately, be sure to document the requirements clearly. Without good documentation, requirements can become unclear as time passes and memories lapse, and the handover of project information from person to person can dilute original intentions. To make matters worse, the analysts responsible for defining the requirements could leave and not be available during the design phase. Undocumented requirements also make it too easy for changes to occur in an uncoordinated manner during later stages of the project, making it difficult to find the correct solution.

Therefore, the team should develop a requirements document containing, at a minimum, an illustration of the organization's high-level business processes (that is, how the company or applicable organization operates) and a definition of each requirement type. The following are the major elements of a requirements document:

- Requirement overview
- Specific requirements
- Constraints
- Assumptions
- Information-elicitation methods
- Issues

Validating and Verifying Wireless LAN Requirements

The importance of requirements can't be overstated: Inaccurate requirements lead to solutions that don't adequately support the needs of the users. Thus, the project team should verify and validate the requirements:

- *Validation* determines whether the requirements fully represent the needs of the users and conform to the company's business processes. It asks the question, are we building the right product?
- *Verification* checks whether the requirements are accurate based on the needs. It asks the question, are we building the product right?

Validating Requirements

The best method to validate requirements is to build a prototype as a model that represents the requirements. This approach will provide effective feedback from potential users by eliciting missed functions and features. For application development, you can build a software prototype using a fourth-generation language that contains the screens and some functionality that implements the requirements, such as Powersoft's Powerbuilder or Microsoft's Visual Basic.

For off-the-shelf applications and hardware, of course, vendors normally will allow enough evaluation time, such as one or two months, to test the application. For either case, you can have the users exercise the prototype and observe whether their needs will be met.

Verifying Requirements

The most important verification point is to be sure that the requirements are complete and unambiguous. Complete requirements describe all aspects of the needs of the users and organization. For example, incomplete requirements might state needs for users and existing systems but not identify anything about the environment, such as the presence of potential electromagnetic interference. For wireline systems, this might not be critical, but it could have serious impact on the operation of radio-based products.

Requirements should be unambiguous, to avoid needing clarification later. Ambiguous requirements force the designer to seek the finer details. To save time, most designers will guess the values of the remaining details, causing the designer to choose inappropriate characteristics.

For most projects, you can verify the requirements by referring to the requirements document and answering the following questions:

- Do the requirements address all user and organizational needs?
- Do the requirements clearly state the needs?
- Do the requirements avoid describing solutions to the requirements?

Baselining Requirements

The *baselining*, or, in other words, standardizing, of requirements involves final documenting and approval of the requirements. This process makes the requirements official, and you should change them only by following an agreed-upon process.

Who approves the requirements? Ultimately, the customer representative should give the final sign-off; however, an analyst should endorse the requirements in terms of their accuracy and efficacy. If you're deploying the system under a contract, other people might need to offer approvals, such as the project manager and contract official. Be certain to indicate that both the organization and the modification team consider the set of requirements as a firm baseline from which to design the network.

Updating the Project Plan

After defining the requirements, it's time to revisit the planning elements that you prepared earlier in the project. At first, you probably based the project work-breakdown structure (WBS), schedule, and budget on incomplete and assumed requirements. The actual requirements, though, might cast the project in a different light. For example, maybe you found during the user interviews that information security was more important than you had expected. This might create a need to modify the WBS—and possibly the schedule and budget—to research security technologies and products. Or, you might have planned to spend three weeks during installation setting up 150 computers, but, during the interviews, you found there will be only 75. This could enable you to cut back the schedule or reallocate the time to a task that might take longer than expected.

Types of Wireless LAN Requirements

When defining wireless LAN requirements, you're building a solid foundation for designing a wireless LAN product or system solution. The following are common requirement types related to wireless network development and system implementations (which are described in the succeeding sections):

- Functional
- Geographical coverage area
- Number of users
- Battery longevity
- Information flow
- Mobility
- End-user device types
- Performance
- Weight and size
- Security
- Integration

- Environmental
- Scalability
- Operational support
- Regulations
- Product availability
- Budget
- Schedule

Functional Requirements

Functional requirements describe what the wireless network is supposed to support. Therefore, functional requirements run parallel to the tasks and actions that users perform. For example, the need to provide wireless connectivity between a handheld bar code scanner and a warehouse-management system is a functional requirement. In addition, a functional requirement might specify that a wireless communications device be worn by patients within a hospital to transmit information on the patient's blood pressure, heart rate, and so on to the nurse's station.

Geographical Coverage Area

The coverage of the wireless network depicts the area where the end users will operate wireless devices, which helps the designer decide the number and location of wireless LAN access points. For example, a requirement dealing with geographical coverage might state that the wireless network must provide radio connectivity throughout all areas in a hospital where resident patients can roam. It's also a good idea to include requirements for the multiple locations where the wireless LAN can operate. Be certain to indicate operation in foreign countries.

Number of Users Requirement

The number of users is a physical count of the number of devices that will require access to the wireless LAN, affecting the amount of hardware that you need to purchase and the utilization of the system. These devices could include bar-code scanners, printers, PCs, and so on. Also be sure to include future expansion possibilities.

Battery Longevity Requirements

For mobile and portable applications, specify the length of time that the end-user devices need to operate from a set of batteries. A mobile patient-monitoring device, for example, might need to operate for at least 72 hours, which is the typical length of an inpatient hospital stay. For a warehouse application, the battery may only need to last for one shift, typically eight hours. This information will indicate whether the wireless LAN components will need to perform power-management functions.

Information Flow Requirements

Business processes within companies depend heavily on communication. To complete their tasks, people need to communicate with other people and systems. Because the network's primary role is to support communication, it is imperative that you fully define information flow requirements. For this requirement, specify the information path flow between people and systems, types and formats of information sent, frequency of information transmission, and maximum allowable error rates. These requirements will provide a basis for the selection of network components, such as the network interface card (NIC) and medium. The wireless network must support network utilization and message latency for the transmission of the defined types of information.

Mobility Requirements

Mobility requirements describe the movement of the users when performing their tasks, distinguishing whether the degree of movement is continuous or periodic.

When the user or network component must have the capability to utilize network resources while physically moving, it is said to be in continuous movement. Examples of users requiring access to network resources while continuously moving include emergency vehicles, military personnel on a battleground, delivery services, and health-care professionals.

Periodic mobility—often referred to as *portability*—implies the utilization of network resources from temporary locations, but not necessarily while the user is in transit between locations. Portability implies a temporary connection to the network from a stationary point, but the interface associated with a portable connection should be easy to move, set up, and dismantle. Examples of users requiring portable interfaces include cashiers, conference organizers, and employees working from a temporary office facility. When specifying mobility requirements, be sure to identify the users needing mobility and the range of movement that each user or component needs.

> **NOTE**
>
> When defining requirements for portability, be certain to indicate the maximum amount of time it will take to set up the wireless connection for operation.

End-User Device Type Requirements

Device types include laptop computers, bar-code data collectors, and mobile patient monitors. You should identify the device's available physical interfaces, such as PC card, PCI, ISA, USB, and so on. Designers will need this information to ensure the proper selection of wireless LAN components.

Performance Requirements

Performance indicates how well a network provides applications and services. You never hear people complain that performance is too high. Low performance, however, means that users cannot do their work as quickly as they want or are accustomed. For performance requirements, identify expected values for reliability, availability, and delay, as follows:

- **Reliability**—The length of time that a system or component will operate without disruption. Most product vendors refer to this as *mean time before failure (MTBF)*.
- **Availability**—The length of time that the system must be operational. As an example, the availability could indicate that a network should be operational 12 hours a day, from 6:00 a.m. until 6:00 p.m.
- **Delay**—The length of time that users or systems can wait for the delivery of a particular service.

Weight and Size Requirements

If the weight and size of the end-user device are a concern, be sure to define applicable requirements. For example, the weight and size of the wireless LAN transceiver would need to fit the comfort and usability needs of a person wearing a device all day when performing his functions. In most cases, smaller and lighter wireless devices are best.

Security Requirements

Security requirements identify the information and systems that require protection from particular threats. The degree of security depends on the severity of the consequences that the organization would face if the system were damaged or if data were lost. Of course, military and law-enforcement agencies require high-level security. Security requirements should address the sensitivity of information processed on the network, the organization's security regulations, and probability of disasters, such as equipment failure, power failure, viruses, and fire.

Integration Requirements

Most likely, the system being developed will have to interface and interoperate with existing systems, such as ethernet networks, client/server systems, and legacy systems. The system interface requirements describe the architectures of these systems and the hardware, software, and protocols necessary for proper interfacing. If the interfacing method is not known, you will need to determine a solution during the design phase.

NOTE

Some systems require nearly continuous connectivity to avoid logouts and errors. Be certain to describe conditions in which end systems require such connectivity so that designers can ensure the that wireless network provides applicable support.

Environmental Requirements

Environmental requirements state conditions such as room temperature/humidity, presence and intensity of electromagnetic waves, building construction, and floor space, all of which could affect the operation of the system. In most cases, you should perform a site survey to inspect the facility and evaluate the presence of potential RF interference. Also consider the degree of durability that the wireless devices must possess. For example, be sure to specify a drop test requirement for radio-based end-user devices. It's best to know these environmental conditions to deploy proper countermeasures.

Scalability Requirements

Scalability requirements indicate the capability to include additional applications and users on the wireless network beyond the initial requirements through the addition of applicable hardware and software. A wireless LAN generally must provide scalability to support the growing number of wireless applications being implemented in companies. For example, the initial intent of the wireless LAN could be only to support relatively light throughput requirements of an inventory application, but future requirements might need higher bandwidth to support voice or video information transmission.

Operational Support Requirements

Operational support requirements define the elements needed to integrate the system into the existing operational support infrastructure. For example, you should require the inclusion of the Simple Network Management Protocol (SNMP) if current network-monitoring stations require SNMP. In addition, you should specify any needs for remote monitoring and configuration of wireless LAN components to centralize operational support.

Regulation Requirements

Some organizations might have to conform to certain local, state, or federal regulations; therefore, be certain to specify these conditions as requirements. Regulations imposing safety and environmental procedures place definite requirements on network implementations. The operation of a wireless radio wave adapter, for example, must conform to Federal Communications Commission regulations.

Another example is the use of radio-based wireless products on military installations within the United States. The military's use of these devices is regulated by a special frequency-management organization, not the FCC. Therefore, radio-based implementations on military bases must conform to the military's frequency-management policies. In addition, the company itself might have policies and procedures, such as strategic plans and cabling standards, that the implementation should follow.

7

PLANNING A WIRELESS LAN

Product Availability Requirements

Sometimes wireless network development and implementation projects require components and products to be available at certain times for prototyping and pilot testing. With the rapid evolution of wireless network technologies, some components and products will most likely lag behind the finalization of standards. In addition, you need to avoid purchasing components that are likely to become obsolete before the end of the expected life of the system. As a result, be sure to define applicable availability dates.

Budget Requirements

An organization might have a certain amount of money to spend on the system implementation. Budget constraints can affect the choice of solution because some technologies cost more than others to implement. The budget requirements should consider the funding plan for the installation project—that is, the availability of funds at specific times. The reason for this is for planning the procurement of components and scheduling of resources.

Schedule Requirements

Schedule requirements should include any definite schedule demands that will affect the project. By their nature, organizations impose scheduling conditions on projects, such as availability of project funds, urgency to begin a return on investment, availability of project team members, and interdependency between this project and other projects. Define schedule requirements so that the team members know the time frames they can work within. For instance, the design team might have a choice of using a current wireless adapter or waiting eight months for the next, faster release. If the organization must have the system operational within three months, then the team would have to choose the existing product.

Questions for Defining Wireless LAN Requirements

To define wireless LAN requirements, you need to determine answers to questions dealing with each requirement type. Consider asking the following questions when developing wireless LAN products and integrating wireless LANs into corporate information systems:

- What functions will the wireless LAN product or system support?
- What geographical area will the wireless LAN need to support?
- What is the maximum number of wireless LAN devices that could be operational within a typical day and at a particular time?
- How long will end users expect to use a wireless device before recharging or changing batteries?
- What battery technologies will provide power for the wireless LAN transceivers?

- What types of information (text, images, voice, video, and so on) will the wireless LAN transmit and receive?

- How often will each information type be sent over the wireless LAN?

- How large are typical information packet/file transmissions?

- How will information flow throughout the wireless LAN (peer-to-peer, point-to-multi-point, bidirectional, and so on)?

- Will the wireless LAN support mobile (continuous movement), portable (temporary location), or stationary (permanent location) operation?

- What form factors will wireless LAN radio cards need to support?

- What types of wireless end-user devices will the wireless LAN need to support?

- What is the expected reliability and availability of the wireless LAN?

- What are the expected information transfer delays?

- What is the maximum weight and size of the wireless LAN interface cards or modules?

- What level of security is needed to protect from potential disclosure of information being transmitted over the wireless LAN?

- What type of encryption (if necessary) is required?

- What back-end information systems (servers, applications, and databases) will the end-user devices need to communicate with over the wireless LAN?

- What communication protocols are necessary to support the interface between the wireless end-user devices and the corporate information system?

- What is the physical location of the back-end information systems?

- What other radio frequency devices and radio/TV stations (specify frequencies) operate close to the intended wireless LAN site?

- What temperature and humidity ranges will the wireless LAN need to operate within?

- What is the physical construction of the facility that will house the wireless LAN?

- What degree of hardening do the wireless LAN components need to support (drop tests, resistance to moisture, and so on)?

- What degree of scalability does the wireless LAN need to support?

- In what country are you going to install the wireless LAN?

- When are wireless LAN components and products needed for prototyping, pilot testing, or system installation?

- What are the budget constraints for the wireless LAN?

- What future requirements is the wireless LAN product or system expected to support?

Case Study 7.7:

Performing a Requirements Analysis for an Enterprise-wide Wireless LAN

At this point in the wireless LAN project, Debra, the project manager, held a kick-off meeting for the project and directed Brian, the business analyst, and Evan, the system analysis, to begin the requirements phase of the project.

Brian scheduled interviews with Denise, the warehouse manager, and a clerk within each of the nine warehouses. Brian also scheduled interviews with several members of the executive staff and company engineers to gain knowledge of the mobility needs in the main office building. The main idea of these interviews was to gain a good understanding of each of the functions within the warehouse and office areas.

Brian found that the operations within the warehouses were very similar. The staff within the warehouses performed receiving, put-away, picking, inventory, and shipping functions manually (using pencil and paper) and then entered the applicable data into the corporate information system via terminals located at certain points within the warehouse. For example, a clerk at the unloading dock writes down a tracking number from a box, goes over to a terminal located near the dock, types the number into the system, retrieves a printed label from a nearby printer, and then walks back over to the box and affixes the label to the box. At one of the warehouses, Brian performed time studies to determine the length of time warehouse staff took to perform various functions, such as receive items from the shipping dock and pick items from the warehouse. This will provide a basis for determining benefits when developing the feasibility study. Discussions with the executive staff and engineers indicated that having wireless laptops would enable them to participate more efficiently in meetings and collaborate with fellow workers.

Evan set up an interview with Chris, the information systems manager, to better understand the existing system. Evan found that the manufacturing company had a mainframe located at the headquarters facility in Atlanta. This mainframe hosted accounting software for managing the company. Each of the 9 warehouses had 10 desktop terminals that clerks used to enter information applicable to each warehouse function. Each of the terminals was connected to the mainframe system at headquarters by a 56Kbps telecommunications line. Evan discovered that the company was planning a migration to a client/server-based system over the next two years.

After eliciting the information, Debra, Brian, and Evan wrote a requirements document addressing the following elements:

- **User profile**—The users are warehouse staff members that have no experience using data-collection equipment, such as handheld scanners and printers. The office staff members have experience using existing laptops, PCs, and associated office applications.

- **Functional**—Warehouse clerks need automated methods for performing receiving, put-away, picking, inventory, and shipping functions within a warehouse. Office staff members need mobility with their laptops to participate more efficiently in meetings and collaborate with fellow workers.

- **Application**—For the warehouse application, the project will need to develop application software that interfaces with the existing corporate information system. The office staff will be capable of continuing to use the existing applications.

- **Information flow**—Each warehouse will have a database for handling information dealing with the AIDC system. Information flow will take place between these databases and the corporate information system at midnight each day. Information flow will also take place between the handheld appliances and databases over a radio network located in each warehouse.

- **Mobility**—The system will need to provide mobility for warehouse clerks to perform functions while carrying handheld appliances. In addition, the system will need to provide mobility for office staff using laptops.

- **Performance**—The system must be capable of providing end-user transactions in less than 3 seconds.

- **Security**—The information that flows through the system must not be available to unauthorized people. All systems and information must be accessible only by user ID and password. It must be possible to invoke encryption for sensitive information transfers.

- **System interface**—The wireless LAN must interface with the existing mainframe and client/server information systems.

- **Environmental**—All hardware must be cable of operating in temperatures between 40° and 110° Fahrenheit.

- **Budget**—A $1.2 million budget is available during the first year, pending approval of the requirements and feasibility analysis.

- **Schedule**—The system must be implemented within the next 12 months.

The completion of the requirements phase of the project didn't require any changes to the project plan.

Analyzing the Feasibility of a Wireless LAN

Implementing a wireless system is generally a costly event. You need to perform a thorough site survey, purchase and install wireless adapters and access points, and possibly procure and install other elements, such as portable computers, handheld terminals, cabling, and servers.

A feasibility study helps organizations decide whether to proceed with the project based on the costs associated with these components and the expected benefits of deploying the system. Before an organization will allocate funding for a project, the executives will want to know what return on investment (ROI) to expect within a particular amount of time. Most companies will not invest a large amount of money, such as $50,000 or more, to deploy a wireless system without the assurance that gains in productivity will pay for the system. Executives should consider the following key factors when making this decision:

- Costs
- Savings
- Impacts on users (such as training and lower initial productivity)
- Effects on existing systems

Humans are notorious for adapting to change very slowly—or not at all. For instance, there are many benefits in replacing paper-based record systems, such as those used in hospitals and warehouses, with handheld wireless devices that provide an electronic means via bar codes of storing and retrieving information from a centralized database. Most people can't make this type of change very quickly, though. Therefore, executives will need to understand how much time and training the current staff might need before realizing the benefits of the wireless system. Some people also resist change when the key concepts of the solution are not their own or if it conflicts with another solution they had in mind. If these people have an impact on the successfulness of the project, then be sure to get their buy-in as early in the project as possible.

Systems managers should be concerned with how the new system will affect the operations and cost of the existing systems. They will ask questions such as these: Will there need to be additional system administrators? Will there be any additional hardware or software maintenance costs? Will we need to interact with new vendors?

This section addresses the steps necessary to analyze the feasibility of a wireless network:

- Performing a preliminary design
- Developing a business case
- Deciding whether to implement

Performing a Preliminary Design

To figure costs for a project, you need to perform a preliminary design to identify the major system components. The preliminary design provides a high-level description of the network, with at least enough detail to approximate the cost of implementing and supporting the system.

For radio LANs, it is very important to perform a site survey to determine the effects of the facility on the propagation of radio waves. This will help you calculate the number of access points if multiple cells are necessary. The preliminary design should indicate enough of the solution as a basis for a cost estimate. Later stages of the design phase will further define the components and configurations necessary to implement the system.

In some cases, the customer might not want to pay for a site survey because he doesn't want to fund the project until he knows all project costs. As a result, it's important to clearly state the benefits of a site survey to the customer. Without the site survey, there's a risk that the number of access points quoted in the preliminary design might be inaccurate and that interference could be present at some locations that would make the wireless network inoperable. If the customer still demands a total system proposal without paying for a site survey, you can estimate the number of access points. Be certain, though, to clearly state in the contract with the customer that the costs associated with the wireless network might escalate and that unforeseen interference could cause network performance problems.

Developing a Business Case

A business case involves conducting a feasibility study to document the costs and savings of implementing a particular system and to offer a recommendation on which direction to proceed. To define costs and savings, you will have to create a boundary for the business case—that is, base it on a specific operating time period. Generally, this operating period is the life expectancy of the system. Most organizations are satisfied with a two- to three-year recovery of benefits on network purchases. Predicting costs and benefits beyond three years can lead to significant margins of error because technologies rapidly change, and most business plans are fairly unstable beyond two years.

The business case contains the following elements:

- **Executive overview**—Provides a concise overview of the business case.
- **Project scope**—Defines the resulting wireless system, assumptions, and constraints.
- **Costs**—Details all costs necessary to implement and support the new system.
- **Savings**—Identifies the savings that result from the deployment and operation of the new system.
- **Return on investment (ROI)**—Describes the difference between the costs and savings of deploying the new system. The ROI is the main factor for basing the decision to proceed with the project.
- **Risks**—Identify the issues that might cause the project to be unsuccessful.

In summary, when developing a business case, you should perform the following activities:

- Recognize applicable feasibility elements.
- Identify costs.

- Identify savings.

- Decide whether to proceed with the project.

Recognizing Applicable Feasibility Elements

The goal of developing a business case is to decide which elements apply to the implementation that you are undergoing and then to assign costs and savings for each element. Some elements are tangible, and some are not. Modification costs, such as the purchase of hardware and software, results in real dollars spent. In addition, increases in productivity result in labor savings or increases in revenue.

The computerized image that a wireless system brings to a company, however, offers intangible benefits. In the eyes of the customers, for example, a company with a state-of-the-art wireless order-entry system might appear to be superior over other companies with older systems. This does not relate to tangible savings; however, in addition to other factors, it might increase the company's level of business.

An oil exploration company operating in Columbia, South America, experienced high expenses when relocating its drilling rigs. The oil drilling setup requires two control rooms in portable sheds separated 5,000 feet from the drilling platform to provide 500Kbps computer communication between the sheds and the drilling rig. The existing communications system consisted of ethernet networks at each of the three sites. Each shed had four PCs running on the network, and the drilling site had one PC for direct drilling-control purposes.

Every time the oil company needed to move to a different drilling site, which occurred four or five times each year, it had to spend $50,000–$75,000 to reinstall optical fiber through the difficult terrain between the sheds and the drilling platform. With recabling expenses reaching as high as $375,000 per year, the onsite system engineer designed a wireless point-to-point system to accommodate the portability requirements to significantly reduce the cost of relocating the drilling operation. The solution includes a spread spectrum radio-based wireless system that uses point-to-point antennae to direct communication between the sheds and the drilling platform.

The cost of purchasing the wireless network components was approximately $10,000. Whenever the oil company now moves its operation, it save the costs of laying new cabling between the sites.

Identifying Costs

When identifying costs, be sure to include everything that the project will require for the implementation and operational support of the system. Do not forget that sustaining the system after it becomes operational will require continual funding. Organizations commonly do not include all costs for operational support, such as training and periodic maintenance.

The best format for identifying costs is to utilize a spreadsheet and layout all cost categories and the prices of each. For the cost elements that apply to your project, determine their associated costs, as shown in the following sections.

Hardware and Software Costs

The cost of hardware and software components is one of the largest expenses when implementing a system. These costs include wireless adapters, access points, ethernet boards, network operating systems, application software, cabling, and other components. Other costs associated with hardware and software costs include maintenance plans and warranties.

Project Costs

Project costs constitute another large percentage of total expenses. Project costs include the labor and materials necessary to complete each phase of the project. These expenses fall into the following categories:

- Planning: Costs for scheduling the modification, establishing an implementation team, and periodically revising plans. Requirements analysis consists of labor costs for the analysts and travel to the customer site.
- Requirements analysis: Labor costs for the analysts and travel to the customer site.
- Network design: Labor costs of the engineers and purchase of any design tools such as network simulators.
- Software development: Costs of programmers and possibly the purchase of compilers or software development kits.
- Operational support preparations: Labor costs of the engineers and operational support staff necessary to analyze support requirements and write a support plan.
- Installation and testing: Labor costs of technicians and testers, but the team also might need to purchase special tools, such as spectrum analyzers and cable testers, to accomplish their jobs.
- Documentation: Costs of creating requirements documentation, design specifications, schematics, users manuals, and so on.
- Training: Labor costs associated with developing the training materials and instructing the courses.
- User inactivity: Costs applying to the decrease in efficiency while the users learn how to use the system effectively. If users are disrupted during the installation of the system, be sure to factor in costs of their inactivity if applicable.

Operational Costs

When the system is operational, it will cost money to keep it running properly; therefore, include operational expenses over the time period you are basing the business case on. The following list describes the costs associated with operating the system:

- **Electricity costs**—The electronic devices within the system, such as computers, access points, network interface cards, servers, and specialized cooling equipment all require electricity; therefore, include a projected cost for the electricity over the applicable time period.

- **System administration costs**—The operational support of the system might require one or more system administrators. These people are needed to maintain usernames and passwords, as well as configure printers and back up the files on the server.

- **Maintenance costs**—An effective system maintenance organization consists of an adequate set of spare components, documentation, employees, and a facility for the maintenance staff.

- **Training costs**—The system might require both initial and recurring training for users and support staff. This results in tuition and possibly travel expenses.

- **Ramp-up costs**—In addition to direct training costs, include other costs associated with migrating to the new system. Initially, user productivity might be low because users normally experience a learning curve when first using the new system.

A staff of accountants, for example, might be accustomed to keeping figures on paper and in spreadsheets. A wireless system might utilize a centralized database, allowing the accountants to input and output data directly from a PC. This changes the way that they manage their information, causing a loss in productivity as they get accustomed to the new system.

Over time, employees will become more productive using the database than they were with pencil and paper, but be sure to include the time lost as a cost.

Identifying System Benefits (Savings)

The objective of identifying system benefits is to show how the new system will reduce or avoid costs and increase revenue. Base the benefits of the system on the following factors:

- Increases in productivity
- Faster service
- Better accuracy
- Lower maintenance costs
- Improved corporate image
- Employee job satisfaction

Some of these benefits result from lower costs in operating the system, an increase in productivity, faster service, lower maintenance costs, fewer changes to network cabling, improved corporate image, and employee job satisfaction. Other elements deal with the implementation itself, such as less expensive installation in difficult-to-wire areas and reduced installation time.

Chapter 1, "Introduction to Wireless Networks," describes several benefits of wireless networks, such as mobility, the capability to install in difficult-to-wire areas, reduced installation times, and fewer changes to network cabling. These benefits convert to cost savings when comparing wireless solutions with Ethernet or other wireline approaches. Review these benefits in Chapter 1, and use them as a basis for comparison.

The following list further describe general networking benefits and associated cost savings that you can also use in justifying a wireless system:

- **Increased productivity**—Applications such as file transfer, email, printer sharing, electronic calendaring, networked fax machines, and mobile access to centralized databases and network services enable users to get their tasks done faster, resulting in lower labor costs and higher profits. Increases in productivity equate to lower task-completion times, resulting in cost savings based on lower labor hours needed to complete the tasks.

  You can easily calculate the cost savings based on an increase in user productivity. Start by determining the amount of time an individual can save by using the new system, and multiply this time by the person's pay rate. This equals the cost savings for that individual. An aggregate cost savings can be calculated by adding the savings from all users.

- **Lower software-upgrade costs**—With a network, software upgrades become much faster and less expensive because of the centralized storage of applications. Imagine having 300 standalone PCs, and assume that someone decides to upgrade an application from one version to another. You could have the users install their own software, but some would not waste their time; others would perform the installation and have trouble, and a few would perform the installation flawlessly.

  Instead, the best method in this case would be for the system administrator to install the new version of software on all 300 PCs. Assuming an average time of 15 minutes to install the software on each computer, it would probably take this person a couple weeks to install the upgrade.

  Upgrading software via networked computers is less expensive and less time-consuming. In a network, the installer simply installs the new version of software on the server, allowing everyone immediate access to the new upgrade. This takes only 15 minutes, which allows the installer to spend his time working on more important items.

  To calculate this type of savings, estimate the number of software upgrades that might occur over the applicable period of time, and figure the amount of time and dollar savings based on the rate that you pay people to install software.

7

PLANNING A WIRELESS LAN

- **Qualitative benefits**—Qualitative benefits are based on elements that cannot be assigned specific dollar values. These types of benefits are very important—they often provide an extra incentive to implement a system. A company that develops software, for example, would want to maintain a good corporate image and retain employees by implementing a state-of-the-art network. Otherwise, clients might not consider the company to be a credible software developer. Also, customers of a retail store who see store staff use wireless terminals to update prices leave with a good impression of accuracy.

> **NOTE**
>
> Be sure to run a time study before finalizing the feasibility study. Time actual users performing existing manual functions that the wireless system will affect. Also time them using a prototype of the wireless system. This will indicate the savings in terms of efficiency gain that you should expect to receive. In addition, you can use the results to verify and validate the wireless system after completing the project.

Documenting the Business Case

Be sure to document all elements of the business case in a form that makes the ROI readily apparent. Before submitting the business case to the executives for review, assess it according to the following criteria:

- Describes realistic and achievable savings
- Describes complete and accurate costs
- Compares costs and savings
- Clearly explains return on investment
- Describes issues and risks associated with realizing benefits
- Is based on a plausible time frame
- Provides a recommendation on whether to implement the system

Making the Decision to Proceed

The final step is to decide whether to proceed with the implementation. Distribute the feasibility study to the appropriate managers, and schedule a meeting to discuss the project. Assuming that the study convinces management that a strong ROI exists, the decision on how to proceed will be based on the availability of money to fund the project and the presence of implementation issues. Funding constraints and implementation issues, such as weak requirements and solutions, can affect the project schedule.

In some cases, managers might want to divide the project into phases and stagger the implementation over a longer period of time to accommodate the following scenarios:

- **Limited funding and no implementation issues**—If there are no implementation issues and complete funding is not possible, the company could agree to the entire project and spread the deployment over a time period that accommodates the future availability of money.

  For example, a company might have 100 salespeople located throughout the United States who need mobile access to the company's proposal and contract databases located at the company's headquarters. The proposed wireless system might consist of 100 mobile portable computers, linked to the headquarters' building via CDPD. Managers might understand the strong benefits in providing wireless access to salespeople; however, the existing budget might be capable of funding only 50 of the connections (CDPD modems and corresponding service) during the current year. The company might decide to deploy the remaining half of the system the following year.

- **Implementation issues but no funding issues**—If plenty of money is available but there is concern about whether the requirements or design is solid, the company should consider funding only the requirements and design phases of the project to better clarify the needs and the solution. This will increase the accuracy of the cost estimate associated with hardware, software, and support. It also ensures the purchase of the right components.

  For example, the business case might do a good job of identifying the benefits and savings that a company will receive by deploying the system, but it might not have been possible to define a solution that would provide assurance of component costs or determine whether a solution even exists. In this case, the company should fund enough of the project to accurately define components necessary to satisfy the requirements. This would enable the company to make a better decision later to allocate money for component procurement and the installation phase of the project.

- **Limited funding and implementation issues**—If funding is limited and there are issues with implementing the system, the company should not continue with the project or proceed with extreme caution.

  For example, there might be fantastic benefits in deploying a wireless patient record system in a hospital, but limited funding and the presence of implementation issues, such as potential interference with medical instruments and the task of migrating existing paper-based records into a database, should cause the organization to think twice before funding the project. In this case, though, the company could fund smaller projects to resolve the issues and then reconsider the implementation of the system at a later date.

7

PLANNING A WIRELESS LAN

Case Study 7.8:

Developing a Feasibility Study for an Enterprise-wide Wireless LAN

Before continuing with the design phase of the project, Debra, the project manager for the wireless LAN project, needed to develop a feasibility study for the project for Bob, the company president. Debra and Brian, the business analyst, spent some time defining the cost-saving benefits that the manufacturing company would realize if it implemented the system.

Based on the time studies that Brian had completed during the requirements phase, they were able to estimate the amount of time that a warehouse clerk would save by using an AIDC-based solution for each warehouse function. This provides a basis for determining labor savings and efficiency gains. For example, Brian found that the time it takes a clerk to receive each item takes approximately 30 seconds. The use of an AIDC system for receiving items will take only 10 seconds. This is a time savings of 20 seconds per item. Each warehouse receives an average of 5,000 items per day, resulting in a time savings of 27.7 man-hours per day. Based on similar analysis techniques, the total time savings per day for all the functions using the AIDC system is 100 hours per day, resulting in 36,500 hours per year. Based on an average pay for warehouse staff of $10 per hour, the annual labor savings for using the AIDC system is $365,000 per warehouse per year. The total labor savings per year for all nine warehouses is then $3,285,000. Of course the company will realize this savings only if it downsizes the warehouse staff, and the savings will begin after the system becomes operational. Other benefits of the AIDC system will include faster deliver times to customers and better accuracy of inventories. The return on investment for this project is positive. The company will need to invest a sizable amount of money, but the resulting labor savings are substantial. The first year of operation of the system will recover the initial investment and still provide some additional savings.

The benefits for implementing a wireless LAN within the corporate offices were very difficult to quantify; however, Brian felt that the implementation of a wireless LAN in the office areas would help foster ideas on how to apply wireless technology in an office. Even though the company already had a wired Ethernet LAN, Brian did some research and found significant cost savings with wireless LANs associated with not needing to install cabling, and the prices for wireless LAN cards were only approximately $75 higher than Ethernet cards with equivalent performance. After doing some comparisons, Brian concluded that a company could install a wireless LAN for nearly the same cost as installing an Ethernet LAN. With similar costs, a wireless LAN seemed to be a preferred alternative, especially if the company utilized mobile end-user devices such as laptops.

Based on the feasibility study results, the executive team decided to allocate the needed capital, and Bob gave approval to Debra to go ahead with the implementation phase of the project. Bob made it clear, though, that capital was available to cover only $1.2 million for the implementation. Additional money would be allocated, though, for the yearly maintenance costs. Thus, the project team decided to focus the first phase of the project on deploying the radio LAN in three of the nine warehouses and implement only the receiving and inventory warehouse functions. In addition, the team would install the wireless LAN in the office areas. The team would propose implementing the other functions, such as picking and shipping, at the beginning of the next year.

Implementing a Wireless LAN

IN THIS CHAPTER

Designing a Wireless LAN

Chapter 7, "Planning a Wireless LAN," addressed defining the requirements and determining the feasibility for a wireless system. The next step is to perform the design. The design phase determines the technologies, products, and configurations providing a solution. As with any engineering activity, the goal of network design is to find a solution that meets requirements and provides the greatest return on investment.

> **NOTE**
>
> A common case study surfaces periodically throughout this chapter to provide real examples of key implementation steps of wireless LAN projects. This case study is a continuation of the case study in Chapter 7.

In some cases, you may have performed a preliminary design as a basis for initial cost estimating and work planning. However, the design phase of the project defines all aspects of the solution, supporting the product procurement, installation, testing, and operational support of the system.

> **NOTE**
>
> If a company or organization has a large internal information system group, it may implement the wireless network itself. Many companies and organizations, though, don't have the necessary resources to perform the implementation. As a result, many outsource the implementation to system integrators or consultants to implement the wireless network and even manage the project.

The design phase of the project produces items such as schematics, building layout drawings, bills of materials (parts list), and configuration drawings. These items are necessary to fully define the design. For most projects, you can complete the design by accomplishing the following steps:

1. Assessing technologies
2. Selecting products
3. Verifying the design
4. Documenting the design
5. Procuring components

The following sections explain how to accomplish each of these steps.

Assessing Technologies

Whether you're developing a wireless LAN product or integrating a wireless LAN into an information system, you need to assess and select the technology that best fits your specific requirements. Figure 8.1 illustrates this approach. The chosen technology will provide the basis for selecting chipsets, product suppliers, and system interfaces that are part of a wireless LAN solution.

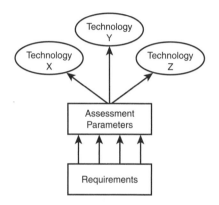

FIGURE 8.1

The technology assessment approach uses assessment parameters as the basis for evaluating the capability of technologies in satisfying requirements.

Consider implementing the following steps when assessing wireless LAN technologies:

1. **Define assessment parameters**   The assessment parameters are technical attributes of the technologies. Carefully define assessment parameters that you can use to evaluate the technologies and determine how well they satisfy your requirements. The next section, "Technology Assessment Parameters," provides examples of common assessment parameters that you can use as the basis for evaluating wireless LAN technologies.

2. **Research potential technologies**   Research potential wireless LAN technologies such as those covered in later chapters of this book. Describe each technology in terms of specific technology assessment parameters.

3. **Evaluate potential technologies**   Evaluate the capability of each technology to satisfy requirements based on the assessment parameters. The section "Technology Evaluation Methodology," later in this chapter, describes a quantitative procedure for evaluating the technologies and identifying a preferred technology.

Technology Assessment Parameters

The requirements of a product or system describe what the wireless LAN is supposed to do. The technology assessment parameters define what each technology is capable of providing. The definition of assessment parameters enables you to better understand wireless LAN technologies as a basis for evaluating their capability to satisfy requirements. The following are common technology assessment parameters for wireless LANs:

- Transmit Frequency
- Transmit Power
- Range
- Transmission Protocols
- Medium Access Protocols
- Data Rates
- Throughput
- Encryption
- Scalability
- Electrical Current
- Power Management
- Product Size
- Standards Maturity
- Product Availability
- Cost

The product or system requirements provide a basis for identifying which technology assessment parameters to use and emphasize. Review the requirements and derive a set of applicable assessment parameters.

Transmit Frequency Parameter

The transmit frequency parameter characterizes the carrier frequencies the technology uses to modulate the data. Standards-based wireless LANs operate in either the 2.4GHz or 5GHz radio frequency band. For example, IEEE 802.11 direct sequence uses 2.4GHz; IEEE 802.11a and HiperLAN/2 use the 5GHz frequency band. Others may operate at lower narrowband frequencies or higher frequencies in the infrared light spectrum. Generally, a higher transmit frequency causes a decrease in transmit range, which increases the number of access points necessary to satisfy geographical coverage area requirements. It also causes an increase in bandwidth and data rates, which increases the capability to satisfy performance requirements. Operation in the 5GHz band exhibits less potential RF interference with other systems.

Transmit Power Parameter

The transmit power parameter describes the power levels that the technology uses when transmitting data and invoking power management processes. The transmit power of wireless LANs generally falls below 1 watt. Transmit power affects requirements for geographical coverage area because higher transmit power increases range. Higher power levels, however, decrease battery longevity, which can be challenging to overcome in portable and mobile devices.

Range Parameter

The range parameter defines the distance to which typical products based on the technology can propagate data. For a wireless LAN, the range is generally the distance between an access point and a radio card installed in a client device, such as a laptop. As an example, the range of 2.4GHz wireless LANs is 150 to 900 feet, depending on the data rate, output power, and facility construction.

If all other attributes are equal, an increase in data rate decreases the effective range (and vice versa). Range affects the requirement for geographical coverage area. A longer range enables the construction of a wireless LAN having fewer access points and covering a wider area. Table 8.1 identifies the affect that specific types of material have on the transmission of RF signals.

8

IMPLEMENTING A WIRELESS LAN

TABLE 8.1   Attenuation Effects of Various Elements

RF Barrier	Relative Degree of Attenuation	Example
Air	Minimal	
Wood	Low	Office partitions
Plaster	Low	Inner walls
Synthetic material	Low	Office partitions
Asbestos	Low	Ceilings
Glass	Low	Windows
Water	Medium	Damp wood, aquariums
Brick	Medium	Inner and outer walls
Marble	Medium	Inner walls
Paper	High	Paper rolls, cardboard boxes
Concrete	High	Floors and outer walls
Bulletproof glass	High	Security booths
Metal	Very high	Desks, office partitions, reinforced concrete, elevator shafts, warehouse shelving

As an example, metal offers very high attenuation to the propagation of radio signals, which significantly limits the range of the wireless LAN. When defining this parameter or particular technologies, be sure to consider attenuation characteristics of the typical environment where the wireless LAN will operate.

Transmission Protocol Parameter

The transmission protocol parameter defines the physical layer of the technology. Wireless LANs use either radio waves or infrared light to transmit data, with varying types of modulation. For example, the 802.11b standard specifies the use of Direct Sequence Spread Spectrum, whereas 802.11a specifies Orthogonal Frequency Division Multiplexing.

This parameter affects the capability of the technology to provide scalability. For example, a wireless LAN based on direct sequence can support up to three non-overlapping radio cells within the same area, but frequency hopping can support as many as 10.

Medium Access Protocol Parameter

The medium access protocol parameter describes how the technology shares the common air medium and provides synchronization. These functions fall within the medium access control (MAC) layer. This parameter affects the capability of the technology to support different types of information flow. For example, the distributed coordination function of the 802.11 protocol provides asynchronous access to the medium, suitable for sending non–time-sensitive data. The optional point coordination of the 802.11 protocol, however, offers synchronous access for supporting time-bounded data, such as video.

Data Rate Parameter

The data rate of a signal is based on the time it takes to send information and overhead data bits when transmitting. Thus, the aggregate data rate is actually much lower because of delays between transmissions. Earlier wireless LANs transmitted data at rates up to 2Mbps, but wireless LANs now transmit at much higher rates. Data rate mostly affects the delay performance of a wireless LAN. The higher the data rate, the lower the delay. As a result, higher data rates can increase the capability to support a larger number of users. Data rate alone is not a good measure for the delay performance of the system, though. You also need to consider the effect of overhead bits, waiting times to access the medium, and the format of the data begin sent.

Throughput Parameter

The throughput parameter is a much better indicator of the delay performance of a wireless LAN than data rate because it is based on the time to send only information bits, not overhead bits. The aggregate throughput of a wireless LAN is 20% to 30% of the data rate. This accounts for the time to transmit overhead bits and the delay between frames due to protocol operation. As with data rates, throughput directly affects the delay performance of a wireless

LAN; however, throughput is a much better measure of the capability to send information through the wireless LAN. For example, an 11Mbps wireless LAN having a throughput of 2Mbps could support the transmission of a continuous video signal at 2Mbps between a pair of wireless LAN stations.

Encryption

The encryption parameter defines the form of encryption that the wireless LAN employs. This parameter directly affects the level of security that the wireless LAN can support. Of course, the use of encryption enables the transmission of information bits that eavesdroppers cannot easily decipher. Wireless LAN standards offer encryption either as a mandatory or an optional feature. For example, encryption is native to the Bluetooth and HomeRF standards, but it is optional with 802.11. The use of encryption greatly increases the security of a wireless LAN, but its use can cause significant delays, especially if it's implemented in software. Hardware-based encryption offers very little degradation in performance.

Scalability Parameter

The scalability parameter defines the extent to which bandwidth can be added to a wireless LAN. In most standards, a wireless LAN may consist of collocated access points to increase the aggregate throughput by having each access point serve a different group of users. This effectively increases the performance of the wireless LAN within a particular area. Even though additional access points increase the cost of the overall system, the capability to scale the wireless LAN makes it possible to support bandwidth-intensive solutions, such as video applications. The scalability parameter indicates the number of collocated access points that can exist in the wireless LAN.

Electrical Current Parameter

The electrical current parameter describes typical power requirements of the wireless LAN components. Wireless LAN radios typically require 250mA to receive, 350mA to transmit, and 10mA for sleep mode. The aggregate power consumption is dependent on use and parameter settings, though. For example, a wireless LAN radio that spends most of its time transmitting could require 350mA of current. One having very little activity would have few transmissions (or receptions), which would significantly decrease current requirements. The current requirements directly affect battery longevity requirements. For example, high current requirements, especially under heavy use, will significantly decrease battery charge longevity.

Power Management Parameter

The power management parameter defines the type of power management, if any, that the technology supports. The existence of effective power management protocols can significantly decrease the electrical current requirements (causing the wireless LAN to enter sleep state whenever possible), which increases battery charge longevity.

8

IMPLEMENTING A
WIRELESS LAN

NOTE

Based on a typical 20 milliamp sleep current, the radio will consume a minimum of 0.48 ampere-hours per day. At this level of power consumption and utilization, a 1.2 ampere-hour battery will last only approximately 2.5 days. The transmission and receive activity of the radio will draw much more current than sleep mode, which will drain the battery faster.

Product Size Parameter

The product size parameter defines the physical dimensions of a wireless LAN component. This parameter is especially important when integrating wireless LAN capability within a user device. For very small user device applications, the most suitable technology may depend much more on the size of the available wireless LAN components, rather than other parameters.

Standards Maturity Parameter

The standards maturity parameter mostly represents a technology's degree of standardization and directly affects schedule requirements. For instance, with a technology having a low degree of standards maturity, such as one under a standard that is not yet finalized, standardized products may not be available in time for a particular product development or system implementation effort. In addition, the use of low maturity standards offers risk because you'll be implementing products that will likely become obsolete when the standard is eventually ratified. The existence of an approved and accepted standard, however, significantly reduces this risk. As a result, technologies having a higher level of maturity lead to longer-lasting solutions that are easier to maintain because of higher compatibility between different vendors.

Product Availability Parameter

The product availability parameter simply indicates whether chipsets, OEM modules, and user devices based on the technology are available. Even with a mature wireless LAN standard, products may still not be available. An example of this is the nonavailability of products based on the IEEE 802.11a OFDM (Orthogonal Frequency Division Multiplexing) standard, which was finalized in December 1999. As of the publication date of this book, chipsets are just becoming available, and user products do not yet exist. As with standards maturity, product availability directly affects schedule requirements.

Cost Parameter

The cost parameter defines the cost of implementing wireless LANs based on a particular technology. Costs include components, development and deployment tools, installation, and support. Of course, the cost parameter directly affects budget requirements.

Technology Evaluation Methodology

The overall goal of evaluating technologies is to measure the capability of each technology to satisfy product or system requirements. The outcome of the evaluation is the selection of a preferred technology that the implementer will use as the basis for product development or system implementation. A project team should follow these steps when evaluating wireless LAN technologies:

1. Grade each technology, as discussed in the next section. The resulting grade for each technology indicates how well the technology satisfies requirements.

2. Based on the grading, select the technology that best satisfies your requirements.

3. Verify the technology chosen. The grading performed in step 1 is not perfect because of human error in estimating—in the absence of actual testing—a technology's performance. It's advisable to verify that the technology chosen satisfies your requirements through testing.

Grading and Selecting Technologies

The goal of grading and selecting technologies is to determine which one best satisfies your requirements. Construct an evaluation matrix in the form of a spreadsheet, as shown in Figure 8.2. One side of the matrix lists the product or system requirements. Each requirement has a weight indicating its relative importance to the overall solution. This ensures that the more important requirements count more in the total score. When assigning weight to each requirement, use a scale from 1 to 5, with 5 representing the highest level of importance.

Requirements	Weight	Technology X	Technology Y	Technology Z
A	5	7	4	2
B	3	9	3	6
C	4	1	5	8
D	2	6	6	9
E	4	7	2	3
F	1	5	8	5
	TOTALS:	111	77	95

FIGURE 8.2

A matrix is a useful tool for evaluating wireless LAN technologies.

The other side of the matrix identifies each of the technologies. Assign a score to each technology, indicating how well it supports each requirement. For these scores, use a scale from 1 to 10, with 10 representing the highest capability to support a particular requirement.

8

IMPLEMENTING A WIRELESS LAN

The total score for each technology is the sum of the weighted scores, as shown in Figure 8.2. When assigning scores for a particular requirement, consider the assessment parameters that affect that requirement (refer to Figure 8.1). Also, be sure to make notes justifying each score for the preferred technology. Keep in mind that in order to facilitate the scoring, you need to have a good understanding of both the requirements and wireless LAN technologies.

In general, the preferred technology for a wireless LAN product or system is the one having the highest score. Be sure to look through the grades given to the technologies, and justify the preferred one over the lower-scoring ones. Ensure that you fully understand the reasons for lower and higher scores. In some cases, there may be several top technologies having similar scores, resulting in multiple preferred technologies. This may take further verification before choosing a technology.

Selecting Products

After you've defined the technologies necessary to support network requirements, you'll need to identify appropriate products. In some cases, such as the NOS and applications, you may have already selected the product as part of the network element definition phase. Regardless, select all products and materials necessary for implementing the network, and create a bill of materials.

In general, select products based on the following criteria:

- Capability to provide necessary degree of functionality
- Product availability
- Level of vendor support after the purchase
- Price

> **NOTE**
>
> Not all 802.11-compliant products provide all 802.11 functions. For example, an 802.11-compliant access point may not include power management and the point coordination function (PCF) modes of operation. In addition, some 802.11-compliant products may have non-802.11-defined features. For example, an 802.11-compliant access point may implement higher bit rates than 11Mbps and provide load balancing.

Also, these criteria are important when selecting wireless products:

- For wireless LANs, compliance with the IEEE 802.11 standard
- Availability of tools that assist with installation (site survey tools, field strength meters, and so on)

- Availability of encryption for higher security
- Availability of power management when using battery-operated devices
- Capability to fit the form factors of your computers (such as PCI, ISA, PCMCIA, and so on)
- Capability to interoperate with the selected operating system (for example UNIX, DOS, Windows CE, Palm, etc.)

> **NOTE**
>
> Most companies implement a wireless LAN backbone using access points from the same product vendor; however, end users will very likely be operating devices using radio cards from different vendors. The 802.11 standard provides interoperability to ensure this is possible; however, there is a possibility that roaming may not work effectively because 802.11 does not specify roaming. Many of the 802.11 vendors, however, have coordinated the development of roaming protocols. In addition, the WECA ensures that roaming between access points functions correctly when testing products for Wi-Fi compliance.
>
> The more serious problem with supporting multivendor interoperability is that some vendor-enhanced performance and security features are lost when end users combine multivendor radio cards on the same network. The network is generally reduced to the lowest common denominator, which is the functions specified by the 802.11 standard. As a result, end users may need to implement wireless middleware (as described in the section "Middleware" in Chapter 6, "Wireless System Integration," in order to regain lost features.

8

IMPLEMENTING A
WIRELESS LAN

Verifying the Design

After selecting a technology and products, the next step before installing a wireless LAN system is to verify that the solution does indeed satisfy requirements. It would be ideal to verify the selected technology's capability to satisfy each requirement; however, this is not always cost effective. The main idea is to verify those elements that are not clear and create significant risk if the solution doesn't operate as expected. Most often it's necessary to verify the capability of the technology to support performance and range requirements.

When verifying the chosen technology, consider the following approaches:

- Simulation
- Physical prototyping
- Pilot testing

Simulation

Simulation uses software models that artificially represent the network's hardware, software, traffic flows, and use. You can run simulations and check results quickly; days of network activity go by in minutes of simulation runtime. There are simulation tools on the market that can assist a designer in developing a simulation model. Most simulation tools represent the network using a combination of processing elements, transfer devices, and storage devices. Simulation tools are generally costly, with prices in the tens of thousands of dollars. You might be better off hiring a company that already owns a simulation tool.

The main attributes of using simulation to verify the technologies are the following:

- Results are only as accurate as the model; in many cases you'll need to estimate traffic flows and utilization.
- After building the initial model, you can easily make changes and rerun tests.
- Simulation does not require access to network hardware and software.
- It does not require much geographical space, just the space for the hardware running the simulation software.
- Simulation software is fairly expensive, making simulation not economically feasible for most one-time designs.
- The people working with the simulation program will probably need training.

Consider using simulation for the following situations:

- When developing a type of wireless LAN product that doesn't yet exist.
- When it's not feasible or possible to obtain applicable wireless LAN hardware and associated software for testing purposes.
- When testing performance requirements based on predicted user activity (it's often not practical to do this with physical prototyping).
- When it's cost effective to maintain a baseline model of a product or system to test changes to the baseline.

Physical Prototyping

A physical prototype is a part of the product or system you want to verify through construction and testing. It consists of the actual hardware and software you may eventually deploy. Prototyping generally takes place in a laboratory or testbed.

The main attributes of physical prototyping are as follows:

- Yields accurate (real) results because you're using the actual hardware and software, assuming you can include applicable user utilization loads.

- Relatively inexpensive as part of a system installation because you can obtain components under evaluation from vendors.

- Takes time to reconfigure the prototype to reflect changes in requirements.

- Requires access to network components, which can be a problem if you don't have easy access to vendors.

- Requires space to lay out the hardware and perform the testing.

Consider using physical prototyping for the following situations:

- When initially testing the design of a new wireless LAN product before going into mass production.

- When testing the system design of a wireless LAN solution prior to vendor selection, especially when the operating environment may have a high degree of signal impairment (such as multipath distortion and RF interference).

Typically, you don't need to physically prototype the entire system, especially those parts that other companies have implemented without encountering problems. Consider prototyping any solutions that have not been tested before, especially those elements dealing with performance and range.

When performing physical prototyping, consider the following tests:

- **Performance Tests**   Performance tests determine associated throughputs of sending information across the wireless LAN. To perform these tests, configure a test network consisting of an access point and multiple radio-equipped user devices. Install application software on each user device that transmits information packets of the size and repetitiveness stated in the requirements. If possible, include the number of user devices indicated in the requirements. Use the monitoring capability that is part of the vendor-supplied management software for the access point and radio cards. This software generally provides a measure of utilization and delay on the network, which can also be used for comparing throughputs of various vendors. Most of these utilities will indicate the time (average, maximum, and minimum) it takes to receive a response from the destination. You can also connect a protocol analyzer to the access point to monitor performance if vendor-supplied monitoring software is not available.

- **Range Tests**   To test the range capability of a wireless LAN, use a laptop equipped with a radio card and vendor-supplied wireless link test software. The wireless link test function determines the quality of transmissions between the radio card in the laptop and the access point. This test sends special control packets to a particular destination, which echoes another packet to the sending station. Based on the sequence numbers of the packets being sent back and forth, the station running the link test knows whether the link corrupts packets on the forward or return leg of the link.

Link test software generally enables the tester to set test parameters such as the type of frames sent, target station address, frame size, and number of frames to send. The link test generally indicates the percentage of frames sent successfully on both forward and return paths, received signal strength at both ends of the link, the number of retries the source accomplishes before actually sending the test frame, and which access point the radio card is associated with.

To test the worst-case scenario, set up the link test software to transmit frames at the required data rate and continuously send full-size frames. The test will begin near an active access point (with other access points turned off or disabled), then the tester will walk away from the access point while monitoring the signal level and association status. Once the association with the access point is lost, the tester measures and records the distance from the access point. This identifies the fringe area (maximum operating distance) of the access point, which indicates the density of access points needed to provide full coverage of an area the size of a plant.

- **Roaming Tests** Most wireless LAN standards don't specify a protocol for handling wireless user devices roaming from one access point to another. Roaming tests will ensure that the access points will properly hand off radio card connections to other access points as the user moves from one part of the facility to the other. This testing is especially important when the radio card and access point vendors are different.

  To accomplish the roaming tests, equip a laptop with a radio card, stand near an access point, and make sure that the radio card is associated with that access point. The tester will walk out of range of the associated access point and closer to another active access point. The radio card should disassociate from the initial access point and reassociate with the next access point. The association information can generally be found via the vendor-supplied management software.

  In addition, consider performing this test while the laptop periodically transmits a file to a laptop or PC connected to the Ethernet switch. After completing this test, the management software should indicate that no packets were lost during the hand-off to the second access point.

- **Multivendor Interoperability Tests** A problem with mixing vendors in a wireless LAN solution is that most vendor-enhanced features are not usable. As a result, the functionality of the network is reduced to the least common denominator, which is the functions specified only by the standard. Test the use of these enhanced features, such as network monitoring tools and performance enhancements, as part of the multivendor testing. This can be done by noting the enhanced features of each vendor and testing whether these features work properly when using a radio card of a different vendor.

Implementing Wireless Link and Carrier Tests

Most radio cards and access points provide wireless link and carrier test functions. Be sure to perform these tests when installing a wireless LAN as a pilot test or operational system. It will save a lot of grief when testing the actual application software.

The wireless link test function determines the quality of transmissions between the station (radio card in the appliance) and the access point. This test sends special control packets to a particular destination, which echoes another packet back to the sending station. Based on the sequence numbers of the packets being sent back and forth, the station running the link test knows whether the link corrupts packets on the forward or return leg of the link. Link test software generally enables you to set test parameters, such as the type of frames sent (multicast or unicast), target station address, frame size, and number of frames to send. The link test provides the following results:

- Percentage of frames sent successfully on both forward and return paths
- Time (average, maximum, and minimum) it takes to receive a response from the destination
- Received signal strength (average, maximum, and minimum) at both ends of the link
- Number (average, maximum, and minimum) of retries at the source before sending the test frame

Most link testers enable you to run a separate signal strength test from a station by sending out a unicast frame (typically one every second) to each individual station within the BSS. The receiving stations send back a response frame that includes received signal strength information. The link test software will display the signal strength at both ends of the link for monitoring purposes.

To test the worst-case scenario of a wireless LAN, transmit frames at the highest bit rate possible and send a large number of full-size frames (typically up to 1,000 frames for most link testers). Keep in mind that performing worst-case tests will take considerably longer than using a smaller number of minimum-size frames. These parameters will result in worst-case results.

A carrier test checks for interference within a wireless LAN. The test works by continuously polling the station's carrier sense functions and displaying the percentage of time the station senses a busy medium. Be sure to run this test, though, when there is no data traffic on the wireless medium. If the test results in activity, then you'll know there's an interfering source nearby. If this occurs, use a spectrum analyzer to pinpoint the frequency of the interfering source.

Pilot Testing

Pilot testing involves installing a real version of the wireless LAN system that users actually operate. This testing enables the evaluation of realistic utilization and long-term performance issues. The results of this testing will also provide a blueprint for the installation of wireless LANs in other common facilities.

The main attributes of pilot testing are as follows:

- Yields the most accurate (real) results because you're using the actual hardware and software under realistic conditions.
- Involves the purchase of applicable hardware and software.
- Depends on relatively firm requirements to minimize costly changes to the installed system.
- Requires a live facility to install and use the system.

Consider using pilot testing for the following situations:

- When testing the design of a new product before going into mass production.
- When testing the system design of a wireless LAN solution prior to installing the system.

The implementation of a wireless LAN pilot test generally involves the installation of multiple access points to cover the facility. Before installing the pilot system, perform an RF site survey to determine the number and location of access points. In addition, the site survey will provide information on the effects of multipath distortion and RF interference within the facility. This data will provide a warning of issues that you may need to consider before installing wireless LANs at other facilities.

To determine the number and location of access points, follow these steps:

1. Obtain a copy of the facility blueprint and verify its accuracy. Blueprints are often outdated because changes, such as the removal of walls or new construction, are not always made to the drawings. As a result, you should walk through the facility before running tests to be sure the building is the same as in the drawing. If not, update the blueprints.

2. Mark user locations. On the blueprint, mark the location of users who will be operating from a fixed location. Also outline potential user roaming areas within the building. In some cases, the roaming area may be the entire facility; however, there may be some areas where users will never roam.

3. Identify obstacles to the radio waves. Observe the construction of the facility, and mark the location of obstacles that may cause a hindrance to radio wave propagation. For instance, high metal racks typically found in warehouses offer a great deal of attenuation.

4. Identify potential sources of RF interference. Discuss sources of interference with the facility's frequency manager, if one exists. If there's doubt on the nature of potential interference, use a spectrum analyzer to record RF transmissions that fall within the frequency band in which your wireless LAN will operate. Be sure to outline on the blueprints the areas that the sources of interference may affect.

5. Identify the preliminary locations of access points based on the vendor's range specifications and information gained from steps 2–4. Ensure that all stationary and roaming users can maintain access to the wireless LAN via an access point. Mark the presumed locations of access points on the blueprints.

6. Verify the location of access points. This is best done by setting up an access point at each location identified in step 5 and testing the signal strength at all corresponding user locations. If possible, be sure to use a device and radio that will be part of the eventual system. This will provide the most accurate results because it will exhibit the same propagation patterns as the eventual system. Most wireless LAN vendors have utilities that run on the user device and record signal levels and packet transmission statistics. With the appropriate tool loaded, walk with a portable computer and record the signal qualities at all applicable locations. If the signal quality falls below suggested values supplied by the vendor, then consider relocating the access point or adding more.

Documenting the Design

As with requirements, you need to document the details of the design to support further implementation activities, such as component procurements, installation, and so on. The final design documentation should include the following:

- A description of each network element
- The location of access points
- Standards
- The products necessary for satisfying specific requirements

Be certain to update any documentation prepared throughout the design with any changes made after verifying the design. Also, update the project documentation, such as the budget, schedule, and resources required to complete the project.

The last step before procuring the components is to obtain approvals for the design. This ensures that applicable managers agree to fund the implementation shown in the design. This normally involves network configuration management, the customer representative, and people with funding authority. For approvals, you can have these people sign a letter having at least the following elements:

- Design document number
- Change control procedures
- Signatures of technical manager, project manager, customer representative, and funding authority

After the approval, consider the design as a baseline that can only be changed by following the stated change control procedures.

Procuring Components

Obviously before installing components you'll need to purchase them and have them delivered to either the staging or installation site. Before doing this, be sure to check on the amount of time it takes for the vendor or supplier to ship the components. In some cases, the provider may have components in stock that can be shipped within a few days. However, it may take several months if the vendor must first manufacture the components. This may be the case for larger orders. Be sure to include this lead time in the schedule when planning the installation dates.

Warranties

When procuring components, you need to understand warranties and maintenance agreements the vendors offer. Most vendors offer excellent warranties and also have maintenance agreements at an additional charge.

Here are some questions you should ask vendors:

- How long is the product covered?
- When does the warranty begin?
- What are the limitations of the coverage?
- How should the product be returned if it becomes defective?
- Does the vendor provide on- or off-site maintenance?

Component Sparing

Be sure to include an adequate level of sparing when purchasing network components. Even though vendors will provide warranties on the hardware, they will not typically be able to respond fast enough with a replacement component if one fails. Spares should be kept near the operational site to provide fast replacement of faulty network components. Of course, sparing will add cost to the project, but this must be weighed against potential downtime if a unit should fail.

> **NOTE**
>
> Because most component warranties begin at time of delivery, be certain each component works properly before putting it in storage. It's difficult to prove the component was bad when shipped from the vendor if you find the component is defective after having it in storage for six months.

Component Storage

Before actually ordering the components, you should plan where the components will be stored after delivery. For small implementations, this may not be significant, but for larger implementations, it's crucial. For example, imagine ordering 75 PCs, 150 radio cards, and 5 printers. Do you know where you'd put all the boxes when they arrive? Since implementations of this size or larger require a great deal of space to store components before they're needed for installation, plan the following items:

- The location to which the components should be delivered
- Storage locations while waiting for installation
- Mechanisms for moving components from the delivery point to the storage area
- Mechanisms for moving the components from the storage area to the point of installation

Case Study 8.1:

Designing an Enterprise-Wide Wireless LAN System

Debra, the project manager for implementing a wireless LAN, began the design phase of the project by having a site survey done at each of the three warehouses and the corporate offices of the parts manufacturing company. Refer to the case studies throughout Chapter 7 to review planning elements of the wireless LAN project. The site survey results showed that each warehouse would require eight access points located throughout the facility to provide enough radio LAN coverage to enable warehouse clerks to work at any point within the facility and around the loading and unloading docks. The corporate offices would require six access points to fully cover the two-floor office facility.

Next, Debra directed Jared, the design engineer for the project, to begin defining the system elements related specifically to the wireless LAN. A preliminary design used for budgeting purposes earlier in the project depicted a system architecture composed of 10 wireless handheld scanners and printers, a radio LAN, and a database and PC application software residing on a server within each warehouse. The wireless

LAN in the corporate offices would require only the installation of access points and radio cards in laptops and PCs. Jared still needed to define the radio network modulation type and other required radio network features, such as power management and security, as well as connectivity software.

Jared decided to utilize wireless LAN products that comply with the IEEE 802.11b direct sequence physical layer because of the need to support existing and future requirements. Jared recommended a single vendor for obtaining the 802.11b wireless components, which would minimize the possibility of incompatibilities and enable them to utilize additional add-on features, such as load balancing.

In addition to the choice of modulation type, Jared specified the use of 802.11b-compliant wireless network components (all from the same vendor) that implement power management to conserve battery power of the handheld appliances. Wired Equivalent Privacy (WEP) was not necessary because security requirements indicate only the need for a user to input a username and password to use the system. This feature would be part of the appliance application software and database, not the wireless LAN. To connect the access points to the server, Jared specified a 10BASE-T ethernet network using ethernet switches.

The choice of connectivity software was the most difficult decision to make concerning the system design. Eric, the software developer, identified three valid alternatives that included terminal emulation, direct database connectivity, and middleware. Refer to Chapter 6 to understand the tradeoffs of each of these connectivity software types. Eric decided to use middleware mainly to enable the AIDC system to interface with both the client/server database that is part of the AIDC system and the existing corporate mainframe system. In addition, middleware would ensure a smooth migration from the existing corporate mainframe system to the future corporate client/server system and provide optimum performance and easier system management. The use of middleware is more expensive than using terminal emulation or direct database connectivity; therefore, the project team had to show that the savings in support costs would outweigh the higher cost of middleware.

Since this project was implementing a complete system (that is, application software and wireless LAN), Eric also needed to design the software for the handheld appliances, PC software, and database. The manufacturing company, however, was not going to implement all system functions during the first year. Instead, it would deploy only receiving and inventory functions. It did agree, though, to design the entire system.

Eric drew flowcharts that describe the appliance software and PC application software. For software development tools, he specified the use of C for the appliance software and Microsoft's Visual Basic for the PC application software. Eric developed a design for the relational database by defining the structure of each table. He also specified the use of Microsoft's Windows NT for the server operating system and Microsoft's SQL Server for the database.

The project team felt confident that the system would work as designed. They were using 802.11b-compliant wireless LAN devices from a reputable vendor, and Jared and Eric had experience in using the chosen middleware to connect appliances software to both databases and mainframes. In addition, this AIDC system wasn't stretching the capabilities of the radio LAN or other system components. Thus, the team didn't feel that they needed to verify the design through simulation or prototyping. They did decide, however, to implement the solution in one warehouse as a pilot test before installing the system at the other two warehouses. If requirements stated that more appliances or performance requirements were stringent, then the team would have performed simulation to ensure the system would operate as expected.

Jared and Eric developed a design specification that described and illustrated all the design elements, including a list of all components the company would need to purchase. Then, Debra scheduled a design review meeting consisting of the entire project team, as well as Chris, the information system manager. At the meeting, Jared and Eric described the system design, and Ron approved the design specification. The outcome of the design phase didn't require any updates to the budget or project plan. At this point, Debra, working with the purchasing department at the manufacturing company, placed orders for all the components to have them delivered to the company headquarters in Atlanta.

Case Study 8.2:

Developing a Wireless System for the Wireless LAN Project

The next phase of the wireless LAN project entails developing the system that the team would install at the warehouses. Eric, software developer, wrote the software for the handheld scanners and printers that implements the receiving and inventory functions. He then had Lola, another software developer, perform unit testing of each software module. While Lola was testing the software, Eric developed the database and PC application software. After Lola was done testing the appliance software, database, and PC application software as individual components, Eric constructed the entire system, including appliances, radio LAN, server, database, and PC application software in a lab at the system integration company. Then, Lola performed system testing to ensure all components would operate together correctly.

The next step was to perform pilot testing of the system at one warehouse to ensure the system operated properly to minimize the amount of rework needed if bugs were found. Eric and Jared installed a couple of access points, the server, database, PC application software, connectivity software, and two appliances at one of the warehouses. They gave some operational training to a couple of the warehouse clerks and asked them to use the wireless LAN system in parallel with their existing manual processes for a period of three weeks. Some bugs were found, and Eric corrected them.

Preparing for Operational Support of a Wireless LAN

As part of the wireless system project, be sure to plan all aspects of operational support. It is advisable to perform this planning in parallel with the design phase of the project. The main goal in support planning is to make certain the system continues to operate effectively during its operational phase. Be sure to prepare for the following support elements before allowing users to use the system:

- **Training** Training provides users, system administrators, and maintenance staff the know-how to effectively operate and support the new system. Training is crucial to the success of a wireless system project. Users will need to know how to use application software, and the system administrator and support staff will need to understand how to manage the network operating system and diagnose system problems. The implementation of proper training will significantly increase the effectiveness of a new system because users will have less of a learning curve, minimizing the drop in productivity normally encountered with new systems. Also, the users will require less support from system administrators and the help desk.

- **System administration** System administration is the liaison between the system and its users. With a network, a system administrator manages the network operating system. Be sure the system administrator understands the configuration of the network (such as IP address assignments of all access points and appliances).

- **Help desk** The help desk is a central point of contact for users needing assistance with the network and its resources. The help desk should concentrate on user satisfaction by providing first-level support via a single phone number. This is an effective method of support because the centralized help desk will not have to redetermine answers to problems when common questions arise. Here are some suggestions in establishing or upgrading a help desk:

    - Establish a single phone number (with multiple call handling) for the help desk, and ensure all users know the phone number

    - Plan for increased call volume as the network grows

    - Incorporate a method to effectively track problems

    - Fully train the help desk team in network operation principles, particularly in user applications

- Use surveys to determine user satisfaction with the help desk
- Review help desk usage statistics to determine optimum staffing
- Periodically rotate network implementation and system administration people into the help desk

- **Network monitoring** Network monitoring seeks to find problems in the network before they arise. Access points and radio cards maintain a management information base (MIB) that stores statistics on the parameters relevant to the radio network, such as the number of duplicate frames, CRC errors, transmit retries, and collisions. Appendix D of the IEEE 802.11 standard describes the MIBs associated with the 802.11 MAC and PHY layers in the ISO/IEC Abstract Syntax Notation (ASN.1). Most access points enable you to monitor these statistics via a network monitoring station conforming to Simple Network Management Protocol (SNMP).

- **Maintenance** Maintenance performs preventative maintenance on the network and troubleshoots and repairs the network if it becomes inoperable. Be sure maintenance technicians are familiar with the wireless network access points and appliances so they can diagnose problems when they arise. An effective method for repairing hardware is to replace the defective component with a spare, then send the defective component back to the vendor for repair or replacement.

- **Engineering/system development** Engineering and system development groups perform enhancements to the system and assist system administrators, help desk, and maintenance staff in troubleshooting difficult network problems. Be sure engineering and system development staff receive adequate training on the wireless system hardware and application development tools.

- **Configuration control** Configuration control procedures make certain proper control procedures exist for making future network and application changes. However, changes to a wireless system, especially those not managed, can cause a lot of headaches. The lack of proper control over changes to the network can result in systems and applications that are not interoperable. It then becomes difficult, expensive, and maybe not possible to provide interfaces that allow the systems and users at these dissimilar sites to share information.

Additionally, the lack of control over network implementations makes it difficult and costly to support the systems. For instance, you may end up with three different types of network operating systems and four different types of wireless LAN adapters to support. Centralized support would need to keep abreast of all of these product types, resulting in higher training costs.

8

IMPLEMENTING A
WIRELESS LAN

Implementing a Configuration Management Process

As you prepare for the operational support of a company-wide system, be sure to establish a configuration control process, shown in Figure 8.3. The design and installation of the system consist of hardware, software, documentation, procedures, and people. It's paramount to consider the system implementation as a baseline, to be changed only when the person initiating the change follows the process. To implement this process, though, you need to identify those elements (configuration items) that are important to control.

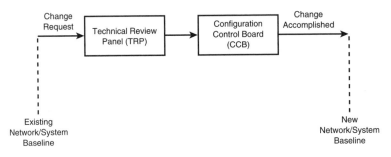

FIGURE 8.3

A configuration control process will help you better manage your wireless system.

The following identifies examples of configuration items you should consider incorporating as a basis for the configuration control process:

- Network interface adapter vendor and type
- Access point vendor and type
- Network operating system release
- Cabling standard
- Switch vendor and type
- Support plans

The description of these elements should be stored in a library accessible by the entire organization.

To make a change to the configuration items, the person wanting to make the change must submit a change request to the technical review panel (TRP), which will assess the technical nature of the change. This includes an evaluation of whether the change complies with company's technical standards.

If the TRP feels the change is technically feasible, it forwards the request to the configuration control board (CCB) for final approval. The CCB mainly evaluates whether the project team has prepared adequate levels of support for the implementation and that the change has been coordinated with the proper organizations. With approval of the change, the project team then must ensure the preparation of support documentation.

Documenting Plans for Operational Support

As with all phases of a project, documentation is important to convey the ideas from that phase to other project phases. In the case of operational support, a support plan is necessary to effectively carry out the support. An operational support plan describes how the organization will support the operational network. This plan should indicate which network elements require support and which organizations are going to support them. More specifically, the operational support plan should describe how the organization will support the following items:

- Network monitoring
- Network troubleshooting
- Hardware maintenance
- Software maintenance

Preparing for the Transfer to Operational Mode

The transfer of the system from project status to operational mode should be very well defined. Otherwise, it's not clear who's supporting the network, and finger pointing will occur if any problems occur. The main task in preparing for the transfer to operational mode is to develop a turnover agreement that will be put into effect after completing the installation and testing phase. At the beginning of the project, the project charter gave the project manager responsibility for implementing the network. The turnover agreement transfers this responsibility to the supporting organizations handling system administration, network management, and so on.

Case Study 8.3:

Preparing Operational Support for the Wireless LAN

Before installing the operational system, Sophie, the operations representative for the wireless LAN project, needed to further define all operational support elements by developing an operational support plan. As stated in the requirements, none of the potential end users had any experience using an AIDC system; therefore, they would require extensive training on how to operate the appliances and system functions. Brian, the business analyst on the project, developed a training course for the end users. The classes would be given to the end users immediately before the system became operational. The class would consist of two half days of hands-on training. Evan, the system analyst on the project, developed the training for the operational support staff, which would run for three full days.

For system administration, Sophie decided to broaden the role of the system administrators located at the headquarter facility in Atlanta to include the new wireless LAN system. The new system, however, required the company to hire an additional system administrator. The system administrator would be able to manage the server, access points, and connectivity software remotely; therefore, there wouldn't be a need to deploy an administrator to each of the warehouses. Someone at each warehouse, though, would be designated to assist the system administrator if needed.

The manufacturing company already had a help desk accessible by a single phone number for users to call if problems arose; however, the help desk staff would need to become very familiar with the wireless LAN functionality to help users understand how to perform certain functions if they'd forgotten from the training. The help desk would also need to know if they should refer a call to a system administrator or to an organization to perform maintenance. If maintenance such as troubleshooting, hardware replacement, or bug fixes were required, then the help desk would hand off the call to the contracted system integrator deploying the system.

Sophie received agreement from Chris, the information systems manager at the manufacturing company, that any change to the wireless LAN system would have to be authorized by her. This would ensure that they could provide proper operational support for the enhancements. Over the next couple of years, there will be many changes to wireless LAN as the company developed and installed additional AIDC functions. Sophie decided to appoint Liza, one of her staff, to manage the changes through the company's configuration management process.

Installing a Wireless LAN

Wireless networks are advantageous because there is less cable to install than with wired networks, such as ethernet. Theoretically, then, a wireless network installation should take less time. Actually, installation time depends on how well you have evaluated the environment before embarking on the installation. If you did not perform a site survey, unseen radio frequency interference might wreak havoc on the operation of a newly installed wireless system, causing significant delays in making the system operate effectively. You want to avoid delays when installing the system. A delay will cause you to not meet schedule constraints and will result in decreased productivity of the system's users. Thus, if you have not performed a site survey at this point in the project, do it now before pressing forward!

The installation of a wireless network requires the following steps:

1. Plan the installation.

2. Stage the components.

3. Install the components.

4. Test the installation.

The following sections cover each of these steps and explain the actions necessary to finalize the project.

Planning the Installation

Before taking components out of the boxes, installing network interface cards, and setting up antennas, spend some time planning the installation. This will significantly reduce the number of problems that might arise. Planning the installation consists of the following actions:

1. Developing an installation plan

2. Coordinating the installation

Developing an Installation Plan

Overall, an installation plan explains how to install the network. Developing an installation plan helps you focus on what needs to be installed. It also provides instructions for installers who might not have been involved with the design of the network and, therefore, do not have firsthand knowledge of the network's configuration. The following identifies the major components of a network installation plan:

- Points of contact
- Safety tips
- Installation procedures
- Tools
- References to design documentation
- Schedule
- Resources
- Budget
- Risks

The project team should assign someone as installation manager who will develop the plan and be responsible for the installation.

8

IMPLEMENTING A
WIRELESS LAN

Points of Contact

The plan should indicate someone as the central point of contact for each installation site if problems arise. This person could be the customer representative or someone who works in the facility where the installation will take place. Be sure this person can provide access to restricted areas and locked rooms. Also, indicate who on the project team can answer questions regarding the installation procedures, network configuration, and frequency usage concerns.

Safety Tips

When network components are being installed, accidents are less likely to happen if you incorporate good safety practices and remind people about them. Here are some safety tips you should list in your installation plan and stress at your preinstallation meeting.

- Insist that no installers work alone—use the buddy system. If a severe accident occurs, the other person can obtain help.

- Recommend that installers remove rings and necklaces while installing hardware components. A metal necklace can dangle into a live electrical circuit (or one that is not connected to a power source, but is still energized by charged capacitors) and provide the basis for electrical shock. Rings also conduct electricity or can catch on something and keep you from removing your hand from a computer or component.

- Use proper ladders and safety harnesses if placing antennas on towers or rooftops. There is no reason to take high-elevation risks.

- Wear eye protection when using saws or drills.

Installation Procedures

The plan should clearly describe the procedures for installing components. In some cases, you can simply refer installers to the manufacturer's instructions. Otherwise, write at least the major steps involved in installing each component. You can use the procedures for installing and testing the network outlined in the next sections as a basis.

TIP

The less cluttered the work environment, the greater the range will be for the wireless LAN. A cluttered office can decrease range as much as 50%.

Tools

Be sure to identify the tools necessary to complete the job. If you have ever constructed a Barbie house, built a patio cover, or worked on a car engine, you certainly realize the need for having the right tools. Not having the proper tools results in time delays looking for the tools or rework needed because you used the wrong tools. Here is a list of tools the installers might require:

- Wireless installation tools and utilities assist in planning the location of access points and testing wireless connections. They are generally available from the applicable wireless product vendor.

- Two-way radios provide communication among the installation team, especially when spread over a large geographical area.

- Specific test equipment verifies the network installation.

- Standard tools, such a flashlights, ladders, and crimping tools, should be readily available for the installation team.

Reference to Design Documentation

The installation will probably require use of design documentation to better understand the overall network configuration. Be sure to indicate the existence of the documentation and how to obtain it.

Schedule

Create a schedule that identifies when to perform each of the installation activities. This helps keep the installation process on schedule. Unfortunately, the best time to install network components is during downtime, such as evening hours and weekends. This minimizes disturbances. Hospitals and warehouses never close, but you should plan the installation activities for when the organization is least active.

Resources

Make certain the plan identifies resources needed to perform the installation procedures. Generally, you will not have a staff of technicians with experience installing wireless networks. If you plan to perform wireless installations as a service to other companies, then you may want to train existing staff to do the implementations. However, in cases where it is a one-time installation, it's best to outsource the work to a company specializing in network installations.

Budget

Create a budget to track expenses related to the installation. The project team has already prepared a budget during the project planning stages. At this time, it may only be necessary to refine the budget to reflect the installation plan.

Risks

Identify any risks associated with the activities and explain how these risks can be minimized. You might be required, for example, to install 200 wireless LAN connections within a two-day time period. With only two installers, you run the risk of not completing the installation on time. Therefore, you will need to look for additional help to keep on schedule. If someone

8

IMPLEMENTING A
WIRELESS LAN

needs to preapprove your plan, it is best to identify risks and solutions before starting any work.

Coordinating the Installation

Most everyday events require you to coordinate activities. For example, before you, your spouse, your four kids, and pet dog leave on a five-day automobile trip from Dayton to Sacramento to stay a week with relatives, you'd certainly want to communicate with someone at your destination to coordinate items such as sleeping accommodations and eating preferences.

Before leaving on the trip, you should let your relatives know that you are on the way. In addition, you would certainly want to hold a predeparture meeting with the family, particularly the kids, and talk about proper behavior while traveling. The installation of a network is probably much easier to pull off than the car trip, but the coordination of activities is similar. The coordination of installation activities includes the following:

- **Communicating with the facility managers**   The person designated as the facility manager for each facility should have a chance to review the installation plan. In fact, he should have been active in developing the schedule to minimize any negative effects on the organization.

- **Giving the organization's employees a heads up**   If you have to install components of the network when the organization's staff is present, announce when, where, and for how long installers will be working within the area. Be sure it's clear to the employees when any existing system resources will not be available. People need time to rearrange their schedules if necessary to accommodate the installation. Have the organization send out a memo or e-mail to announce the installation.

- **Holding a preinstallation meeting**   The preinstallation meeting gathers together everyone involved in the installation to review procedures. Be sure everyone knows who to contact if problems occur. This meeting is also the best time to remind people about good safety practices.

With an installation plan in hand and coordination behind you, it's time to begin the installation.

Staging the Components

If you are implementing a wireless system at multiple sites, be certain to use a staging function to ensure the most effective pretesting and distribution of components to the intended operating locations. The staging process essentially puts the system together in a single non-user location to verify it works as expected. It's best to do this testing before rolling it out to many sites because it significantly reduces the amount of rework necessary if a defect is found in the design or one or more of the components.

Staging involves the following functions:

- Warehousing bulk components, such as boxes of radio cards and access points
- Unpacking bulk components
- Sorting components for each installation site
- Installing and testing software on appliances
- Packing and shipping components destined for specific installation sites

The benefits of staging include reduced installation time at the users' sites, assurance that all necessary components are available at the installation site, and having all subcomponents properly installed and tested.

Installing the Components

The installation of network components should follow a bottoms-up approach. When installing, first construct and configure individual components, such as servers, user worksta-tions, and cabling, then connect the components together, implement communications soft-ware, and install and link the applications. Consider installing the network from the ground up as follows:

1. Install NICs in the computers.
2. Install cabling from ethernet repeaters/switches to the access point installation locations.
3. Install access points using applicable mounting brackets,
4. Establish wide area network connections if necessary.
5. Assemble server hardware.
6. Install and configure the network operating system.
7. Install client software on the user appliances.

8

NOTE

Be sure to follow installation procedures supplied by the vendor when installing net-work components.

In most cases, the team can install some components in parallel to decrease installation time. There's nothing wrong, for example, with installing network interface cards, cabling, and access points at the same time. Just be sure to test each component properly, as described later in this chapter in the section "Performing Unit Testing," before connecting the pieces together.

You can't fully access or operate the network operating system and applications until after lower-level components such as cabling, network installation cards, and access points have been installed.

Installing Wireless NICs

If you are installing wireless NICs, follow these recommendations:

- Be sure to acquire the correct NIC driver software before attempting to bind the appliance's application software to the NIC.

- Some appliances require the vendor's service staff to install wireless NICs to ensure the antenna is properly connected. Be sure to follow these policies to ensure the appliance will operate correctly and will be covered under warranties.

- Perform the installation of wireless NICs as part of a centralized staging process of the system.

> **NOTE**
>
> You can set parameters within the wireless NIC by writing specific instructions in a configuration file that is part of the wireless NIC installation process.

Installing Access Points

If you are installing access points within a facility, follow these recommendations:

- Clearly mark the cables connecting the access points to the corresponding ethernet repeater or switch. Ensure that these cable markings are present on network diagrams.

- Follow vendor instructions on configuring the access point with an applicable IP address and protocol settings.

- Mount the access points as high as possible to increase transmission range; however, ensure there is some way to reach the device to provide periodic servicing of the unit.

> **NOTE**
>
> Most access points have a variety of interfaces, such as RS-485 and RS-232, for connecting a console (terminal or PC running terminal emulation software) to the access point for configuration purposes. Some access points even enable you to change configuration parameters via a Web browser or telnet session if wired network connectivity exists between the access point and the PC running the Web browser software or telnet software. Be sure to set passwords on the access points to enable access to only those who need to manage the access points.

> **TIP**
>
> For best performance, follow these tips when installing access points:
>
> - Place antennas as high as you can to increase range between the access point and wireless stations.
> - Position the units above office partitions and away from metal objects, such as furniture, fans, and doors.
> - Install the unit in a central location, such as the center of a large room or corridor.

Installing Laser Links Between Buildings

If you're installing laser links between buildings, follow these recommendations:

- The beam should not be directed near or through electrical power lines or tree branches. Consider tree growth, wind load on trees, and power lines. Power lines also sag during warm weather and tighten up during cold weather. Make provisions to discourage nest building in the optical path by birds and insects.

- Make sure the transmission path is at least 10 feet above pedestrian or vehicular traffic. This both prevents accidental viewing of the laser beam and keeps the signal from being interrupted. Make allowances for any unusual effects that traffic may cause, such as dust clouds.

- Make sure the transmission path is not shooting through or near exhaust vents that can cause steam to be blown into the path. This has the same effect as fog on the laser beam.

- Most outdoor point-to-point components are fully weatherproof. These units may also be mounted inside buildings and the signal passed through glass windows. When light particles hit a glass surface, some of the light is reflected. With a clear glass window, approximately 4% of the light is reflected per glass surface. If the glass is tinted, the amount of light reflected and absorbed increases. In the case of reflective coatings, the laser light will reflect off the coating, and the light will never be detected at the receiver.

  Another problem when shooting through glass occurs when it rains. Water droplets on the glass in front of the transmit lens act as additional lenses and can cause the beam to diffuse. Mounting the laser near the top of the window will reduce this problem somewhat, especially if there is an awning over the window. Figure 8.4 illustrates the proper critical angle when operating through glass. As the angle of the beam with the glass increases, more and more light is reflected until the critical angle is reached (approximately 42 degrees). Above the critical angle, all of the light is absorbed into the glass, and no transmission occurs.

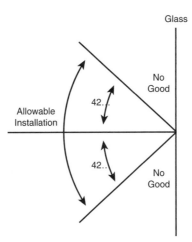

FIGURE 8.4

When passing signals through glass, it is advisable to keep the beam as close to perpendicular to the glass as possible to minimize reflection losses, which can reduce signal strength.

- Avoid east-west orientations. Although LCI uses optical filters in the receiver and has a small angle of acceptance, direct sunlight can overload the units for several minutes a day for a few days per year.

- Heat from roof tops, air duct vents, air conditioners, glass-faced buildings, and so on can cause a condition known as *shimmer*. Shimmer will cause the light beam to bend and appear to dance around the receiver. If sufficient heat is present, the beam will deflect enough to miss the receiver altogether, usually for a few milliseconds at a time, and burst error will occur. When mounting on rooftop locations, the preferred location is at the leading edge of the roof, with the front of the laser at least six inches over the edge. This minimizes the effect of roof heating, heat rising up the side of the building, and snow accumulation in front of the unit. This also provides access to the rear of the unit for easier setup and alignment.

- The movement of laser units caused by a strong mechanical vibration could cause the system to go in and out of alignment intermittently. It is advisable to avoid mounting laser equipment near vibrating machinery such as air conditioning units, compressors, motors, and so on.

- The laser beam produced by laser units is not subject to the interference produced by EMI sources. However, if laser units are placed within proximity of such sources, the unit's electronics may pick up this interference, which would then be impressed on the signals to and from the equipment. It is advised that laser units be mounted away from large microwave dishes, antennas, radio stations, or any unusual electronic equipment that may be radiating electromagnetic signals.

- Laser units are normally designed to project a two-meter diameter beam at the receiver. This provides some latitude for beam movement. It is essential, however, that unit movement be kept to an absolute minimum to ensure peak performance. A movement of only 1mm at the transmitter can divert the beam off of the receiver if the units are installed one kilometer apart.

- Ideally, a laser unit should be mounted on the corner of the building to which it will be attached and preferably to masonry construction. This will provide the most stable arrangement. When transmitting signals more than 300 meters, it is not advisable to mount LACE units anywhere except at the corner of the structure. On buildings with a thin metal skin, the base for the mounts must be attached to the supporting structure or to the metal substructure.

- Do not mount laser units on structures that can sway, such as trees, fences, towers, poles, or buildings exceeding 40 stories in height. Always avoid movable camera mounts.

- Do not mount laser units to wooden structures. The expansion/contraction properties of these materials through precipitation and temperature make them good sources for movement and should be avoided. For example, high humidity will cause the units to go out of alignment due to the wood expanding.

- Make sure that when laser is mounted there are no ledges in front of the laser that could be used by roosting birds. Ledges can also cause a problem in rain or snow. Water bouncing up from the ledge onto the optics or snow buildup in front of the optics will diminish performance.

Testing the Installation

In the software world, testing is extremely important—countless problems have resulted from defects in software. You might have heard, for example, about the farmer in a remote area of Nebraska who one day received thousands of the same copy of *Time* magazine? Apparently, the publisher's label printing software had a defect that made it spend hours printing the same address. Defects in networks might not cause similar incidents, but improper configurations and unforeseen propagation impairments can easily discontinue the network's operation. This is especially serious in hospitals where a doctor's or rescue person's access to information can create a life-or-death situation.

There are several definitions for testing. Some people say that testing is for checking if the system offers proper functionality, and others say the reason for testing is to find conditions that make the system fail. Actually, testing is a combination of the two—it ensures that the network behaves as expected and that no serious defects exist.

Test Cases

A test case represents an action you perform and its expected result. For example, one test case might determine whether access to a database meets performance requirements. The action would be to run a particular query, and the expected result would be the maximum time it takes for the query to return the corresponding data.

How do you write test cases? First, be sure to review the later sections on performing unit, integration, system, and acceptance testing before writing test cases. Then, referring to the network requirements and design defined earlier in the project, describe the tests necessary to ensure a network that behaves adequately. The following are attributes of a good test case:

- Has a good chance of uncovering a defect.
- Can be performed with attainable test equipment.
- The expected result is verifiable.

Test Execution

With a complete set of test cases, you're ready to run the tests. As you'll see later, testing takes place throughout the installation phase. You might have noticed that building contractors must carefully inspect the foundation before building the structure on top; otherwise, the building itself could hide support structure defects that could later cause a disaster. Network testing is similar; you should fully test the radio connectivity and cabling before installing and testing their interaction with the network operating system and application.

Test Results

The outcome of performing test cases is test results. Of course, you hope everything checks out okay. Poor results indicate the need for rework, meaning a design modification is necessary and components need to be reinstalled or reconfigured. This will take time to complete, possibly extending the project. It's a good idea to record test results for observation later when supporting the network. Test results offer baseline measurements that support staff can use to aid in troubleshooting future problems.

> **TIP**
>
> A wireless link test that results in a relatively large number of retries at a particular station indicates a problem. The cause of the problem could be interference from a nearby source or collisions resulting from excessive network utilization.

Evaluation Comments

After obtaining the test results related to the portion of the network under testing, compare them to the expected values identified in the test case. The evaluation comments should explain any differences and, if necessary, recommend corrective action.

Corrective Actions

Corrective actions provide baseline information for later testing. When problems arise during the network's operational life, you can run tests again and compare them to those run during installation. This can help pinpoint problems.

TIP

If a wireless station fails to establish a connection with the access point, consider the following corrective actions:

- Ensure that the antennas are securely attached to the radio card and access point, and ensure that the antenna cable is connected to the correct antenna port.
- Try moving the antenna several feet.
- Ensure that the radio card is firmly seated in the PC Card or ISA slot.
- Check for properly set parameters at the station and access point.

Performing Testing

The best method of testing the network installation is to follow a bottom-up approach by performing the following types of tests:

1. Unit testing
2. Integration testing
3. System testing
4. Acceptance testing

Performing Unit Testing

Unit testing verifies the proper internal operation or configuration of individual network components, such as network interface cards, access points, servers, cables, printers, and so forth. You should unit test each component before trying to make it work with other parts of the system to ensure it is not defective. Knowing that individual parts work makes it easier to troubleshoot problems later.

Ideally, you want to fully test all possible functions and configurations of each unit; however, that's usually not feasible. The following sections offer examples of unit tests you should perform.

8

IMPLEMENTING A
WIRELESS LAN

Testing Individual Components

Be sure to test the operation of each component, such as printers, servers, and access points, before integrating it with other components. Most components have built-in self-tests that run whenever you turn the device on, or they have test utilities that you can run manually; therefore, you usually won't need to develop specialized test cases for most individual units. Proxim's wireless LAN products, for example, come with a utility that verifies whether you've chosen an I/O address, IRQ, or memory window that conflicts with other hardware.

Testing Category 5 Cable Installations

Cable problems within the backbone of a wireless system rank high as causes of networking troubles. Mechanical elements, such as cabling, connectors, and wall plates, tend to fail more often than active electronic devices such as network adapters and switches. Approximately 85% of cable problems arise from the installation; therefore, be sure to fully test cable installations. Cable faults result from improper splices, improper connector attachments, lack of termination, and corrosion.

The good news is that cable problems are relatively easy to find, especially if you use an effective cable tester conforming to TIA's Technical Service Bulletin (TSB) 67, published by the Link Performance Task Group of the Telecommunications Industry Association (TIA). This TSB is not a standard; however, it describes how to test Category 5 twisted-pair cable. You should definitely consider TSB-67 when selecting a cable tester.

TSB-67 addresses two link configuration models: Channel Link and Basic Link. The *Channel Link* consists of the patch cords that connect the access points to the horizontal wiring, and the horizontal wiring itself can span a total of 100 meters. Channel Link testing covers a range that verifies wiring connections up to the user's interface. The *Basic Link* includes only the horizontal wiring to the building ceiling and two 2-meter tester equipment cords and can be 90 meters long. Installation crews commonly perform Basic Link testing after laying the cabling.

The authors of TSB-67 chose two levels of accuracy for testing links: Level I for low accuracy and Level II for high accuracy. These two accuracy levels take into consideration the test configurations you implement for testing the Basic and Channel Links. For instance, Channel Link testing almost always requires the use of an RJ45 interface attached directly to your tester. The problem is that the RJ45 interface offers unpredictable crosstalk and affects the accuracy of crosstalk measurements. This type of test, therefore, would need only Level I testing. On the other hand, Basic Link testing enables you to interface the tester to the cable via a connector having much lower crosstalk, such as a DB-9 or DB-25 connector. Thus, with Basic Link testing, it is possible to run the more accurate Level II tests.

After installing Category 5 cabling, test the installation by performing the following tests that TSB-67 recommends:

- **Wiremap**   The wiremap test ensures that a link has proper connectivity by testing for continuity and other installation mistakes, such as the connection of wires to the wrong connector pin. For example, if you don't wire an RJ45 connector exactly according to a standard, such as EIA/TIA 568A's T568A or T568B wiring scheme, then you might produce split pairs.

  A *split pair* occurs when you attach the connector in a way that a wire pair consists of one lead from one twisted pair and another lead from a different twisted pair, creating a pair of wires that are untwisted. The split pair might result in an excessive amount of external noise interference and crosstalk, which will cause transmission errors. Most cable testers perform wiremap tests to detect this type of cable problem.

- **Link Length**   Link length measurements identify whether a cable meets the length limitations. Cable testers use a Time-Division Reflectometer (TDR), which measures the length of a cable. The operation of a TDR is shown in Figure 8.5. Several products on the market run TDR tests on metallic or optical-fiber cable. Tektronix TS100 Option 01 Metallic TDR, for example, tests LocalTalk, Type 1 and 3; Category 3, 4, and 5; and thin and thick coax cables. This test set finds shorts, opens, and breaks in the cable. The Tektronix TFP2A Fibermaster OTDR tests single-mode and multimode fiber-optic cables.

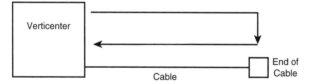

FIGURE 8.5

The TDR emits a pulse at one end of the cable that travels to the opposite end of the cable and then reflects back to the TDR. The TDR measures the propagation time and calculates the cable length based on an average wave propagation rate.

- **Attenuation**   Attenuation tests ensure that the cabling will offer acceptable attenuation over the entire operating frequency range. If too much attenuation is present, digital signals sent throughout the cable will experience rounding, resulting in transmission errors. Cable testers examine attenuation by measuring the effects of sending a series of signals that step through the cable's operating frequency bandwidth.

  For Category 5 testing, most cable testers cover bandwidth of 1MHz to 100MHz by taking readings in 1MHz increments, and this certifies whether the cable meets

8

IMPLEMENTING A
WIRELESS LAN

specifications in the part of the frequency spectrum where the signal mostly resides. The Microtest Pentascanner is an example of a cable tester that measures attenuation on Category 3, 4, and 5 cable.

- **Near-End Crosstalk (NEXT)**   Crosstalk is the crossing of current from one wire to a nearby wire, causing transmission errors. Near-End Crosstalk (NEXT) is a specific case in which signals at one end of the link interfere with weaker signals coming back from the recipient. The amount of NEXT varies erratically as you sweep through the operating bandwidth of a cable. For an accurate measurement, cable testers record NEXT by stepping though the cable's operating frequency range at very small increments.

  For Category 5 cable, TSB-67 recommends a maximum step size of 0.15MHz for lower frequencies and 0.25MHz for higher frequencies within the 1MHz through 100MHz frequency range. This requires a fast instrument to take the hundreds of samples necessary. Fluke's DSP-100 handheld cable tester is an example of an incredibly fast NEXT tester. The DSP-100 uses digital signal processing to increase its speed and enable samples to be taken at close 100KHz intervals. The DSP-100 performs all tests required by TSB-67 for a 4-pair cable in under 20 seconds. The DSP-100 not only identifies the presence of crosstalk, it also locates its source.

If any defects are found through unit testing, correct the problems of each unit before integrating them with other components.

Performing Integration Testing

The concept of integration testing is shown in Figure 8.6. Although unit testing guarantees the proper functioning of individual components, that is not enough to certify a network. Integration testing goes a step further and ensures that these components operate together. For example, you may have unit tested a PC containing a wireless network interface card, an associated access point, and a server located on the wired network and found all of them operating sufficiently.

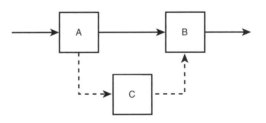

FIGURE 8.6

Integration testing would verify that components A and B work together okay. Then, after component C is installed, integration testing would verify that all three components work together acceptably.

However, performing an integration test, such as attempting to log in to the server from the PC via the access point, may fail. The reason could be because the network interface card and access point were set to different channels, not allowing a connection.

TIP

It's important that you perform integration testing constantly as you add components to the network. You can then find problems before they become buried. If you were to finish the entire implementation first, then run tests, it would be more difficult to find the problems.

If the final configuration of the preceding example included TCP/IP access to an application residing on the server via a WAN as well, troubleshooting would be much more complex because of the additional components. Thus, be sure to include integration testing *as* you build the network.

As with unit testing, the ideal is to verify all possible functions across the set of components you're testing; however, that's not feasible in most cases. To help you narrow possibilities to a workable set, here are some examples of integration tests you should consider performing:

- Capability to roam from one radio cell to another
- Capability to roam throughout the designated coverage area
- Capability of a remote host at the end of a TCP/IP connection to respond to a continuity test, such as a Ping

As with unit testing, correct any defective installations before pressing on with further integration or system testing.

Performing System Testing

System testing determines whether the completed network installation is capable of satisfying the requirements specified at the beginning of the project. Thus, system testing requires you to first install all components (and perform appropriate unit and integration tests). System testing is the final testing done before handing the system over to the users for acceptance. For example, after installing all network components, such as the clients' terminals, access points, ethernet networks, WAN, servers, and applications, you should check whether the software on the client workstation communicates correctly with the application on the server.

The scope of system testing depends on the potential for disaster if the network fails. As an example, if you're building a network to support an information system onboard a manned spacecraft destined for Mars, you'd want to perform exhaustive testing to discover and fix any defects so that unfixable problems don't arise en route. The main reason for the thoroughness is because human lives are at stake if the system fails. Most Earth-based systems without human lives on the line will not require this extreme testing. Be sure, however, to develop test cases that exercise the system from one extreme to another. The goal is to develop and execute system tests that verify, at the minimum, the following system attributes:

- Capability of users to access appropriate applications from terminals and PCs
- Capability to support all security requirements
- Capability to meet performance requirements
- Capability to interface with all external systems

If the testing of these attributes provides unfavorable results, take corrective actions, then retest the portions of the system that required modification.

TIP

If you've just installed an 802.11-compliant network having radio cards from one vendor and access points from a different vendor, and it doesn't operate correctly, then check to ensure that the radio cards and access point all comply with the same version of the 802.11 standard. Many radio network vendors initially released products that complied with draft versions of the 802.11 standard. If the radio card is based on a draft version, and the access point is based on the official version, then the network will probably not operate correctly. In some cases, the radio card and access point may associate, but they won't exchange data. In other cases, the radio card and access point will not even associate. If you find some of your 802.11 wireless components do not comply with the official version of the 802.11 standard, then the vendor should be able to change firmware on the card to bring it up to date.

Performing Acceptance Testing

After the project team fully tests the system, it's time for the customer to perform acceptance testing, which involves actual users running tests to determine whether the implementation is acceptable. These tests should focus on verifying whether the system functions as specified in the requirements. This does not require the same level of detail as system tests do. Acceptance testing is done at a much higher level to ensure that users can run the appropriate applications while performing their jobs. For example, Mary will be using a wireless terminal tied to a central database to access inventory records as she stocks the shelves. Acceptance testing will determine whether she can actually enter and retrieve data from the database while handling the stock.

It is best not to deploy the network or system to the entire population until a cross section of users performs the acceptance tests. Most people refer to this as a *system pilot*. It's advisable to perform acceptance testing as a pilot of the implementation if either of the following conditions is true:

- The implementation spans multiple geographic locations.
- The network supports mission-critical applications.

In these cases, there is great risk in losing productivity and valuable information if there are defects in the system. For instance, if you deploy a wireless inventory system at six warehouses and find that other existing devices interfere, then all warehouses stand to lose some productivity until the problem can be resolved. A pilot system at one of the warehouses would have identified the problem, and you could have fixed it before deploying the system to the remaining sites. The drawback of pilot testing, though, is that it delays the deployment of the system to the users not participating in the pilot. This could make it impossible to meet schedule deadlines. However, if the conditions above exist, running a pilot test will be worth the wait.

Finalizing the Project

After the user organization accepts the system, the project might seem to be over, right? Actually, there are still some tasks left, including the following:

- Updating documentation
- Training the users
- Transferring the system to operational support
- Evaluating the outcome of the project

Updating Documentation

During the installation and testing phase, the team may have made changes to the design or layout of the network as a result of corrective actions to failed tests. Therefore, the team might need to update documentation, such as design specifications. In some extreme cases, requirements might need updating if it's found that the installed system can't support desired requirements as expected. Most companies refer to these updated documents as *installed* or *red-lined* drawings. These provide an accurate set of documentation for support staff to use when troubleshooting or modifying the system.

Training Users

The training of users and support staff is extremely important. Training strengthens the interface between the system and the users. If possible, offer the training before or during the system installation. This prepares specific users for performing the acceptance testing and ensures that all users are ready to start using the system when it's operational. You can perform a small implementation of the system in a classroom and teach people how to use the system before it is actually deployed to the rest of the company.

In many cases, the implementation team can develop training in the form of a train-the-trainer course. The idea of this form of training is to teach other instructors how to teach the material to the end users. This case is common when system integrators implement a system for another company.

Transferring the Network to Operational Support

While implementing the network, the project team provides support for the network, such as the creation of user accounts, and troubleshooting and repair actions. In fact, during the requirements phase and acceptance testing, potential users generally assume that members of the project team will always be providing support. In some cases, this might be true. Regardless of whether the team will be providing operational support, be sure to clearly transfer support of the operational network from the project team to applicable people and organizations.

This clearly marks the end of the project and ensures that users having problems with the system will call upon the right people for assistance. Be certain as part of the transfer that the operational support staff have copies of network documentation, such as designs and support plans. Figure 8.7 illustrates the concept of transferring the network to operational support.

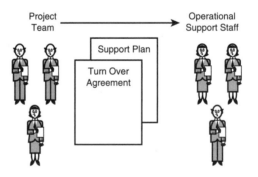

Figure 8.7

Transferring the network to operational support is crucial for properly supporting the installed system.

This transfer should mark the completion of a successful wireless network implementation. Soon, the numerous benefits of wireless networking will be apparent, and your efforts will be justified.

Evaluating the Outcome of the Project

After the project is finished, the project manager should congratulate the team and review the lessons learned throughout the implementation. Gather one last time as a project team and discuss the activities that took place from the beginning of the project through the requirements, design, operational support preparation, and installation phases. What did the team learn as a result of completing the project? You can answer this by thinking of what the successes were and why they occurred. Also identify any problems that happened that would be beneficial to solve before undertaking another project.

Here are some questions the team should consider for analyzing the lessons learned:

- Did upper management continue to support the project to the end?
- Did the requirements phase go smoothly?
- Did all members of the team communicate effectively within the team and with other individuals and groups?
- Were there any problems associated with the mechanics of product procurement?
- Was operational support in place before users began using the system?
- Did the training properly prepare users to operate the system?
- Was the project completed on schedule and within budget?
- Do the users feel the system will enhance their performance?
- Does the implemented system perform as expected by the project team and the users?

For the *yes* responses, identify why that particular aspect of the project went well. If any answers to these questions are *no*, then determine what went wrong and why. If you treat problems and successes as lessons, your future projects will go much smoother.

8

Case Study 8.4:

Installing the Wireless LAN

Debra, the project manager for the wireless LAN system deployment, was ready to install the operational system at each of the nine warehouses. Debra called in Lindsey, the installation manager from her company, to plan the installation based on the design. Debra introduced Lindsey to Morris, the company's facility manager of all the warehouses. Morris would be the point of contact for Lindsey when needing to schedule the installations and gain access to certain parts of the facilities. Lindsey would need to plan around events such as active periods and construction.

Before sending all the components out to each warehouse, Lindsey set up a staging area at the manufacturing company's headquarters facility, which is where the components had been delivered. During the staging process, the installation crew configured the components for each warehouse to ensure that all components were available and that they worked together properly. After testing each system, the installation crew packed the components destined for each warehouse in individual sets of boxes for shipment to the respective warehouses.

Three installers then traveled to each warehouse and the corporate offices sequentially over a 10-week period to install the systems. Lola, the system tester on the project, went with them to perform quality assurance inspections after the installation took place at each warehouse. Brian, the business analyst on the project, also traveled to each location to provide training to the end users. Meanwhile, Evan, the system analyst on the project, delivered the operational support training to each of the support staff members back in Atlanta.

The final two steps of the wireless LAN project included acceptance testing and transfer of the system to operational status. Debra and Denise, the warehouse manager, visited each site to observe the completion of acceptance testing by warehouse staff. After they completed this testing, Denise officially accepted the completion of this phase of the project for deploying the wireless system with receiving and inventory functions. Sophie, the project operations representative, then announced to all support staff that the wireless LAN system was operational, and the users began utilizing the system.

Summary

As you can see from this chapter, the implementation of a wireless LAN is much more involved than wired networks such as Ethernet. Wireless LANs require a more in-debth understanding of requirements, such as range and potential interference, and additional thought on the number and placement of access points. If you follow the steps that this chapter has discussed, then you should be able to inmplement a succuessful, high performance wireless LAN.

Glossary

Symbols

10Base-2   IEEE standard (known as thin ethernet) for 10Mbps baseband ethernet over coaxial cable at a maximum distance of 185 meters.

10Base-5   IEEE standard (known as thick ethernet) for 10Mbps baseband ethernet over coaxial cable at a maximum distance of 500 meters.

10Base-F   IEEE standard for 10Mbps baseband ethernet over optical fiber.

10Base-T   IEEE standard for 10Mbps baseband ethernet over twisted-pair wire.

10Broad-36   IEEE standard for 10Mbps broadband ethernet over broadband cable at a maximumdistance of 3600 meters.

100Base-T   IEEE standard for a 100Mbps baseband ethernet over twisted-pair wire.

802.2   IEEE standard that specifies the Logical Link Control (LLC) that is common to all 802-series LANs.

802.3   IEEE standard that specifies a carrier-sense medium access control and physical-layer specifications for wired LANs.

802.4   IEEE standard that specifies a token-passing bus access method and physical-layer specifications for wired LANs.

802.5   IEEE standard that specifies a token-passing ring access method and physical-layer specifications for wired LANs.

802.10   IEEE standard that specifies security and privacy access methods for both wired and wireless LANs.

802.11   IEEE standard that specifies medium access and physical-layer specifications for wireless connectivity between fixed, portable, and moving stations within a local area at data rates of 1 and 2 Mbps.

802.11a   IEEE standard for orthogonal frequency-division multiplexing (OFDM) operation in the 5GHz frequency band at up to 54Mbps.

802.11b   IEEE standard for direct sequence modulation as an extension to the initial 802.11 standard for data rates up to 11Mbps in the 2.4 GHz frequency band.

802.11e   IEEE standard that defines quality-of-service (QoS) mechanisms for IEEE 802.11 products.

A

acceptance testing   Type of testing that determines whether the network is acceptable to the actual users. The users of the network should participate in developing acceptance criteria and running the tests.

access point (AP)   An interface between the wireless network and a wired network. Access points combined with a distribution system (such as ethernet) support the creation of multiple radio cells (BSSs) that enable roaming throughout a facility.

acknowledged connectionless service A datagram-style service that includes error-control and flow-control mechanisms.

ad hoc network   A wireless network composed of only stations and no access point.

adaptive routing   A form of network routing in which the path that data packets traverse from a source to a destination node depends on the current state of the network. Normally with adaptive routing, routing information stored at each node changes according to some algorithm that calculates the best paths through the network.

Address Resolution Protocol (ARP) A TCP/IP protocol that binds logical (IP) addresses to physical addresses.

analog cellular   A telephone system that uses radio cells to provide connectivity among cellular phones. The analog cellular telephone system uses frequency modulation (FM) radio waves to transmit voice-grade signals. To accommodate mobility, this cellular system switches your radio connection from one cell to another as you move between areas. Every cell within the network has a transmission tower that links mobile callers to a mobile telephone switching office (MTSO).

analog signal   An electrical signal with an amplitude that varies continuously as time progresses.

appliance   Runs applications and is a visual interface between the user and the network. There are several classes of user appliances: the desktop workstation, laptop, palmtop, pen-based computer, personal digital assistant (PDA), and pager.

application layer   Establishes communications with other users and provides services such as file transfer and electronic mail to the end users of the network.

application process   An entity, either human or software, that uses the services offered by the application layer of the OSI reference model.

application software   Accomplishes the functions users require, such as database access, electronic mail, and menu prompts. Therefore, application software directly satisfies network requirements, particularly user requirements.

ARP   See *Address Resolution Protocol*.

ARQ   See *automatic repeat-request*.

association service   An IEEE 802.11 service that enables the mapping of a wireless station to the distribution system via an access point.

Asynchronous Transfer Mode (ATM)   A cell-based connection-oriented data service offering high-speed (up to 2.488Gbps) data transfer. ATM integrates circuit and packet switching to handle both constant and burst information. Frequently called *cell relay*.

asynchronous transmission   Type of synchronization in which there is no defined time relationship between transmission of frames.

ATM   See *Asynchronous Transfer Mode*.

attachment unit interface (AUI) A 15-pin interface between an ethernet network interface card and a transceiver.

AUI   See *attachment unit interface*.

authentication   The process a station uses to announce its identity to another station. IEEE 802.11 specifies two forms of authentication: open system and shared key.

automatic repeat-request (ARQ)   A method of error correction in which the receiving node detects errors and uses a feedback path to the sender for requesting the retransmission of incorrect frames.

B

bandwidth   Specifies the amount of the frequency spectrum that is usable for data transfer. In other words, it identifies the maximum data rate that a signal can attain on the medium without encountering significant attenuation (loss of power).

baseband   A signal that has not undergone any shift in frequency. Normally with LANs, a baseband signal is purely digital.

Basic Service Set (BSS)   A set of 802.11-compliant stations that operate as a fully connected wireless network.

Basic Service Set Identification (BSSID) A 6-byte address that distinguishes a particular access point from others. Also known as a network ID or network name by some product vendors.

baud rate   The number of pulses of a signal that occur in one second. Thus, baud rate is the speed that the digital signal pulses travel.

bit rate   The transmission rate of binary symbols (0 and 1). Bit rate is equal to the total number of bits transmitted in one second.

Bluetooth   A specification published by the Bluetooth Special Interest Group (SIG) for 1Mbps data rates in the 2.4GHz band at relatively short ranges. Bluetooth doesn't constitute a wireless LAN. Instead, it fits the profile of a wireless personal area network (PAN).

bridge   A network component that provides internetworking functionality at the data-link or medium access layer of a network's architecture. Bridges can provide segmentation of data frames.

broadband   A signal that has undergone a shift in frequency. Normally with LANs, a broadband signal is analog.

BSS   See *Basic Service Set.*

BSSID   See *Basic Service Set Identification.*

bus topology   A type of topology in which all nodes are connected to a single length of cabling with a terminator at each end.

C

carrier current LAN   A LAN that uses power lines within the facility as a medium for the transport of data.

category 1 twisted-pair wire   Old-style phone wire, which is not suitable for most data transmission. This includes most telephone wire installed before 1983, in addition to most current residential telephone wiring.

category 2 twisted-pair wire   Certified for data rates up to 4Mbps, which facilitates IEEE 802.5 Token Ring networks (4Mbps version).

category 3 twisted-pair wire   Certified for data rates up to 10Mbps, which facilitates IEEE 802.3 10Base-T (ethernet) networks.

category 4 twisted-pair wire   Certified for data rates up to 16Mbps, which facilitates IEEE 802.5 Token Ring networks (16Mbps version).

category 5 twisted-pair wire   Certified for data rates up to 100Mbps, which facilitates ANSI FDDI Token Ring networks.

CCITT   See *International Telegraph and Telephone Consultative Committee.*

CCK   See *Complementary Code Keying.*

CDDI   See *Copper Data Distributed Interface.*

CDPD   See *Cellular Digital Packet Data.*

CDRH   See *Center for Devices and Radiological Health.*

cell relay   See *Asynchronous Transfer Mode.*

Cellular Digital Packet Data (CDPD) Overlays the conventional analog cellular telephone system, using a channel-hopping technique to transmit data in short bursts during idle times in cellular channels. CDPD operates in full duplex in the 800MHz and 900MHz frequency bands, offering data rates up to 19.2Kbps.

Center for Devices and Radiological Health (CDRH)   The part of the U.S. Food and Drug Administration that evaluates and certifies laser products for public use.

centronics   A de facto standard 36-pin parallel 200Kbps asynchronous interface for connecting printers and other devices to a computer.

clear channel assessment   A function that determines the state of the wireless medium in an IEEE 802.11 network.

coaxial cable   Type of medium that has a solid metallic core with a shielding as a return path for current flow. The shielding within the coaxial cable reduces the amount of electrical noise interference within the core wire; therefore, coaxial cable can extend to much greater lengths than twisted-pair wiring. Commonly called coax, it is used in older ethernet (10Base-2) networks.

collocation   The concept of operating multiple access points tuned to different channels in the same area to support additional throughput.

Complementary Code Keying (CCK)   A modulation technique that the IEEE 802.11b standard specifies for delivery of 5.5Mbps and 11Mbps data rates.

connection-oriented service   Establishes a logical connection that provides flow control and error control between two stations needing to exchange data.

connectivity   A path for communications signals to flow through. Connectivity exists between a pair of nodes if the destination node can correctly receive data from the source node at a specified minimum data rate.

connectivity software   A wireless system component that provides an interface between the user's appliance and the database or application software located on the network.

Copper Data Distributed Interface (CDDI)   A version of FDDI specifying the use of unshielded twisted-pair wiring (category 5).

CRC   See *cyclic redundancy check*.

cyclic redundancy check (CRC)   An error-detection process that (at the transmitting station) divides the data being sent by a particular polynomial and appends the resulting remainder to the transmitted data. Then (at the receiving station) the process divides the received data by the same polynomial and compares the resulting remainder to the remainder appended to the data at the transmitting station. If the remainders are equal, there is very high probability that no errors are present in the data. If they don't match, then errors are present.

D

Data Encryption Standard (DES)   A cryptographic algorithm that protects unclassified computer data. DES is a National Institute of Standards and Technology (NIST) standard and is available for both public and government use.

data link layer   Provides the synchronization of frames between two entities (for example radio card and access point).

data service unit/channel service unit (DSU/CSU)   A set of network components that reshape data signals into a form that can be effectively transmitted over a digital transmission medium, typically a leased 56Kbps or T1 line.

datagram service   A connectionless form of packet switching in which the source does not need to establish a connection with the destination before sending data packets.

DB-9   A standard nine-pin connector commonly used with RS-232 serial interfaces on portable computers. The DB-9 connector will not support all RS-232 functions.

DB-15   A standard 15-pin connector commonly used with RS-232 serial interfaces, ethernet transceivers, and computer monitors.

DB-25   A standard 25-pin connector commonly used with RS-232 serial interfaces. The DB-25 connector will support all RS-232 functions.

DES   See *Data Encryption Standard*.

DHCP   See *Dynamic Host Configuration Protocol*.

diffused laser light   Type of laser transmission in which the light is reflected off a wall or ceiling.

direct sequence spread spectrum (DSSS)   Combines a data signal at the sending station with a higher data-rate bit sequence, which many refer to as a chip sequence (also known as processing gain). A high processing gain increases the signal's resistance to interference. The minimum processing gain that the FCC allows is 10, and most products operate under 20.

disassociation service   An IEEE 802.11 term that defines the process a station or access point uses to notify that it is terminating an existing association.

Distributed Queue Dual Bus (DQDB)   A technology that provides full-duplex 155Mbps operation between nodes of a metropolitan area network. The IEEE 802.6 standard is based on DQDB.

distributed routing   A form of routing in which each node (router) in the network periodically identifies neighboring nodes, updates its routing table, and, with this information, sends its routing table to all its neighbors. Because each node follows the same process, complete network topology information propagates through the network and eventually reaches each node.

distribution service   An IEEE 802.11 station uses the distribution service to send MAC frames across a distribution system.

distribution system   An element of a wireless system that interconnects Basic Service Sets via access points to form an Extended Service Set.

DQDB   See *Distributed Queue Dual Bus*.

DSSS   See *direct sequence spread spectrum*.

DSU/CSU   See *data service unit/channel service unit*.

Dynamic Host Configuration Protocol (DHCP)   Issues IP addresses automatically within a specified range to devices such as PCs when they are first powered on. The device retains the use of the IP address for a specific license period that the system administrator can define. DHCP is available as part of the many operating systems, including Microsoft Windows NT Server and Unix.

E

EDI   See *electronic data interchange.*

EIA   See *Electronics Industry Association.*

electronic data interchange (EDI)
A service that provides standardized inter-company computer communications for business transactions. ANSI standard X.12 defines the data format for business transactions for EDI.

Electronics Industry Association (EIA)
A domestic standards-forming organization that represents a vast number of U.S. electronics firms.

ethernet   A 10Mbps LAN medium-access method that uses CSMA to allow the sharing of a bus-type network. IEEE 802.3 is a standard that specifies ethernet.

ethernet repeater   Refers to a component that provides ethernet connections among multiple stations sharing a common collision domain. Also referred to as a shared ethernet hub.

ethernet switch   More intelligent than a hub, this switch has the capability to connect the sending station directly to the receiving station.

Extended Service Set (ESS)   A collection of Basic Service Sets tied together via a distribution system.

F

FDDI   See *Fiber Distributed Data Interface.*

FEC   See *forward error correction.*

FHSS   See *frequency hopping spread spectrum.*

Fiber Distributed Data Interface (FDDI)
An ANSI standard for token-passing networks. FDDI uses optical fiber and operates at 100Mbps.

File Transfer Protocol (FTP)   A TCP/IP protocol for file transfer.

firewall   A device that interfaces the network to the outside world and shields the network from unauthorized users. The firewall does this by blocking certain types of traffic. For example, some firewalls permit only electronic-mail traffic to enter the network from elsewhere. This helps protect the network against attacks made to other network resources, such as sensitive files, databases, and applications.

forward error correction (FEC)
A method of error control in which the receiving node automatically corrects as many channel errors as it can without referring to the sending node.

fractional T1   A 64Kbps increment of a T1 frame.

Frame Relay   A packet-switching interface that operates at data rates of 56Kbps to 2Mbps. Actually, frame relay is similar to X.25, minus the transmission error control overhead. Thus, frame relay assumes that a higher-layer, end-to-end protocol will check for transmission errors. Carriers offer frame relay as permanent connection-oriented (virtual circuit) service.

frequency hopping spread spectrum (FHSS)   Takes the data signal and modulates it with a carrier signal that hops from frequency to frequency as a function of time over a wide band of frequencies. For example, a frequency-hopping radio will hop the carrier frequency over the 2.4GHz frequency band between 2.4GHz and 2.483GHz. A hopping code determines the frequencies it will transmit and in which order. To properly receive the signal, the receiver must be set to the same hopping code and "listen" to the incoming signal at the right time at the correct frequency.

FTP   See *File Transfer Protocol*.

fully connected topology   A topology in which every node is directly connected to every other node in the network.

G

gateway   A network component that provides interconnectivity at higher network layers. For example, electronic-mail gateways can interconnect dissimilar electronic mail systems.

Gaussian frequency shift keying
A frequency modulation technique that filters the baseband signal with a Gaussian filter before performing the modulation.

Global Positioning System (GPS)
A worldwide, satellite-based radio navigation system providing three-dimensional position, velocity, and time information to users who have GPS receivers anywhere on or near the surface of the Earth.

GPS   See *Global Positioning System*.

H

HDLC   *See High-level Data Link Control*.

hierarchical topology   A topology in which nodes in the same geographical area are joined together and then tied to the remaining network as groups. The idea of a hierarchical topology is to install more links within high-density areas and fewer links between these populations.

High-level Data Link Control (HDLC)
An ISO protocol for link synchronization and error control.

HiperLAN   Developed by the European Telecommunications Standards Institute (ETSI) Broadband Radio Access Network (BRAN) organization. HiperLAN/1, the current version, operates in the 5GHz radio band at up to 24Mbps. ETSI is currently developing HiperLAN/2 under an organization called the HiperLAN/2 Global Forum (H2GF). HiperLAN/2 will operate in the 5GHz band at up to 54Mbps using a connection-oriented protocol for sharing access among end-user devices.

HTML *See Hypertext Markup Language.*

Hypertext Markup Language (HTML)
A standard used on the Internet for defining hypertext links between documents.

I

IBSS Network See *Independent Basic Service Set Network.*

IEEE See *Institute of Electrical and Electronic Engineers.*

Independent Basic Service Set Network (IBSS Network) An IEEE 802.11-based wireless network that has no backbone infrastructure and that consists of at least two wireless stations. This type of network is often referred to as an *ad hoc network* because it can be constructed quickly without much planning.

industrial, scientific, and medicine bands (ISM bands) Radio frequency bands that the Federal Communications Commission (FCC) authorized for wireless LANs. The ISM bands are located at 902MHz, 2.400GHz, and 5.7GHz.

infrared light Light waves that have wavelengths ranging from about 0.75 to 1000 microns, which is longer (lower in frequency) than the spectral colors but much shorter (higher in frequency) than radio waves. Therefore, under most lighting conditions, infrared light is invisible to the naked eye.

Institute of Electrical and Electronic Engineers (IEEE) A United States–based standards organization participating in the development of standards for data transmission systems. IEEE has made significant progress in the establishment of standards for LANs, namely the IEEE 802 series of standards.

Integrated Services Digital Network (ISDN) A collection of CCITT standards specifying WAN digital transmission service. The overall goal of ISDN is to provide a single physical network outlet and transport mechanism for the transmission of all types of information, including data, video, and voice.

integration service Enables the delivery of MAC frames through a portal between an IEEE 802.11 distribution system and a non-802.11 LAN.

integration testing Type of testing that verifies the interfaces between network components as the components are installed. The installation crew should integrate components into the network one by one and perform integration testing when necessary to ensure proper gradual integration of components.

interframe space Defines spacing between different aspects of the IEEE 802.11 MAC access protocol to enable different transmission priorities.

Intermediate System-to-Intermediate System Protocol An OSI protocol for intermediate systems exchange routing information.

International Standards Organization (ISO)   A nontreaty standards organization active in the development of international standards such as the Open System Interconnection (OSI) network architecture.

International Telecommunications Union (ITU)   An agency of the United States providing coordination for the development of international standards.

International Telegraph and Telephone Consultative Committee (CCITT) An international standards organization that is part of the ITU and that is dedicated to establishing effective and compatible telecommunications among members of the United Nations. CCITT develops the widely used V-series and X-series standards and protocols.

internetwork   A collection of interconnected networks. Often it is necessary to connect networks together, and an internetwork provides the connection between different networks. One organization with a network might want to share information with another organization that has a different network. The internetwork provides functionality needed to share information between these two networks.

inward interference   Interference coming from other devices, such as microwave ovens and other wireless network devices, that results in delay to the user by either blocking transmissions from stations on the LAN or causing bit errors to occur in data being sent.

ISDN   See *Integrated Services Digital Network*.

ISM bands   See *industrial, scientific, and medicine bands*.

ISO   See *International Standards Organization*.

isochronous transmission   Type of synchronization in which information frames are sent at specific times.

ITU   See *International Telecommunications Union*.

J

JAD   See *joint application design*.

joint application design (JAD)   A parallel process simultaneously defining requirements in the eyes of the customer, users, salespeople, marketing staff, project managers, analysts, and engineers. You can use the members of this team to define requirements.

L

LAP   See *Link Access Procedure*.

laser   A common term for Light Amplification by Stimulated Emission of Radiation, a device containing a substance in which the majority of its atoms or molecules are put into an excited energy state. As a result, the laser emits coherent light of a precise wavelength in a narrow beam. Most laser MANs use lasers that produce infrared light.

LED   See *light emitting diode*.

light emitting diode (LED) Used in conjunction with optical fiber, it emits incoherent light when current is passed through it. Advantages to LEDs include low cost and long lifetime, and they are capable of operating in the range of megabits per second.

Link Access Procedure (LAP) An ITU error-correction protocol derived from the HDLC standard.

local bridge A bridge that connects two LANs close to each other.

Logical Link Control Layer (LLC) The highest layer of the IEEE 802 reference model. It provides similar functions of a traditional data-link control protocol.

M

MAC Layer See *Medium Access Control Layer*.

MAC protocol data unit (MPDU) The unit of data in an IEEE 802 network that two peer MAC entities exchange across a physical layer.

mail gateway A type of gateway that interconnects dissimilar electronic mail systems.

management information base (MIB) A collection of managed objects residing in a virtual information store that extend the SNMP system for controlling, monitoring and configuring devices.

MAU See *multistation access unit*.

medium A physical link that provides a basic building block to support the transmission of information signals. Most media are composed of either metal, glass, plastic, or air.

medium access A data-link function that controls the use of a common network medium.

Medium Access Control Layer (MAC Layer) Provides medium access services for IEEE 802 LANs.

meteor burst communications A communications system that directs a radio wave, modulated with a data signal, at the ionosphere. The radio signal reflects off the ionized gas left by the burning of meteors entering the atmosphere and is directed back to Earth in the form of a large footprint, enabling long-distance operation.

MIB See *management information base*.

middleware An intermediate software component located on the wired network between the wireless appliance and the application or data residing on the wired network. Middleware provides appropriate interfaces between the appliance and the host application or server database.

MIDI See *Musical Instrument Digital Interface*.

Mobile IP A protocol developed by the Internet Engineering Task Force to enable users to roam to parts of the network associated with a different IP address than what's loaded in the user's appliance.

mobility   Capability to continually move from one location to another.

mobility requirements   Describe the movement of the users when performing their tasks. Mobility requirements should distinguish whether the degree of movement is continuous or periodic.

modulation   The process of translating the baseband digital signal to a suitable analog form.

MPDU   See *MAC protocol data unit*.

multistation access unit (MAU) A multiport wiring hub for token ring networks.

multiplexer   A network component that combines multiple signals into one composite signal in a form suitable for transmission over a long-haul connection, such as leased 56Kbps or T1 circuits.

Musical Instrument Digital Interface (MIDI)   A standard protocol for the interchange of musical information between musical instruments and computers.

N

narrowband system   A wireless system that uses dedicated frequencies assigned by the FCC licenses. The advantage of narrowband systems is that if interference occurs, the FCC will intervene and issue an order for the interfering source to cease operations. This is especially important when operating wireless MANs in areas that have a great deal of other operating radio-based systems.

NETBIOS   See *Network Basic Input/Output System.*

Network Basic Input/Output System (NetBIOS)   A standard interface between networks and PCs that allows applications on different computers to communicate within a LAN. It was created by IBM for its early PC Network, was adopted by Microsoft, and has since become a de facto industry standard. It is not routable across a WAN.

network file system (NFS)   A distributed file system enabling a set of dissimilar computers to access each other's files in a transparent manner.

network interface card (NIC)   A network adapter inserted into a computer so that the computer can be connected to a network. It is responsible for converting data from the form stored in the computer to the form transmitted or received.

network layer   Provides the routing of packets from source to destination.

network management   Consists of a variety of elements that protect the network from disruption and provide proactive control of the configuration of the network.

network-management station   Executes management applications that monitor and control network elements.

network monitoring   A form of operational support enabling network management to view the inner workings of the network. Most network-monitoring equipment is unobtrusive and can determine the network's utilization and locate faults.

network re-engineering   A structured process that can help an organization proactively control the evolution of its network. Network re-engineering consists of continually identifying factors that influence network changes, analyzing network modification feasibility, and performing network modifications as necessary.

network service access point (NSAP)
A point in the network where OSI network services are available to a transport entity.

NFS   See *network file system.*

NIC   See *network interface card.*

node   Any network-addressable device on the network, such as a router or a network interface card.

NSAP   See *network service access point.*

O

ODI   See *Open Data-Link Interface.*

ODBC   See *Open Database Connectivity.*

OFDM   See *orthogonal frequency-division multiplexing.*

Open Database Connectivity (ODBC)
A standard database interface enabling interoperability between application software and multivendor ODBC-compliant databases.

Open Data-Link Interface (ODI)
Novell's specification for network interface card device drivers, allowing simultaneous operation of multiple protocol stacks.

Open Shortest Path First (OSPF)
Routing protocol for TCP/IP routers that bases routing decisions on the least number of hops from source to destination.

open system authentication   The IEEE 802.11 default authentication method, which is a very simple two-step process. First the station wanting to authenticate with another station sends an authentication-management frame containing the sending station's identity. The receiving station then sends back a frame stating whether it recognizes the identity of the authenticating station.

Open System Interconnection (OSI)
An ISO standard specifying an open system capable of enabling the communications between diverse systems. OSI has the following seven layers of distinction: physical, data link, network, transport, session, presentation, and application. These layers provide the functions necessary to allow standardized communications between two application processes.

orthogonal frequency-division multiplexing (OFDM)   A modulation technique that divides a high-speed serial information signal into multiple lower-speed subsignals that the system transmits simultaneously at different frequencies in parallel. OFDM is the basis of the IEEE 802.11a standard.

OSI   See *Open System Interconnection.*

OSPF   See *Open Shortest Path First.*

P

packet radio   Uses packet switching to move data from one location to another across radio links.

PCF   See *point coordination function.*

PCM   See *pulse code modulation.*

PCMCIA form factor   See *Personal Computer Memory Card International Association form factor.*

PCS   See *Personal Communications Services.*

peer-to-peer network   A network in which there are communications between a group of equal devices. A peer-to-peer LAN does not depend upon a dedicated server, but it allows any node to be installed as a nondedicated server and share its files and peripherals across the network. Peer-to-peer LANs are normally less expensive because they do not require a dedicated computer to store applications and data. They do not perform well, however, for larger networks.

performance modeling   The use of simulation software to predict network behavior, enabling you to perform capacity planning. Simulation enables you to model the network and impose varying levels of utilization to observe the effects. Performance monitoring addresses performance of a network during normal operations. Performance monitoring includes real-time monitoring, in which metrics are collected and compared against thresholds that can set off alarms; recent-past monitoring, in which metrics are collected and analyzed for trends that might lead to performance problems; and historical data analysis, in which metrics are collected and stored for later analysis.

Personal Communications Services (PCS)   A spectrum allocation located at 1.9GHz; a new wireless communications technology offering wireless access to the World Wide Web, wireless e-mail, wireless voice mail, and cellular telephone service.

Personal Computer Memory Card International Association form factor (PCMCIA form factor)   A standard set of physical interfaces for portable computers. PCMCIA specifies three interface sizes: Type I (3.3 millimeters), Type II (5.0 millimeters), and Type III (10.5 millimeters).

physical layer   Provides the transmission of bits through a communication channel by defining electrical, mechanical, and procedural specifications.

physical-layer convergence procedure sublayer (PLCP)   Prepares MAC protocol data units (MPDUs) as instructed by the MAC Layer for transmission and delivers incoming frames to the MAC Layer.

physical medium-dependent sublayer (PMD)   Provides the actual transmission and reception of physical-layer entities between two stations via the wireless medium.

plain old telephone system (POTS)   The original common analog telephone system, which is still in wide use today.

PLCP   See *physical-layer convergence procedure sublayer.*

PMD   See *physical medium-dependent sublayer*.

point coordination function (PCF)   An IEEE 802.11 mode that enables contention-free frame transfer based on a priority mechanism. It enables time-bounded services that support the transmission of voice and video.

Point-to-Point Protocol (PPP)   A protocol that provides router-to-router and host-to-network connections over both synchronous and asynchronous circuits. PPP is the successor to SLIP.

portability   Defines network connectivity that can be easily established, used, and then dismantled.

portal   A logical point at which MSDUs from a non-IEEE 802.11 LAN enter the distribution system of an extended service set wireless network.

POTS   See *plain old telephone system*.

PPP   See *Point-to-Point Protocol*.

presentation layer   Negotiates data transfer syntax for the application layer and performs translations between different data types, if necessary.

processing gain   Equal to the data rate of the spread direct sequence signal divided by the data rate of the actual data.

project charter   Formally recognizes the existence of the project, identifies the business need that the project is addressing, and gives a general description of the resulting product.

project management   Overseers needed to make sure that actions are planned and executed in a structured manner.

prototyping   A method of determining or verifying requirements and design specifications. The prototype normally consists of network hardware and software that support a proposed solution. The approach to prototyping is typically a trial-and-error experimental process.

pseudo-noise   An actual signal that has a long pattern that resembles noise.

pulse code modulation (PCM)   A common method for converting analog voice signals into a digital bit stream.

pulse position modulation   The varying ofthe position of a pulse to represent different binary symbols. The changes in pulse positions maintain the information content of the signal.

R

real time location system (RTLS)   A system that combines the use of wireless LAN and positioning technology.

reassociation service   Enables an IEEE 802.11 station to change its association with different access points as the station moves throughout the facility.

Red Book   A document of the United States National Security Agency (NSA) defining criteria for secure networks.

relay node   Implements a routing protocol that maintains the optimum routes for the routing tables, forwarding packets closer to the destination.

remote bridge A bridge that connects networks separated by longer distances. Organizations use leased 56Kbps circuits, T1 digital circuits, and radio waves to provide long-distance connections between remote bridges.

repeater A network component that provides internetworking functionality at the physical layer of a network's architecture. A repeater amplifies network signals, extending the distance they can travel.

requirements analysis A process of defining what the network is supposed to do, providing a basis for the network design.

ring topology A topology in which are joined in a closed loop.

RIP See *Routing Information Protocol*.

router A network component that provides internetworking at the network layer of a network's architecture by allowing individual networks to become part of a WAN. It routes using logical and physical addresses to connect two or more separate networks. It determines the best path by which to send a packet of information.

Routing Information Protocol (RIP)
A common type of routing protocol. RIP bases its routing path on the distance (number of hops) to the destination. RIP maintains optimum routing paths by sending out routing update messages if the network topology changes. For example, if a router finds that a particular link is faulty, it updates its routing table and then sends a copy of the modified table to each of its neighbors.

RS-232 An EIA standard that specifies up to 20Kbps, 50-foot, serial transmission between computers and peripheral devices.

RS-422 An EIA standard specifying electrical characteristics for balanced circuits (that is, both transmit and return wires are at the same voltage above ground). RS-422 is used in conjunction with RS-449.

RS-423 An EIA standard specifying electrical characteristics for unbalanced circuits (that is, the return wire is tied to ground). RS-423 is used in conjunction with RS-449.

RS-449 An EIA standard specifying a 37-pin connector for high-speed transmission.

RS-485 An EIA standard for multipoint communications lines.

RTLS See *real time location system*.

S

SAP See *service access point*.

Serial Line Internet Protocol (SLIP)
An Internet protocol used to run IP over serial lines and dial-up connections.

server-oriented network A network architecture in which the network software is split into two pieces, one each for the client and the server. The server component provides services for the client software; the client part interacts with the user. The client and server components run on different computers, and the server is usually more powerful than the client. The main advantage of a server-oriented network is less network traffic. Therefore, networks that have a large number of users will normally perform better with server-oriented networks.

service access point (SAP)   A point at which the services of an OSI layer are made available to the next-higher layer.

service primitive   A communications element for sending information between network architectural layers.

session layer   Establishes, manages, and terminates sessions between applications.

shared key authentication   A type of authentication that assumes that each station has received a secret shared key through a secure channel independent from an 802.11 network. Stations authenticate through shared knowledge of the secret key. Use of shared key authentication requires implementation of the 802.11 Wireless Equivalent Privacy algorithm.

Simple Mail Transfer Protocol (SMTP)   The Internet electronic mail protocol.

Simple Network Management Protocol (SNMP)   A network-management protocol that defines the transfer of information between Management Information Bases (MIBs). Most high-end network-monitoring stations require the implementation of SNMP on each of the components that the organization wants to monitor.

SLIP   See *Serial Line Internet Protocol*.

SMDS   See *Switched Multimegabit Digital Service*.

SMTP   See *Simple Mail Transfer Protocol*.

SNA   See *Systems Network Architecture*.

SNMP   See *Simple Network Management Protocol*.

SONET   See *Synchronous Optical Network*.

spectrum analyzer   An instrument that identifies the amplitude of signals at various frequencies.

spread spectrum   A modulation technique that spreads a signal's power over a wide band of frequencies. The main reason for this technique is that the signal becomes much less susceptible to electrical noise and interferes less with other radio-based systems.

SQL   See *Structured Query Language*.

ST connector   An optical fiber connector that uses a bayonet plug and socket.

star topology   A topology in which each node is connected to a common central switch or hub.

station   In IEEE 802.11 networks, any device that contains an IEEE 802.11-compliant Medium Access Control layer and physical layers

Structured Query Language (SQL)   An international standard for defining and accessing relational databases.

Switched Multimegabit Digital Service (SMDS)   A packet-switching connectionless data service for WANs.

Synchronous Optical Network (SONET)   A fiber-optic transmission system for high-speed digital traffic. SONET is part of the B-ISDN standard.

synchronous transmission   Type of synchronization in which information frames are sent within certain time periods. It uses a clock to control the timing of bits being sent.

system testing   Type of testing that verifies the installation of the entire network. Testers normally complete system testing in a simulated production environment, simulating actual users to ensure that the network meets all stated requirements.

Systems Network Architecture (SNA)
IBM's proprietary network architecture.

T

T1   A standard specifying a time-division multiplexing scheme for point-to-point transmission of digital signals at 1.544Mbps.

TCP   See *Transmission Control Protocol.*

TDR   See *time-domain reflectometer.*

Technical Service Bulletin 67 (TSB 67)
Describes how to test category 5 twisted-pair cable. TSB 67 was published by the Link Performance Task Group, a subcommittee of the Telecommunications Industry Association's TR41 Standards Committee.

technology-comparison matrix   A documentation method that compares similar technologies based on attributes such as functionality, performance, cost, and maturity.

telecommuting   The concept of electronically stretching an office to a person's home.

Telnet   A virtual terminal protocol used in the Internet, enabling users to log in to a remote host.

terminal node controller (TNC)
Interfaces computers to ham radio equipment. TNCs act much like a telephone modem, converting the computer's digital signal into one that a ham radio can modulate and send over the airwaves using a packet-switching technique.

test case   An executable test with a specific set of input values and a corresponding expected result.

thicknet   A term used to refer to the older 10Base-5 (coaxial cable) standard for cabling ethernet LANs.

thinnet   A term used to refer to the older 10Base-2 (coaxial cable) standard for cabling ethernet LANs.

time-domain reflectometer (TDR)   Tests the effectiveness of network cabling.

TNC   See *terminal node controller.*

token ring   A medium access method that provides multiple access to a ring-type network through the use of a token. FDDI and IEEE 802.5 are token-ring standards.

top-down design   First defines high-level specifications directly satisfying network requirements, and then defines the remaining elements in an order that satisfies the most specifications already determined.

topography   A description of the network's physical surface spots. Topography specifies the type and location of nodes with respect to one another.

topology   A description of the network's geographical layout of nodes and links.

TP0   OSI Transport Protocol Class 0 (Simple Class), useful only with very reliable networks.

TP4   OSI Transport Protocol Class 4 (Error Detection and Recovery Class), useful with any type of network. The functionality of TP4 is similar to that of TCP.

transceiver   A device for transmitting and receiving packets between the computer and the medium.

Transmission Control Protocol (TCP)   A commonly used protocol for establishing and maintaining communications between applications on different computers. TCP provides full-duplex, acknowledged, and flow-controlled service to upper-layer protocols and applications.

transport layer   Provides mechanisms for the establishment, maintenance, and orderly termination of virtual circuits, while shielding the higher layers from the network implementation details.

TSB 67   See *Technical Service Bulletin 67*.

twisted-pair wire   Type of medium using metallic type conductors twisted together to provide a path for current flow. The wire in this medium is twisted in pairs to minimize the electromagnetic interference between one pair and another.

U

UDP   See *User Data Protocol*.

unacknowledged connectionless service   A datagram-style service that does not involve any error-control or flow-control mechanisms.

unit testing   Type of testing that verifies the accuracy of each network component, such as servers, cables, hubs, and bridges. The goal of unit testing is to make certain that the component works properly by running tests that fully exercise the internal workings of the component.

User Data Protocol (UDP)   A connectionless protocol that works at the OSI transport layer. UDP transports datagrams but does not acknowledge their receipt.

user profile requirements   Identify the attributes of each person who will be using the system, providing human factors that designers can use to select or develop applications.

V

V.21   An ITU standard for asynchronous 0–300bps full-duplex modems.

V.21 FAX   An ITU standard for facsimile operations at 300bps.

V.34   An ITU standard for 28,800bps modems.

W

WBS   See *work breakdown structure*.

WECA   See *Wireless ethernet Compatibility Alliance*.

WEP   See *Wired Equivalent Privacy*.

Wi-Fi   A standard for "wireless fidelity" sponsored by the Wireless ethernet Compatibility Alliance (WECA). Wi-Fi is actually a brand that signifies 802.11 inter-operability with other Wi-Fi certified prod-ucts.

Wired Equivalent Privacy (WEP)
An optional IEEE 802.11 function that offers frame transmission privacy similar to that of a wired network. The Wired Equivalent Privacy generates secret shared encryption keys that both source and desti-nation stations can use to alter frame bits to avoid disclosure to eavesdroppers.

Wireless ethernet Compatibility Alliance (WECA)   WECA provides for certification of interoperability of IEEE 802.11 products and promotes Wi-Fi as the global wireless LAN standard across all market segments.

wireless metropolitan area network
Provides communications links between buildings, avoiding the costly installation of cabling or leasing fees and the downtime associated with system failures.

wireless network interface   Couples the digital signal from the end-user appliance to the wireless medium, which is air.

Wireless Middleware   See *middleware*.

wiremap test   Ensures that a link has proper connectivity by testing for continuity and other installation mistakes, such as the connection of wires to the wrong connector pin.

work breakdown structure (WBS)
Shows how the team will accomplish the project by listing all tasks that the team will need to perform and the products they must deliver.

X

X.12   An ITU standard for EDI.

X.21   An ITU standard for a circuit-switching network.

X.25   An ITU standard for an interface between a terminal and a packet-switching network. X.25 was the first public packet-switching technology, developed by the CCITT and offered as a service during the 1970s; it is still available today. X.25 offers connection-oriented (virtual circuit) service and operates at 64Kbps, which is too slow for some high-speed applications.

X.75   An ITU standard for packet switch-ing between public networks.

X.121   An ITU standard for international address numbering.

X.400   An ITU standard for OSI messag-ing.

X.500   An ITU standard for OSI directory services.

INDEX

SYMBOLS

A